Renovating the Victorian House

Renovating the Victorian House

Katherine Knight Rusk

101 Productions
San Francisco

TECHNICAL DRAWINGS Nancie West Swanberg
COVER AND TEXT DESIGN Patricia Glover

Printed and bound in the United States of America.

Distributed to the book trade in the United States
by Charles Scribner's Sons, New York.

Published by 101 Productions
834 Mission Street
San Francisco, California 94103

1 3 5 7 9 11 13 15 17 19   20 18 16 14 12 10 8 6 4 2
Library of Congress Cataloging in Publication Data

Rusk, Katherine Wright
   Renovating the Victorian house

   Bibliography: p.
   Includes index.
   I. Dwellings--Remodeling.   2. Architecture,
Victorian--Conservation and restoration.   I. Title.
TH4816.R86   1982   643'.7   82-12397
ISBN 0-89286-187-8 pbk
ISBN 0-89286-217-3

COVER NOTES

FRONT COVER A bay-windowed Italianate in San Francisco,
designed in the late 19th century by architect Henry Geilfuss
and later converted into apartments. Renovated in 1980 by
architect Roy Killeen. The free-standing colonnettes around
the window are a rare detail. Photograph: Rik Olson.

BACK COVER Another San Francisco Italianate sorely in need
of repair. Photograph: Patricia Glover.

Contents

Introduction

The historic preservation movement is growing, and house renovation has become a nationwide fad. People are moving back into the core cities where Victorian houses are plentiful, drawn by an appreciation for America's heritage and spurred by exorbitant commuting costs.

A well-made house of natural materials is a welcome departure from the shoddy, synthetic techniques that characterize much modern construction. Even the two-by-fours in a Victorian house are 2 inches by 4 inches! Economically, also, older homes are a good bet. Victorian houses can still be purchased for a fraction of their renovated value. Federal and state governments offer tax benefits and subsidies in certain cases. And, in this era of volatile economics, financing an old home has become easier than obtaining a mortgage on a new dwelling.

Emotional attachments to Victorian homes can be strong as well. Some people have a nostalgia for the house where grandma lived. Others love the lofty ceilings, spacious rooms, and majestic fireplaces of those grand madams.

House renovation isn't for everyone, however, and there are compelling reasons to avoid it. Weigh them carefully. Rehabilitating a Victorian home takes a lot of time, work, and (no matter how much labor you do yourself) a certain amount of money. Renovation never proceeds as quickly as you planned, and, during the process, you will find yourself wistfully coveting your friends' new (and completed) homes.

What you have envisioned as a project soon becomes a way of life. Renovating an old home means dirt under your fingernails (what's left of them); tools, nails, and electrical paraphernalia bulging from your purse or pockets; sawdust in your hair; paint specks on your glasses; and plaster dust everywhere. It means returning home to such unpleasant surprises as several inches of water on the kitchen floor. It often means poor plumbing, inadequate wiring, and nonexistent heating. Treasure hunts for rare fixtures and hardware can be fun, but if you have to scour a dozen plumbing stores before you find that essential, obsolete washer, the treasure hunt disintegrates into a frustrating search for the holy grail.

Consider the challenge one Maryland couple faced:

> Soon after we were married, Nancy and I had the opportunity to purchase an old house and a few acres. The house had not been cared for properly for about 15 years, and needless to say, was in rather poor condition. There was no heating or septic system, the water pipes had all burst during previous winters, only three electrical outlets worked, windows had been broken, and the front porch floor had rotted into oblivion. The lawn had become a tall pasture and the shrub border consisted of lilacs supported primarily by honeysuckle, brambles, and poison ivy.
>
> In thinking back, I believe the main reason we fell in love with this place was because it had been neglected so long.[1]

Definitely crazy. But, then, when you're hooked, you're hooked.

A single volume cannot begin to relate everything there is to know about Victorian houses and house renovation. I hope you will use this book as a springboard and consult the resources mentioned throughout for in-depth study in areas of interest to you.

ACKNOWLEDGMENTS

This book is the outgrowth of the many hours I have spent digging for answers to the problems and tasks I faced renovating my own Victorian-era houses. During this quest, I not only gathered a wealth of knowledge, but also came to know an even greater wealth of people who love and have owned or worked on Victorian-era houses. These people—grandfathers of friends, acquaintances of acquaintances, retired craftspersons—have imparted to me tidbits of knowledge and nearly lost skills. They have made this book possible and unique.

The book wouldn't be complete without the input of Sean Fitzpatrick, a contractor who has worked on scores of old-house renovations in central and northern California. Sean's comments and philosophy run throughout this book, from the analyses of Victorian social customs to demolition techniques to wallpapering. Specifically, his expertise is the foundation for the chapters on tools; siding; working with a contractor; appeasing the building inspector; and roofs, gutters, and eaves. He also made significant contributions to the chapters on plumbing, electricity, heating, painting, structural integrity, and moving houses.

Despite my six years of renovation experience, I learned a lot working with Sean on this book. He has gently mocked me at times for not knowing about a particular material or technique—or for spending hours on a task that would have taken him only a few minutes. More than once I learned from him—after the fact—how I should have done a particular job. Behind the respect I have developed for Sean is my conviction that, even though he earns his living renovating old houses, his motivation emanates from a commitment to doing a job the right way—a commitment tempered with a genuine appreciation of old materials and craftsmanship and a sensitivity to preserving each house's individual character and heritage. If you work with a pro, don't settle for less.

Many of the photographs in this book were taken by John Burrows of Bradbury and Bradbury Wallpapers. I feel a deep gratitude towards John and towards Bruce Bradbury (mentor of Bradbury and Bradbury and self-proclaimed Victorian wallpaper fanatic) for their information and assistance.

I would also like to thank Mac the Antique Plumber (who could always manage to find that obsolete washer); Ken Marr of Marr-Schaefer Associates; Michael Mattis, editor of the "California Life" section of the *Sacramento Bee*; Dave Whitlock, proprietor of the Moulding Mart; Marion Mitchell-Wilson of the California State Office of Historic Preservation; David R. Simmons of the Insurance Information Institute; Nancie West Swanberg, the book's illustrator; Frederick W. Stephenson; and Brian Reardon, alias Jack the Stripper.

Thanks also to Kathryn Lehman, my typist and also my oldest friend, and to John A. Tosney, my husband, for their support and infinite patience; and to Ted Knight, my father, who printed the photographs for the book.

And finally, I wish to dedicate this book to my dear friend, Lori McMahan, who has given me motivation and glasses of wine—and whose beautifully renovated 1889 Queen Anne home has been a constant inspiration to me.

Historical Perspective

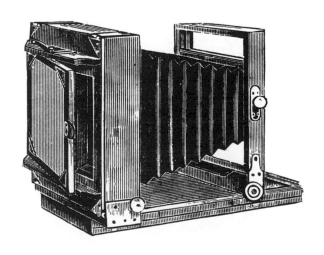

PART I

CHAPTER 1

Victorian Domestic Architecture

Victorian architecture ranges from the opulence of the antebellum Southern mansions to the austerity of the bungalow; from the symmetry of the Greek Revivals to the cacaphony of the Queen Annes. Despite their variations, row houses, Stick houses, Gothic Revivals, and Craftsmans are all "Victorians": homes built from 1837 through 1901, during the reign of Queen Victoria in Britain.

Just how many original Victorian houses have survived is presently unknown, although the preservation movement and federal subsidies have prompted local resource surveys, which the bureaucrats hope will yield reliable figures "by around 1989."

The Victorian period in this country, in the opinion of many, is an architectural embarrassment. Books on great American architecture gloss over it with a bland paragraph or two; architects change the subject in conversation.

This, though, is not a book about great American architecture. If it were, it would dwell on mansions. The majority of Victorian homes—those you or I would be likely to renovate—are common peoples' dwellings: row houses and company houses, homes of bureaucrats and bankers, shopkeepers and accountants.

The Victorian period was one of staggering growth and development. The American population grew from 17 to 50 million people, twelve states were admitted to the Union, and the Civil War was fought. Technology mushroomed, yielding such inventions as electricity, the railroad, the telephone, the steam and internal combustion engines, running water, and central heating.

When Victoria Regina received her crown in Britain in 1837, formally marking the beginning of the Victorian era, the United States was still fighting its reputation as a bunch of squabbling ex-

colonies with nothing but a paper alliance. A wave of patriotism and a desire for unity that had been brewing since the beginning of the nineteenth century would soon develop into a full-blown nationalism, complete with American heroes, legends, songs, flags, and monuments.

Consistent with this, American architects discarded traditional Colonial styles (saltbox, Georgian, Federalist), which they believed were British influenced, seeking instead a uniquely American style. Consequently, beginning in the 1820s, the Greek Revival style came into prominence. Greece was a kindred democracy, and, as Thomas Jefferson's home at Monticello showed, was an embodiment of grace, purity, harmony, and democratic ideals (designed in 1771, Monticello served as the model for the Greek Revivals). Although not exclusively an American phenomenon (Greek Revival houses were built in England and Europe also), Americans touted the style as exclusively their own.

The Greek Revival style was simple and uncluttered and could be readily replicated in wood, brick, or stone. The classic Greek Revivals are the huge, opulent mansions in the East and on the Southern plantations. These resemble Greek temples, with massive porticos and columns. Many lower- and middle-class dwellings were also rendered in the Greek Revival style. These maintain the proportions and harmony of their splendid counterparts, but are often completely unadorned.

The Greek Revival style enjoyed several decades of exclusive popularity, but, by the middle of the nineteenth century, the United States was ready for a change of style. Critics challenged that the temple style of architecture was unsuited for residential dwellings and should be reserved for public buildings.

An attack on the exclusive use of the Greek order in the building trades came from Andrew Jackson Downing, an American architect and landscape specialist. Downing stressed the architectural contributions of many different cultures. He praised Greece for order, Egypt for exoticism, Roman architecture for power and grandeur, and Renaissance styles for splendor, wealth, and sophistication. Downing's philosophy, espoused in *Cottage Residences* (1842) and *The Architecture of Country Houses* (1846), called for harmony, beauty, and truth in architecture, and for an integration of the house and its surroundings.

America was expanding her horizons, as a result of improved methods of communication and transportation. Trade with Asia and the Middle East was initiated. Admiral Perry's treaty with Japan in 1854 kindled interest in the Orient. Exotic goods from around the world and tales of exciting and hitherto unknown places influenced fad and fashion.

Subsequently, American architectural fashion simply exploded to include Downing-inspired "revivals" of nearly every international style and tradition. This trend seemed less a product of historical reverence than a mania for eclecticism and uniqueness. In 1850, for example, Philadelphia sported an Egyptian jail, a Greek bank, medieval cottages, and Moorish churches. What other period could create a Jewish synagogue with a Gothic tower and Greek columns?

Downing himself preferred the Gothic Revival style, with its tall gables and medieval-inspired tracery that was easily translated into wood or wrought iron. The Gothic influence permeated Victorian architecture, and many characteristics—particularly the steep gables and "gingerbread"—are found in various styles until the turn of the century.

Sharing the mid-century limelight with Downing and his disciples (who were identified as members of the Hudson River school of architecture) were two European-inspired styles, both contemporary renditions of Renaissance architecture. The Italianate style, derived from sixteenth- and seventeenth-century Italian villas, took many forms in residential architecture. In the 1850s and 1860s, Italianate details (cupolas, bracketing, quoins, and cornices) were frequently added to essentially boxlike structures reminiscent of the Greek Revivals.

Italianate villas, rendered usually for wealthy suburbanites, featured tall, flat-topped towers and cupolas. Later, in the 1870s and 1880s, the style sprouted five-sided slanted bay windows, which are considered a hallmark of later Italianates.

The Mansard style (also known as the Second Empire or French Academic style) was a revival of a French seventeenth-century style. Reputedly first inspired by an addition to the Louvre Museum in Paris, Mansard is named after the French architect François Mansart (who reached the peak of his career in 1650) and his nephew Jules Hardouin Mansart, the latter of whom was commissioned in the 1670s to extend and adorn the Palace of Versailles for Louis XIV. The unusual roof design of the Mansard style is its distinguishing characteristic: the house has an entire story above its eaves. During the seventeenth century, French property taxes were assessed according to the number of stories a house had, with the exception of the attic area, which was exempt. The Mansard style afforded a way of adding a story of living space to a house—tax free.

By the 1860s, the United States had turned out some powerful architects, including William Morris Hunt; Henry Hudson Holly; the firm of McKim, Mead, and White; and Henry Hobson Richardson. Richardson, especially, made an impact upon Victorian architecture. His huge, castlelike buildings, constructed of massive fieldstones, became known as Richardsonian Romanesques. Residential use

This pattern, from Andrew Jackson Downing's Cottage Residences, *shows a typical Gothic-style cottage. Downing's volumes contained not only illustrations and floor plans for actual houses but also offered philosophy on architecture and advice on furnishing, decorating, and landscaping.*

of this style predominated in the East and Midwest, where stone is less costly and more abundant than in other regions, but the style was used widely throughout the country for public buildings.

The Stick style developed during the 1870s. These houses were characterized by thin, ornamental wooden strips that outline the structural framing of the house. Although probably rooted in the revival movement, the Sticks developed independently of it. The exact origin of the Stick style is debated, but it resembles English half-timbering, French country cottages, and Swiss chalets.

The wave of Victorian eclecticism reached its epitome during the 1880s and 1890s with the Queen Anne style. Originated by Britain's Richard Norman Shaw, this style was based on English middle-class architectural fashion during the reign of Queen Anne (1702–14). It represented a veritable fruit salad of almost every known material, architectural characteristic, and mode of embellishment. At first severely denounced—critics warned that Queen Anne houses would depreciate the land on which they were built—the style ultimately flourished.

The demand for housing was tremendous throughout the Victorian era. The wealthy sought more and more opulence. High Victorian, or Chateauesque, homes were built for these magnates. These houses were imposing dwellings of immense proportions that really have no middle-class counterparts. The burgeoning middle class, however, demanded elegance and style at affordable prices. Many of the large railroad and manufacturing companies built fashionable homes for their higher-level employees.

Industrialism created a market for cheap labor, and the poor, tired, huddled masses immigrated from Europe, Asia, and the Orient to make their fortunes or escape political or religious persecution. During the 1850s, for example, 130,000 Irish came to Boston. Many of the immigrants (and many natives, as well) could not afford the down payments to purchase homes, and multifamily dwellings were erected to house them.

The Civil War had taken its toll of buildings, and Reconstruction gave the South a hefty share of Victorian houses. Fires, such as those that devastated Chicago in 1871 and Boston in 1872, necessitated major reconstruction of towns throughout the country. The Gold Rush drew hundreds of thousands of people—all of whom needed shelters—West.

Land in large cities was appreciating so rapidly as a result of this building boom that many homeowners in eastern cities sold relatively new homes for profit to real estate entrepreneurs who then razed or moved the buildings and subdivided the lots for several smaller houses. This was a rich harvest for speculative builders, but it also gave rise to the first large-scale slums in the country. Real estate companies flourished, though, and profit was the name of the game. In the cities where land was scarce, hundreds and hundreds of row houses—each touching its neighbors' walls—were built. These were primarily mass-produced and often had identical floor plans: the first tract homes, so to speak.

By the late 1870s America and much of the rest of the world was saturated with Victorian pretense and excess. It was time for a change. The Aesthetic, or Arts and Crafts, Movement had arisen, entreating a return to naturalness and simplicity. This movement, which began in Britain, was evangelical in nature and sought to enlighten the masses about what its proponents believed to be good taste. Critic and writer Oscar Wilde, for example, traveled throughout the United States, lecturing about the Arts and Crafts Movement and securing converts.

One of the chief spokesmen for the Arts and Crafts principles was English architect Charles Locke Eastlake, whose book of new furniture styles, *Hints on Household Taste* (1868 and 1872), was an outstanding success in the United States. Although the furnishings in Eastlake's book are still ornate by today's standards, they represented a welcome departure from the extremely ornamented earlier Victoriana.

An Eastlake chair, from Hints on Household Taste.

Eastlake's popularity, however, took an ironic turn in the West, where the carvings and decorations from his furniture were copied liberally and were used as exterior house ornamentation. This practice was a perversion of Eastlake's precepts—he advocated simplifying dwellings and furnishings, not embellishing them—but aspiring real estate developers and house owners who perhaps misunderstood Eastlake's philosophy were determined to capitalize on a fad. A mania developed on the West Coast for sawn and incised wood ornamentation "in the Eastlake tradition."

Eastlake was horrified at the westerners' use of his decorations, denouncing it in a letter in the *California Architecture and Building News:*

> I now find, to my amazement, that there exists on the other side of the Atlantic an "Eastlake" style of architecture, which, judging from the [California] specimens I have seen illustrated, may be said to burlesque such doctrines of art as I have ventured to maintain. . . . I feel greatly flattered by the popularity which my books have attained in America, but I regret that their author's name should be associated there with a phase of taste in architecture and industrial arts with which I can have no real sympathy and which by all accounts seems to be extravagant and bizarre.[2]

So numerous were houses bespangled in this fashion that "Eastlake" is erroneously referred to by some authors as an architectural style. Actually, Eastlake-inspired ornamentation was perhaps first added to Queen Anne houses, but the development companies soon adopted a style adapted for economy and speed of construction: the Italianate slanted bay window was reduced to a more economical flat, three-sided version, and was combined with the gables and the eclectic ornamentation of the Queen Annes. Like the Stick-style houses, flat wooden strips outlined the structural framing of the house, giving this "style" its proper name: Stick-Eastlake or San Francisco Stick.

Virtually all parts of a Stick-Eastlake house were machine made, and the Stick and Eastlake types of ornamentation consisted of simple, mass-produced wood strips and baubles, often used to conceal mediocre construction.

Raw materials were cheap and plentiful during the Victorian era, but labor was scarce and expensive.

Traditional mortise and tenon construction required six to eight people to raise. Each story first had to be entirely assembled on the ground, then raised into place with ropes and pulleys. The new balloon-frame construction (made possible during the mid-nineteenth century by the development of inexpensive, machine-made nails and mass lumber milling techniques) required only three or four men. A San Francisco Stick house could be constructed in hours.

Although probably not what the early architects had envisioned, the San Francisco Stick was perhaps the first true American architectural style. It was the logical outcome of the combination of early Victorian styles, the sociological changes created by massive urban growth, and the development of manufacturing technology.

The Philadelphia Centennial Exposition of 1876 had a profound impact upon American Victorian taste, spawning a patriotic nostalgia that enveloped the country and resulted in the revival of the Colonial Federalist and Georgian styles. During the 1880s, also, the Shingle style emerged. It was a simpler, less formal version of the Queen Annes, and bore a resemblance to early Colonial rural architecture. So prevalent was the use of natural or dark-stained wood shingle cladding in this and other subsequent styles that the late nineteenth and early twentieth centuries were termed "the brown decades."

Later pattern books lacked the moral essays of Downing and his contemporaries but offered more complete house patterns, including sections, elevations, and even specifications for decorative trim.

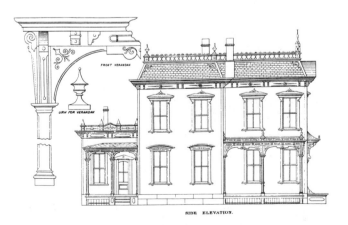

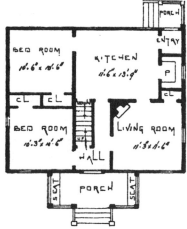

Above: *A plan, from Palliser's* American Architecture *(1888). The house in the photograph was built from this plan in Dell Rapids, South Dakota. (Photograph by John Burrows.)*

During the last decade of Queen Victoria's reign, ornateness gave way to austere simplicity and ostentation changed to conservatism, in keeping with the principles of the Arts and Crafts Movement.

Until the late 1880s, American architectural fashion emanated from the East Coast and Chicago, but thereafter the West—ridiculed only a few years earlier for its so-called lack of taste—would, along with Frank Lloyd Wright's Prairie school, become the architectural trendsetter.

The Craftsman style, developed at the end of the nineteenth century by the Bay Tradition that included architects Bernard Maybeck, Ernest Coxhead, and Julia Morgan, was a radical deviation from its predecessors. Homes were built on a horizontal, rather than a vertical, plane; and they featured simple, uncluttered decoration using natural hand-carved wood and leaded glass. These homes were also engineered to harmonize with the California climate: they were built on posts several inches above the ground to allow the air to flow underneath them. Wide, overhanging eaves protected the interiors from hot summer rays. Picture windows encompassing California's vistas let the warming winter sunlight inside the house; windows were opened during the summer months for fresh air circulation.

In Los Angeles, architects Charles and Henry Greene popularized another new style: the bungalow. These single-story houses, with low-pitched roofs and wide verandas, had their origins in India and Ceylon, and the name "bungalow" is an Anglicization of "Bengali." Although high-priced versions of the bungalow were built for wealthy clients, this was essentially a middle-class house style, and once it caught on (which took more time in the cold-climate East than in other places), this "home for the masses" retained its popularity for decades.

RECOGNIZING VICTORIAN STYLES

Naming and precise dating of individual Victorian-era styles is often difficult—as difficult as attaching labels to modern middle-class dwellings can be. The dates for some styles may vary by as many as twenty years, so any dates given for Victorian architecture should be used as guidelines only.

Until the last decade of the nineteenth century, when West Coast architecture came into its own,

American architectural styles developed on the East Coast and in Chicago and traveled south and west, often along railroad or riverboat lines. Several years were often required for a style to take hold, and many "transitional" versions appeared in the interim.

Construction materials also differed in different parts of the country, and styles were translated into the vernacular materials that were popular and available in each particular area. Builders in the East and Midwest preferred traditional stone and masonry; in New York between 1830 and 1860, hundreds of homes were built from the field-stones that had been left in the wake of prehistoric glaciers. Building with cobblestones was a fad in Michigan, Illinois, and Wisconsin. Another popular material on the East Coast was brownstone: brown-colored sandstone applied over brick. Redwood emerged in the West as a cheap, abundant resource. Ornamental ironwork was produced almost exclusively in the industrial North after the Southern iron foundries closed during the Civil War, but it was shipped throughout the country.

Actually, there is an impressive amount of standardization of Victorian architectural styles, con-sidering the vastness of the United States. Although this was partly a product of communication and transportation systems developed during the nineteenth century, it was due also to the popular house-pattern books that were published during the Victorian era. These incorporated illustrations of finished houses, floor plans, sections, elevations, and even suggestions for interior finishing and decorating. Among the best known are Downing's volumes, which have been reprinted by Dover Press; Orson Squires Fowler's *A Home for All,* 1848, which created a fad for octagons (this book has also been reprinted by Dover); George and Charles Palliser's *Model Homes* (1878), *American Cottage Homes* (1878), and *New Cottage Homes and Details* (1887)—all reprinted by the American Life Foundation in one volume entitled *The Palliser's Late Victorian Architecture*—and Thomas Walter's *200 Designs for Cottages and Villas* (1848).

The architectural-parts catalogs were companions to these house-plan books. Owners and builders could order prefabricated house parts and orna-mentation, and thereby create houses from bits and pieces out of these books.

THE GREEK REVIVALS (1820–50) Right: *A classic Greek Revival, this house on St. Charles Street in New Orleans, Louisiana, features large columns; a wide portico; a wide, flat gable; a prominent pediment; and a massive yet symmetrical form.*

Above: *This relatively simple farmhouse in Walworth County, Wisconsin, is a middle-class Greek Revival. It is symmetrical, with small columns over a modest portico suggesting its Classical heritage. (Photograph by John Burrows.)*

GOTHIC REVIVAL/CARPENTER GOTHIC (1885–80) Left: *A characteristic Gothic Revival cottage in Ferndale, California. Note the steeply pitched gable, pointed arches, lancet windows, finial, and ornamental bargeboard. Decorative tracery, copied originally from medieval tracery, was often translated in these houses into iron or wood; the latter made good use of the newly developed power band saw and jigsaw. (Gothic Revival frame houses decorated with wood are often known as Carpenter Gothics.)*

THE ITALIANATES *These three very different houses are all Italianates. An early version of the Italianate style (right) is this essentially boxlike structure in New Haven, Connecticut, crowned with a cupola, which was a common characteristic of the more opulent Italianates.*

Below left: A paradigm Italianate villa house located in Galena, Illinois. Note the wide brackets under the eaves and the tall, flat-topped tower.

A hallmark of later Italianate houses, such as this example in central California (below right), is the five-sided bay window, which often adorned the fronts and sides of the house; these either extended to the ground or were supported by a bracket (the latter are known as oriel bay windows). (Photographs at left and upper right by John Burrows.)

THE MANSARDS (1860–80) Left: *The sole characteristic of a Mansard house is its roof, which, irrespective of any other styling or ornamentation on the house, gives it its name. The specific shape of the roof may be square, curved, or conical. Most Mansards also feature dormer windows; all have a full story above the eaves. (Photographs by John Burrows.)*

THE STICK STYLE (1865–90) Below: *This style derives its name from the vertical, horizontal, and diagonal stickwork that adorns the outside of the house, suggesting the structural framing. This house is located in Dell Rapids, South Dakota. (Photograph by John Burrows.)*

SAN FRANCISCO STICK/STICK EASTLAKE (1885–1900). Above: *Essentially a West Coast phenomenon, these San Francisco houses are characterized by their flat, three-sided bay windows, "stickwork," and by the ornamentation copied from furniture designed by Sir Charles Locke Eastlake.*

RICHARDSONIAN ROMANESQUE (1860–95) Left: *Richardsonian houses, exhibiting French, Spanish, and Roman influences, are instantly recognizable by the large earth-colored fieldstones used in constructing them. Other features include huge porches, crenelation, turrets, and massive fireplaces; Richardsonian homes are often emblazoned with gargoyles. This house pictured above is located in Sioux City, Iowa. (Photograph by John Burrows.)*

THE QUEEN ANNES (1880–95) *This home in Sacramento, California (right) is a classic Queen Anne, with tall, pointed gables; a turret; a recessed porch; stained glass; turned wood ornamentation; and combinations of different sidings on the exterior.*

The middle-class version (far right) is simpler and less adorned than its opulent counterpart, but retains the wood ornamentation, decorative shingles, and tall pitched gables that characterize it as a Queen Anne.

HIGH VICTORIAN/CHATEAU-ESQUE (1870–90) *This was really an upper-class style: a huge, massive house built with ostentation for the very wealthy, a tribute to the excesses that could be achieved with money. There were High Victorian examples of many different styles of the era: Gothic (such as the house on the right in Washington, D.C.), Richardsonian, Stick, and Queen Anne (such as the house on the far right, in Eureka, California). (Photograph at left by John Burrows.)*

SHINGLE (1885–1900) *Many Shingle-style houses resemble stripped-down versions of Queen Annes, devoid of ornamentation and totally clad, roof and sides, in brown shingles. It was also perhaps the first Victorian-era style to utilize natural, unfinished wood.*

COLONIAL REVIVAL (1880–1900) *There were essentially two different types of Colonial Revival houses, although the style actually incorporated facets of various different architecture styles that were popular from 1776 to 1820. One type, shown above (in Sacramento, California), adopted Georgian, Federalist, and Greek Revival elements; huge mansions (the Beaux-Arts Revivals) in this mode were built for the very rich. Distinguishing characteristics include fanlights, regular symmetry, columns, and pilasters. The other type of Colonial Revival resembles the saltbox and Dutch Colonial styles, with tall pointed or gambrel roofs.*

CRAFTSMAN (1895–1910) *A style representing a wide deviation from its predecessors. Note the use of natural wood; wide, overhanging eaves; simple, rusticated styling; large picture windows; and a low profile in this house in Berkeley, California.*

THE BUNGALOW (1895–1925) *These small informal houses (Sacramento, California)—the mass-produced version of the Craftsman house—have low-pitched roofs; broad, gabled front porches; and wide, overhanging eaves. Built on a raised foundation, the bungalow is usually only one story high, rarely more than two.*

ROW HOUSES *In the cities, nearly every Victorian style was translated into row houses. Above are examples from San Francisco, California (*Queen Annes, *left and center), and Washington, D.C. (right). (Photograph at right by John Burrows.)*

A Queen Anne house with Greek Revival columns, Dubuque, Iowa. (Photograph by John Burrows.)

An octagonal house in Wisconsin. (Photograph by John Burrows.)

A Mansard house? No, it's an Italianate; the Mansard roof on this house, built in the 1850s in Sacramento, California, was added some twenty years after initial construction.

Many Victorian-era houses, especially those built during the last quarter of the nineteenth century, were not really any recognizable style, but were built for comfort in whatever manner was least expensive, such as this "vernacular Victorian" in rural central California.

A Moorish arch on an Italianate porch, California.

CHAPTER 2

Victorian Interiors

The early and middle Victorian eras were characterized by a preference for classical French furniture and decorative styles. Exceptions, however, were found in houses built in the revival styles. Owners often attempted to decorate these to correspond with the particular period, such as medieval-like furnishings for Gothic Revival houses.

Imitation was the byword of mid-Victorian interior design and many materials were treated to look like what they were not. *Graining* and *marbleizing* were two common imitations. In graining, one kind of wood (often fir) was painted with a different grain—even fake knotholes—to resemble different kinds of wood. Marbleizing is a technique of painting wood or cast iron to resemble marble.

In England, a revolution in design known as the Arts and Crafts or Aesthetic Movement—began brewing in the 1860s. During the 1880s, the Aesthetic Movement broke forth on both sides of the Atlantic, severely denouncing the imitations, excesses, and pretense of the Victorian era.

The Aesthetic principles were gradually accepted in interior (as well as exterior) house fashion. Natural and finished woods replaced graining and marbleizing; wallpaper patterns were drawn from

nature. Simple and comfortable furniture replaced the carved. By the turn of the century, interior fashion had done a complete about-face, becoming so plain and simple that it was practically austere.

INTERIOR COLORS AND STYLES

The interiors of the American Victorian-era home developed along the same lines as the evolution of nineteenth-century architectural styles, although architectural innovation preceded interior fashion throughout the era.

The old-house owner has a wealth of different styles from which to choose, since perhaps no other period of history has featured as wide a diversity of furnishing styles, colors, modes, and moods (see Chapter 25 for a discussion of Victorian use of color). And because much of the Victorian sense of style revolved around eclecticism, even ultramodern furnishings can successfully blend with Victorian architecture. It's up to you.

Following is a rough list to help you determine how the rooms in your house were originally decorated. Remember that, as with architectural styles, pure paradigms rarely existed, and styles

Above: *"Eastlake" sofa from* Hints on Household Taste.
Left: *Patterns designed by Dr. Christopher Dresser, characteristic of Arts and Crafts styling.*

PERIOD/STYLE	PREVALENT COLORS	SIGNIFICANT DECOR/FURNISHINGS
Greek Revival	Green and white (exteriors), pastels and beiges (interiors).	Rosewood and marble (early houses), wallpaper, gilding, ornamental plasterwork, stenciling.
Downing Revivals	Earth colors—rust, greens, browns, ochre—for both interiors and exteriors.	Furnishings generally matched the type of revival; graining and wainscoting popular; wallpaper, stenciling.
High Victorian (Mansard/Italianate)	Rich reds, browns, purples, peacock blue—often many colors were mixed in one room.	Graining and marbleizing, ornate furnishings, heavy upholstery and draperies, wallpaper, stenciling, carpeted floors, decorative tile.
Queen Anne/Richardsonian, Romanesque/Colonial Revivals	Generally same colors as High Victorian period—some trend towards lighter shades.	Stained glass, more use of natural wood dadoes and boxed-in beams, fad for Oriental furnishings, screens and murals, wallpaper, area rugs, decorative tile.
Brown Decades (Shingle/Craftsman), Bungalows	Greens, rusts, browns, ochres, and other earth tones; white and cream colors towards the end of the century.	More subdued and sparsely furnished, use of natural wood (oak or redwood, especially); later styles featured wicker and bamboo furniture, earlier styles used dignified Mission-style furniture; small area rugs, linoleum, decorative tile.

were most often mixed and blended. Also, the Victorians, eager for the latest fads and fashions, loved to redecorate, and the interior of your house probably underwent a series of "modernizations"—even when first built.

LIVING SPACE

The word parlor derives from the French *parler,* to speak, and the parlor has signified, for at least seven or eight centuries, a room where "parleys" take place. The origin of the Victorian parlor fad is uncertain. A. J. Downing's volumes label the living spaces in large villas "drawing rooms" and those in small cottages "parlors." Wherever it came from, by 1860, virtually every house had—or claimed to have—its parlor.

One of the chief social pastimes during the 1860s was socializing, and callers were usually received into the parlor. Each individual of any social stature whatever—real or pretended—had his or her own calling card: a small white or ivory card engraved with the person's name—the forerunner of modern business cards.

In most of the modest Victorian homes, the parlor was the only room available for socializing, and it had to suffice for every occasion from large parties to intimate twosomes. Small groups of chairs, tables, and sofas dotted the room, creating conversation areas to accommodate many people

or just small gatherings. One parlor could have as many as twenty different types of lamps (table, floor, hanging, wall sconces), and this versatility provided an almost infinite variety of lighting combinations.

The parlor flaunted all the period's fads and fashions: elaborately arranged flowers, musical instruments, early photographs, figurines, trinkets under glass domes. Here, too, the women of the house displayed needlework, paintings, and shell pictures.

The Victorian era represented a transition from the "olden times" to the modern era of mechanization, mass production, and transglobal travel. Not everyone could be an inventor or an explorer, but anyone could have a parlor to display the latest mechanized toys, silks brought from India, or (for the brazen) fossils supporting the theories of Charles Darwin. Expanding travel and trade brought rugs, curios, screens, and paintings from the Orient, the Middle East, and Asia. The affluent bought these treasures to display in their parlors; the middle class dauntlessly followed suit with a plethora of copies rendered, not always successfully, by enterprising domestic manufacturers.

Some houses had two parlors: a front parlor (open to anyone) and a rear parlor (reserved for more intimate acquaintances). Because the parlor was usually so elaborately furnished and decorated, it was often painted and papered with a lighter, simpler color scheme than other rooms.

By the 1870s, the parlor had become so excessively cluttered that it became an object of ridicule:

> Most people who live in the country have experienced the discomfort of being "received" into a cottage parlor [by] a polite village hostess. . . . She insists on her visitor having the honor of sitting on the sofa, covered with horsehair, and the privilege of seeing the precious bugle mats and the stuffed weazel [sic]. Those who laugh at her mistaken notion of hospitality often subject their own visitors to a precisely similar ordeal, though their sofa cushions may be covered with yellow satin and their tables set out with Paris knickknacks.[3]

After 1876, the Aesthetic/Arts and Crafts Movement grew, and proponents chose the parlor as a primary target, for it embodied everything they detested about the Victorian era: pretense, cheap imitations, clutter, eclecticism, vanity, and lack of taste.

By this time, entertaining had also become less important, and fewer people "went calling"—especially since many homeowners were working-class people with little spare time. If the women of the house did not work, they were usually busy with domestic issues and civic reforms—some even went to college! The house was becoming a sanctuary for the family, rather than a showplace to impress others. Perhaps this is why the parlor eventually evolved into the "living room," where the family could relax together: comfortable, sparsely furnished, often with large windows, books, and a radio.

EVOLUTION OF THE BATHROOM

Although cleanliness, hygiene, and hot and cold running water are taken for granted by modern America, only during the last century has bathing really become an accepted and common practice here. Colonial America considered bathing to be hazardous to the health (and it may well have been since houses were cold and drafty). Many communities, incited by conservative Puritans who protested the fact that bathing requires nudity, even passed laws restricting or prohibiting bathing. The Victorian era, however, saw a reversal in the attitudes towards bathing. This was due partly to growing knowledge about germs and human health and the role dirt plays in carrying and causing diseases.

Cleanliness became important years before running water was common in America. Bathrooms became status symbols for the few who were wealthy enough to afford them. In 1851, the first bathroom in the White House was installed by President Millard Fillmore. Those first bathrooms—"boudoirs"—were actually converted bedrooms and were usually located adjacent to the bedroom

A typical mid-nineteenth-century parlor. Note the proliferation of furniture, decorations, and knickknacks. (Photograph courtesy of the University of California, Berkeley, Bancroft Library.)

A turn-of-the-century Arts and Crafts living room. Furnishings are sparse and rustic. Note the use of natural wood. (Photograph courtesy of the University of California, Berkeley, Bancroft Library.)

of the hostess of the house. Taking a bath in one of these early bathrooms must have been a delightfully relaxing and decadent experience: the bathtub, which was portable, reposed before the fire (for warmth), and the bather was invariably attended (and even bathed) by servants. The surroundings were ornate, with beautiful hand-carved and gilded furnishings, and decorated with rich silks and velvets and plants.

Most people could not afford this luxury, however, and they bathed in rude tin tubs set in the kitchen. City dwellers also usually had access to public baths (many of which were operated by reform groups), where, for five cents, a bather received a hot bath, complete with soap and towel.

Technological innovations in the 1860s and 1870s increased the popularity of the bathroom. In 1872, Thomas Crapper, an English inventor, introduced the flush toilet to the western world. Crapper didn't exactly invent the loo, since the Minoans had a version of it in 1100 B.C., but he is credited with the concept. Many of the original pull-chain "crappers" are still in use today. Among the fads of the day were custom-sculpted china toilet bowls, which often carried exquisite designs. A toilet bowl might be shaped like a fish or ornately sculpted with flowers or leaves.

Another important invention was the hot water heater, which usually sat in the kitchen and was prone to exploding. Rainwater was collected in a cistern on the rooftop of the house, then piped to a tank where it was heated by a coal-fed fire. Finally, mass-produced bathtubs, sinks, and toilets became readily available during the 1880s, enabling more and more households to afford private bathrooms.

The first shower

For the poor and much of the middle class, however, hot and cold running water remained a pipe dream, and until the 1900s, fewer than 20 percent of city houses, and even fewer rural dwellaings, had indoor plumbing. Many Victorian-era houses—especially those in the country—still have outhouses.

Most Victorian homes built before 1880 (and many built thereafter) had their plumbing added years after initial construction. Water and waste pipes were usually run up the back or side wall, and the bathroom, like the kitchen, was often located at the rear of the house.

Early bathrooms epitomized the Victorian penchant for modesty. Toilets were enclosed in cupboards, hence the term "water closet" (this was done also to shut off offensive and deadly sewer gas before P-traps—bends in either the bottoms of toilet bowls or in drainage pipes to trap the gas—were invented); marble-topped bureaus hid basins; wooden cabinets were specially constructed to encase piping.

Bathrooms in even the smallest city houses were pleasant. Chairs, sofas, and stained glass created a relaxing and inviting atmosphere. Floors were usually painted wood, and wainscoting, stenciling, and wallpaper were common wall treatments. Through the 1880s, fixtures were usually marble, although tin, copper, and other metals were used. Most bathrooms also had several mirrors, a footbath, scales, and a medicine chest.

Comfort was not as prevalent in rural areas, especially where winters were cold. Outhouses and even indoor bathrooms were seldom heated, and special "freeze toilets" were necessary. Water was activated in them only when someone sat on the toilet—so that water could not freeze solid in the bowl.

By the last two decades of the Victorian era, bathing was being touted as a cure-all for everything from liver ailments to melancholy. Doctors prescribed such bizarre bathing remedies as the "ascending douche bath" and the "electric light bath"; and many gullible patients had to purchase special bathing contraptions in which to take the "cure." Among these were the individual steam baths, which resembled huge tin cans. Many of the mineral baths, spas, hot springs, and mud baths enjoying current popularity were originally built during the Victorian era.

This renovated bathroom in San Francisco, California, is elegant and comfortable: the tub reposes before the fire (the original fir floor has been painted and stenciled); the sink sits in an ornate cupboard; the commode is hidden behind a screen and underneath a stained glass window.

The 1890s saw the beginning of a revolution in hygiene, and the bathroom became one of its first targets. Germ-conscious for the first time, society saw the bathroom as a primary transgressor: wooden floors that could trap moisture and dust and were difficult to clean were replaced with scrubbable ceramic tile (the small, hexagonal tiles were most common). Water pipes that had been so discreetly shut away in little cupboards were exposed so they could be cleaned; sinks were elevated on pedestals or legs; and bathtubs sprouted claw feet to raise them off the unsanitary floors. Polished porcelain enamel replaced marble. The bathroom, along with many other places in later Victorian homes, took on an antiseptic aura, resembling a hospital room: white walls, white fixtures, white floors—even white towels.

CREATING A "VICTORIAN-LOOKING" BATHROOM
Restoration purists may have a difficult time replicating the bathroom. Many Victorian-era homes had *no* bathroom, and who wants to restore the outhouse? Also, although anyone who has luxuriated in a footed bathtub will agree that it can't be beat, the first shower apparatus looks more like a torture chamber than a place of cleanliness and refreshment. Elegant fixtures in mansions built by the affluent may remain; in most cases, however, the bathroom has probably undergone several "remuddlings" to keep pace with modernization (a phrase coined by Clem Labine and the staff at the *Old-House Journal*). The earliest bathroom fixtures—many of which were uncomfortable, rudimentary, and inefficient—are rare and prohibitively expensive to replace. The claw-foot tubs and pedestal sinks of the late Victorian era are plentiful, however, since they were manufactured as late as the 1940s. These are currently enjoying a renaissance of popularity, and pull-chain toilets, wooden seats, and Victorian towel bars are being widely reproduced. Using a combination of reproductions and antiques, you can create an old-fashioned atmosphere that, although technically unauthentic, blends with the rest of a Victorian house.

Buying reproductions may also be, in the long run, more economical and practical than searching for antiques. This is especially true of old toilets (see Chapter 15), where buying a reproduction for $300–$700 may be more practical than spending that much on an antique perpetual headache.

Another beautiful touch (although again, not authentic) is to strip the plating from your plumbing fixtures. Most faucets, supply valves, drains, overflows, etc. made before 1950 are plated cast brass. Beneath that old, peeling chrome finish could be a beautiful, solid brass faucet. Check it with a magnet—brass does not attract it.

Have brass pieces stripped of their coatings at a commercial plating establishment. This is usually not expensive (about $10 to $20 per fixture) and it is too dangerous a process, involving strong acids, for the do-it-yourselfer.

Once the brass is stripped, it can be polished or given an "antique" finish (painted black, then wire brushed). Lacquering the pieces (spraying them with a clear finish) will retard tarnishing, as will rubbing the pieces with tung oil varnish. Lacquered or oiled brass is never as shiny as unlacquered pieces, however, and the brass will eventually tarnish, even under the protective coating.

THE VICTORIAN KITCHEN

The early Victorian kitchen is another room you might not want to replicate. Dark, gloomy, and dirty, it was frequently located in the basement, where cooking odors, grease, and soot would not bother the family. All but the poorest households had kitchen servants, who cooked on wood-burning

An early kitchen in New Orleans, Louisiana. This house was built with running water, an innovative phenomenon for the mid-nineteenth century, when the house was constructed. The sink and hot water heater (in the far right corner) are copper; cooking was done over the open fire. Probably only the servants ate in the kitchen, and the family was served in the dining room.

cast-iron stoves. Frequently, the dining room was served by a dumbwaiter: a shaft running from the basement to the first floor, with a platform on pulleys for hoisting food and dishes from the kitchen to the dining room.

Until the 1860s, little attention was accorded to kitchen fashion. Several factors, however, combined in the late nineteenth century to elevate the lowly kitchen from a dungeonlike servants' domain to the core of the household. The first was the loss of servants and slaves. After the Civil War, slavery no longer existed in the South, and indenture lost favor in the North. Fewer and fewer families could

afford to pay servants, and many of the growing class of middle-income homeowners were themselves serving people. Kitchen tasks, therefore, fell to the family. A second factor in the kitchen revolution was the development of gas and electric cooking ranges. Dirt and soot became less of a problem, and the kitchen could be located upstairs without fear of soiling the rest of the house. After the advent of plumbing, kitchens were often located at the rear of the house, near the pipes that usually ran up the back of the structure.

The acceptance of the kitchen onto the main floor of the house brought interest in its decoration and atmosphere. In 1869, Harriet Beecher Stowe and her sister, Catharine Beecher, wrote in *The American Woman's Home* that the kitchen should be the "core of the household" and should let the outside in as much as possible, using plants for decoration and eliminating curtains, which weren't necessary and which collected unsanitary dirt and grease.[4] Other suggestions the authors made included painting the walls and floors of the kitchen and placing food and pans on open shelving for convenience and attractiveness.

But the kitchen was still just a work place, decorated with dull, drab, institutional grays and greens, until 1876, when the first refrigerators appeared and the Philadelphia Centennial changed the kitchen in yet another way. At the exposition, a Revolutionary-era kitchen was displayed beside a "new, modern kitchen" to compare and laud the fruits of progress. Ironically, the American people, caught in a wave of patriotic nostalgia, preferred the Colonial kitchen, and fashion thereafter attempted to recreate this cozy room.

Less than fifty years later, the kitchen had changed dramatically, as evidenced by this award-winning room from a 1900 Ladies' Home Journal. Note the decorative touches, hanging utensils, and "new linoleum."

The Colonial Revival–style kitchens that evolved during the 1870s and 1880s were, like their predecessors, large, cheerful rooms, with fireplaces and colorful patterns. Other features included stenciling, hanging pot racks, and open shelving.

The role of the American woman also changed during this time, thanks to the contributions of manufacturing. Modern techniques emancipated her from such time-consuming tasks as making soap and cheese, canning, and butchering and curing meat. Elevated to a new position of authority, she became mistress of the kitchen, responsible for the family's health and nutrition. She also became the purchasing agent in the home, and prided herself in running an orderly, organized, and efficient household. She took special interest in the kitchen. Magazines such as the *Ladies' Home Journal, House Beautiful,* and *House and Garden* were published to give her ideas, apprise her of inventions for the home, and bring her into the mainstream of progress. At the turn of the century, she led the country in the campaign for cleanliness (and hundreds of other reforms) and began to move out into the world and demand her rights.

Unfortunately, the germ-conscious fin de siècle robbed the new Victorian kitchen of its open shelving, plants, and much of its charm. The turn-of-the-century kitchen, like the turn-of-the-century bathroom, was white and antiseptically clean.

THE BEDROOM

The bedrooms were the private areas of the Victorian house. They were individual domains, where the younger set kept their prized collections, where husband and wife shared intimacies, where lovesick youths went for solitude. Not ostentatious and showy like the parlor, nevertheless the master bedrooms and guest suites of the wealthy, in particular, were majestic and spacious.

In larger, early Victorian homes, the master bedroom suite included a separate "boudoir" or dressing room (the forerunner of the first bathrooms), where the lady of the house could rest, relax, and perform her "toilette." Even the smallest house had a boudoir corner, perhaps a dressing table screened off from the rest of the bedroom—well lit and complete with a washstand, a bowl, and a pitcher for water.

Children's bedrooms, on the other hand, even in the larger houses, were frequently plain and often sported cast-off furnishings and decorations from other rooms. The nursery was often adjacent to and connected by a door to the master bedroom.

During the mid-Victorian era, people began to realize the need for fresh air in the bedroom, and this dictated the way bedrooms were decorated. Fireplaces were important not only for winter warmth, but for ventilation as well. Curtains and draperies in the bedrooms tended to be of lighter weight than in other rooms, so air could enter through the windows. Fresh air, unfortunately, brought dirt with it, so bedroom decorations were usually scrubbable: woodwork and floors were painted, and wallpaper was varnished so walls could be scrubbed. Throw rugs were often used instead of area rugs.

Many Victorian bedrooms were built without closets. Where there were no closets, clothes were kept in large wardrobe chests or armoires. These pieces of furniture were often so large that they actually had to be constructed or assembled in the bedroom.

Victorian-era bedrooms invariably included some sort of table and chairs, a fainting couch (a couch built with only one arm, so that a lady feeling faint could easily fall upon it), or other furnishings where occupants could read, write, or just relax. Early bedroom furnishings, like those in other rooms of the house, were heavy, carved, ornate, and draped with valances. Later styles were light and airy and made of wicker, plain iron and brass, and simple oak.

A typical late nineteenth-century bedroom from a house (now demolished) in Portland, Oregon. (Photograph courtesy of the Portland Historical Society.)

DINING ROOMS AND HALLWAYS

THE DINING ROOM: CENTER OF FAMILY ACTIVITY
Throughout most of the Victorian era, while the parlor was reserved for entertaining and the kitchen was a servants' domain, the dining room was the center of family activity. As such, it was probably the precursor of the modern family room.

Parents and children usually came together only at mealtimes. The family would gather for breakfast and meet after the day was done to share their daily tribulations and anecdotes. Because of this impor-

A typical Queen Anne hall, with a decorative wood dado, wooden spindles on the transom, and stained glass. Note the conversation area, where the woman of the house could receive callers.

tant function, the *Ladies' Home Journal* and other women's magazines of the time preached that the dining room should be cheerful, light, warm, with a cozy fire, fresh flowers on the table, and bright colors used throughout to lend a gay atmosphere. Silverware and linens for the table were usually kept in a sideboard or china closet, especially in the early Victorian-era homes, where the kitchen was located at some distance from the dining room.

THE GREAT HALL: AN AMERICAN INNOVATION
Towards the close of the Victorian era, the use of space within the home had changed dramatically— a change that reflected not only an evolving American lifestyle, but an emerging uniquely American architecture. This change was manifested, among other ways, in the manner in which the rooms of the house were organized.

Gone was the need to copy English and other European styles. Henry Hobson Richardson (see Chapter 1) experimented with opening the living floor of the house. He connected the rooms on the main floor via archways—a unique departure from the European-derived custom of having each room a separate entity connected by long, narrow hallways. Richardson's rooms, which seemed to flow into each other, were usually joined by a large, coaxial hallway.

Many Queen Anne– and Colonial Revival–style houses boast great, Richardson-inspired hallways. They are large, usually paneled with wood dadoes, and often adorned with stained glass windows. Some have benches built into the space below the stairway to the upper floors, and there is often a conversation area with small tables and chairs. Some of the hallways in the larger houses boast huge, baronial fireplaces.

These large hallways were often used by the lady of the house, who, during a few hours each day, would receive drop-in visitors who'd stay for only a few minutes. Because little time was spent in either the dining room or in hallways, they were often decorated in bolder colors or with bolder prints than other areas of the house.

PART II

Before You Begin

CHAPTER 3

Buying The House

CHOOSING THE RIGHT LOCATION

My father maintains that the three most important considerations in any real estate investment are location, location, and location.

One of the financial enticements of renovating an old house is that you can purchase a relatively inexpensive house and, by putting some money, creativity, and a lot of sweat into it, turn it into a lucrative investment. To accomplish this, however, the house should be located in an area where it can realize an accelerated appreciation—for example, among other houses that are already renovated (and worth much more), or in a neighborhood that will undergo mass renovation in the next few years.

Obviously, Victorian-era houses do not grow everywhere, and this limits your choices. Many are, however, located in run-down neighborhoods where preservation programs will upgrade the neighborhood and multiply the value of the homes. On the other hand, you might purchase a house in a run-down area and spend time, money, and effort to renovate it, only to be left with a beautiful gem in a forever-derelict neighborhood—a house that will never return to you the money and effort you've invested.

Knowing which properties will appreciate is a subjective matter, based on intuition and familiarity with a geographical area and its political climate. Although each person has his/her own criteria, and only you can determine when you've found "the right buy," here are a few guidelines to use when assessing a neighborhood of old houses:

● Look for development and renovation in the area. The neighborhood should show some signs of recent improvement.

● Close proximity to low-income government housing and/or industrial and warehouse sites indicates that the neighborhood may remain low income.

● Know the area. If you're moving to a new city, take some time to familiarize yourself with the area and the local real estate market. Talk with other old-house owners for their viewpoints.

● Know the political climate. A strong historic preservation movement is evidenced by articles in local newspapers, active local historical societies, classes and lectures on historic preservation, and local government concern and involvement in historic preservation. Contact local historical societies, city planning departments, and state historic preservation officers (see Appendix C for a list of the latter).

● Play it safe. Don't be either the first or the last renovation project in the neighborhood. If you're the first, there is no guarantee the rest of the neighborhood will follow suit. If you're the last, chances are you are going to pay a top dollar, inflated price for the property.

WORKING WITH A REALTOR

A realtor who is knowledgeable about old houses and local renovation can be a boon, especially if you are unfamiliar with the area. S/he should be able to steer you towards good investment areas and tell you what neighborhoods to avoid. A realtor may also know people who would like to sell their homes but have not listed them.

Most realtors maintain communications with banks, savings and loan associations, and mortgage companies and can also advise you and help you seek financing for your house.

To locate a realtor knowledgeable about old houses, contact the local board of realtors or local historical and preservation societies and ask for referrals. Also, note on real estate signs agents who list Victorian-era houses.

A realtor also usually has access to a *multiple-listing book*, which shows pictures and gives specifications about properties listed for sale by the area's real estate firms. Many times this information is computerized, and the realtor can obtain in minutes a list of houses for sale in specific areas that are within your price range and that possess the characteristics you seek.

The multiple-listing book contains many additional statistics. It lists the houses that have sold in the recent past in a given area, including list prices and final sales prices, which will give you concrete price comparisons. In addition, the multiple-listing book indicates how long properties have been listed, which can help you judge whether to make an immediate offer on a piece of property (so someone else will not snap it up), or, if the property has sat on the market for a while, to wait and negotiate for a lower price.

Sometimes you can save money by purchasing a home directly from an owner, without the involvement of realtors, since a seller might raise the price of a house to cover the real estate commission.

If the seller has listed the house with a real estate agent, however, you should have your own agent to represent you, since the seller's agent is the seller's advocate—not yours. Also, having your own agent will not cost you, the buyer, anything, since the seller pays the real estate commission. The listing (seller's) agent will, if s/he has the chance, probably discourage you from having your own agent, since then s/he will have to split the commission with another realtor.

Also, for this same reason, if you are working with a realtor attempting to find a house, the realtor will attempt to interest you in the properties s/he has listed for sale. No matter whom s/he represents, any realtor is ultimately working for a commission, and, beyond that, owes no allegiance to you. Thus, as always, look out for your own interests—"buyer beware"—and make sure the terms of any purchase suit *you*.

After you have located a house you wish to buy, a realtor can be an important buffer between you and the seller. Buying a house involves myriad negotiations and paperwork—both in the offer/acceptance and escrow phases. If a realtor assumes these responsibilities for you, you can be free to make a thorough investigation of the house.

ASSESSING THE CONDITION OF THE HOUSE

You may believe you've found your dream house, but examine it carefully before you buy, so you'll know what major work will be required. One midwestern couple did not. The seller assured them that the house was "in great shape"—and they believed him and looked no further. One day, as the new owner was sitting on the toilet, it fell through to the story below—right into the kitchen sink—and he was left in a pile of debris, dishes, and dry rot. Some dream house.

If you do not feel comfortable making your own assessment, coax or hire a contractor to accompany you. S/he can also give you a rough estimate of how much it would cost to fix up the house. Make sure you assess the following:

● *Structural integrity* A certain amount of sagging and settling is to be expected in a Victorian-era house—you'll sag, too, when you're a centenarian. If the house requires a lot of structural work, however, renovation may not be worthwhile, since replacing or repairing the foundation or structural members is a major undertaking necessitating considerable expense.

● *Plumbing* Replumbing a house costs thousands of dollars and usually requires tearing out floors, walls, and ceilings.

● *Electrical system* As many as 70 percent of houses over fifty years old have inadequate or unsafe electrical systems. The cost of a total rewiring job may exceed $10,000.

● *Heating and cooling* Many houses have inadequate or nonexistent heating and cooling systems. Many options exist for adding new systems and living with old ones—check this out before you buy.

● *Termites and dry rot* Insist on a termite inspection, even if the seller will not pay to fix the damage. This will also give you some idea of the extent of dry rot in the house. Remember that a structural pest report only discloses visible insect and fungal damage, and usually contains disclaimers about hidden deterioration.

If you are in the market for a bargain fix-it-upper, you are bound to encounter these and many other problems. Anything can be fixed, repaired, or replaced—for a price. What you should know before you crash head-first into disaster (or, like our midwestern friend, rear-first into the kitchen sink) is what you're getting yourself into, and whether it falls within the price and headache ranges you are willing to endure. You may get a bargain—or more than you bargained for.

THE CONTRACT OF SALE

Don't expect a realtor to act as your attorney. Although many realtors are conversant with the legal terminology required to write an offer to purchase a house, you shouldn't expect them to know all the legal nuances and ramifications of a contract of sale. When you purchase a house, you enter into a legal contract; have an attorney look it over before you sign.

Unsuspecting house purchasers do not prepare themselves for the seller who guts the house before he or she moves out. When one of my friends moved into her old house, she discovered that the former owner had removed a wall air conditioner, an antique stove, windows, two light fixtures, the front gate, and the mailbox! Although these items rightly belonged with the house, and my friend could have sued, that would have required the time and expense of a lawsuit—meanwhile, the seller had moved out of state.

Many *deposit receipts* (offers to purchase property) state that fixtures that are on the premises shall remain with the house upon sale. Exactly what is "part of the house" may not be clear; when in doubt, specify in the contract of sale what is to remain. Some things you might want to retain:
- salvage materials and fixtures that are not installed but were originally part of the house.
- artifacts such as old bottles, magazines, documents, and photographs that date the house.
- building materials that you can use in the renovation.

CHAPTER 4

Getting Ready To Renovate

One of the joys of living in an old house is discovering and becoming a part of its heritage, for an old house is a living chronicle of all who have lived there and the love or neglect they gave the house.

Unearthing your house's past will help you determine what your house originally looked like: who built and lived in it, when and how it was remodeled, where the original walls stood, even what colors and fixtures were used. Additionally, whatever you discover about the house's previous owners, such as their occupations or the number of children they had, provides a good clue to the families who occupied the house, their social status, lifestyles, etc. From this information you can extrapolate how they decorated, furnished, and used the house.

THE INSIDE

The treasure hunt begins with the structure itself. For starters, to determine when your house was built, look for dates or manufacturers' names stamped on bricks, cast-iron pipes, and old plumbing fixtures (inside the tanks of old toilets, under the bathtub or sink drain). Every footed bathtub has the manufacturer's name and date stamped on it, usually on the bottom or back. Some knobs for old knob and tube wiring (Chapter 16) were installed with *date nails*: nails stamped with the last two digits of the year in which they were made.

Some indicators of remodelings are obvious: aluminum sash windows, aluminum siding, plastic pipes, conduit and cable wiring, and modern plumbing and lighting fixtures. Watch for such things as a parquet floor or a ceiling molding that is interrupted by a wall (which probably is not original), a door or window that does not match the others in the house, or closets that were tacked on to a bedroom (Victorians, for the most part, kept their clothes in armoires).

Many times you will pick up clues to your house's past while you are working on a room. I removed some floorboards in my attic to wire a ceiling fixture for a room below. Underneath the attic floor, I discovered not only old gas supply pipes, but also a newspaper printed in 1910, suggesting that some of the early wiring had been done in that year.

Other indications of remodeling: wider stud spacing and different construction materials and techniques in an area of your house; use of round nails in part of your house if the house was originally built with square nails.

UNCOVERING OLD WALLPAPER AND PAINT Among the great "finds" you might come across during your renovation activities, under layers of paint on walls and ceilings, is the original wallpaper, paint, graining, or stenciling. Unearthing these specimens should be one of your first tasks; otherwise they could be damaged or forever hidden during a sanding, stripping, or painting binge.

You will probably not be able to uncover the original paint or wallpaper without destroying it, but if you are careful, you should be able to reveal enough of a pattern or color to be able to replicate it.

Begin your search in a logical place. For ceilings, start where the ceiling meets a wall. This is not only an unobtrusive spot that can be easily patched later, it is an area that was routinely stenciled. The center of a room, especially around a ceiling fixture, is also a good bet. For walls, start near the

Patterns designed by Dr. Christopher Dresser, characteristic of Arts and Crafts styling.

baseboards. Wallpaper tends to loosen there first, and, again, patching afterwards will be less noticeable. You will need a surgeon's scalpel or a sharp razor-blade scraper. Working slowly and carefully, scrape a small (1-1/2 inches in diameter) crater with sides sloping in at the middle to about 3/8 inch in diameter. This will expose all the layers on the wall. If you think you have reached some stenciling, stop the scraping process and proceed carefully with cotton balls dampened (not saturated) with acetone-based stripper. You will need to be extremely careful to avoid damaging the stencil pattern beyond recognition. Take slides of what you uncover, match the colors to paint chips, and, if possible, trace the pattern.

If you find an old wallpaper layer, remove it (and any paint that might be on top of it) carefully with the use of a hand-held wallpaper steamer, which you can find at most rental yards. After the paper has been dislodged, use the cottonball-acetone method to remove old paint layers and expose the paper surface.

You will know that you have reached the original coat of paint, obviously, when there is nothing but plaster or white primer beneath it. Again, match the color to a paint chip. Chip down to the original paint in several areas of a room in case the room was painted with a pattern or with several different colors.

If you find a grained surface underneath several layers of paint and paper, you may be able to remove carefully the paint on top of it and save the original graining. Use a fast-acting but mild stripping agent, such as acetone, and don't let it penetrate the surface of the graining. Once the old paint has softened, scrape it off the surface with the scalpel or razor-blade knife and neutralize immediately with warm water.

OUTSIDE THE HOUSE

Although I don't advise digging up the whole yard, if you are planning some landscaping you should do some extra, exploratory spading. Not only could this tell the locations of the house's original out-buildings (outhouse, smokehouse, carriage house, etc.), but you could unearth such treasures as old hardware, bottles, or tools.

OTHER RESOURCES

- *Previous owners* Former owners or their families could be the best source of information about your house.
- *Historical surveys and societies* If your house is located in an area that is either historically preserved or has an active historic preservation movement, some research work might have already been done on your house's past. Check your local historical society, preservation department of the county or city government, or historical museum. If research has not been compiled and you are interested in conducting a historical resources survey, the secretary of the interior has published standards for such surveys and has grants available (see Appendix B). There are also professional organizations that conduct these surveys.
- *Assessor's maps and tax rolls* These can show you when your house was built and can trace successive owners. Choose the book for the approximate year your house was built. The first year that the assessment rolls indicate improvements on the property is probably the year the house was built (unless it replaced an existing structure that was demolished, in which case you will have to do further detective work). Remember, however, that

the owners may not have lived in the house if it was rental property.

Records—or lack of them—can also tell you if your house has been moved. You can probably approximate the date of construction by the style of your house and the construction method used. If there are no improvements listed on the tax assessor's rolls until a date much later than you believe the house was built, the house was probably constructed at an earlier date, then moved to the property the year that the improvements first show on the tax rolls.

● *The county recorder's office* This is the repository for deeds, mortgages, and birth, death, and marriage records. If there are no early tax records on your house (i.e., if it was located outside a municipality) this might be a good way to determine when it was built and when it changed hands. Most recorder's records are filed chronologically, however, and looking through decades worth of records can be tedious and time-consuming.

● *City directories* These usually list both husband and wife and their occupations. If any children who worked lived at home, they are also listed. City directories usually also list the locations of the businesses for which the occupants worked and indicate if the family rented or owned the house.

● *Old businesses* Sometimes a business that employed a previous owner will still be operating. If so, they may have archives and perhaps old photographs or other information about your house's previous owners.

● *Old local newspapers* A good source of vital statistics. Some papers have cataloged their past stories, which will save you hours of digging through issues.

● *Building department* This and other city or county offices may have on file permits for your house and its additions, unless your house was built before permits were required.

● *Utility companies* These may have records showing when gas, water, electricity, and sewers were hooked up to your house and may also have service records showing successive owners.

● *Libraries, museums, state and county archives, private collections, neighbors, graveyards, church records* Use your imagination—you'll just have to keep following tips and hunches—and who knows what you'll find.

DEVELOPING YOUR RENOVATION PHILOSOPHY

Before you even start planning what you are going to do to your old home, decide how you are going to approach the task. Are you going to renovate your house? Rehabilitate it? Restore it? What is the difference, anyway?

To *renovate* is to clean up, replace, or repair a house, returning it to a good and useful condition. Rehabilitation and restoration are both renovation activities.

To *restore* means to return the house authentically to a specific period and condition. Authenticity has charm, but I have no desire to restore the outhouse. Larry Martin of Ferndale, California, for example, has restored his Stick-style home. The lighting is exclusively kerosene; a wood cookstove sits in the kitchen. This is definitely the purist approach. Technically, restoration implies that everything in the house will conform to a specific time period, usually the one in which the house was originally built. Although this is fine for museums, most homeowners retain modern conveniences, especially in bathrooms and kitchens.

To *rehabilitate* (being an English language purist, I refuse to use the vernacular "to rehab") is the philosophy of the current preservation movement. According to the secretary of the interior's *Standards for Rehabilitation* (see Appendix B), this means:

> the process of returning a property to a state of utility, through repair or alteration, which makes possible an efficient contemporary use while preserving those portions and features of the property which are significant to its historic, architectural and cultural values.

The phrase "state of utility" suggests that needed repairs will be made to the house; "efficient contemporary use" connotes modernizing of at least bathrooms and kitchens. Within these parameters, however, rehabilitation encompasses a wide range of philosophies. Many of the houses in New Orleans' French Quarter, for example, seem to be held together by their coats of paint, but these are considered to be "rehabilitated." On the other hand, many of the buildings that have been rehabili-

valued only in wines and cheeses, but character lines and "crow's feet" cracks are an antique house's heritage; and, over the years, the well-loved home becomes an amalgam of those who have lived in it, and the chronicle of an era.

RENOVATION GUIDELINES

Since each renovation project and each owner are unique, I can't really advise you the best place to start on your home, but I will offer some general guidelines.

To obtain ideas for your home, look at houses in your area that have been rehabilitated, scour the bookshelves for Victoriana picture books, and read the Victorian history chapters in this book. Don't limit yourself to volumes on older houses, though. Two good idea books for any home are *The House Book* by Terence Conran (New York: Crown Publishers, 1976) and *Inside Today's Home* by Ray and Sarah Faulkner (New York: Holt, Rinehart, and Winston, 1975).

If you are undertaking a major remodeling project, an architect or building designer should be consulted. He or she can draw your house plans and give you ideas, and has a working knowledge of applicable code requirements. Look for someone who has experience with older homes; the local chapter of the American Institute of Architects or the American Institute of Building Designers can provide a referral.

And don't forget to take "before" pictures of your house!

tated in Old Sacramento, California, were literally torn down and rebuilt with reproduction materials and ornamentation. Some old-house owners even gut the interiors of their houses to make way for ultracontemporary furnishings.

There are certain dos and don'ts concerning rehabilitation. Basically, preservationists maintain a general abhorrence of anything aluminum, vinyl, asbestos, fiberglass, or plastic. Any remodeling you do should blend with and complement the original structure and any older additions. Don't, as Clem Labine, editor of the *Old-House Journal,* quips, "remuddle" your house. The secretary of the interior's *Standards for Rehabilitation* (quoted above and reprinted in full in Appendix B) offers succinct guidelines.

Many purists insist that the old-house owner should not impose his or her personality on the house. I disagree strongly. You are not embarking upon a research or demonstration project necessitating professional distance and dispassion. This is your home, a part of you and your lifestyle. As such, it should reflect the love, attitudes, and gifts of materials and labor you bestow upon it—just as it reflects those of owners before you.

Think twice before you replace a worn floorboard or remove a weathered cornice. Aging is usually

LIVING IN THE HOUSE WHILE YOU ARE WORKING ON IT

I don't recommend this although I've done it several times, due to financial constraints. Obviously, you cannot live in a house while it is being moved or jacked up for foundation work. Also, if possible, have the major structural, plumbing, and wiring work done before you move in. Not only do these tasks tear up the house, they can leave you without water and/or power for several days.

Establish, for your living area, one part of the

house that is not being torn up. Perhaps, for this purpose, you can renovate one wing or floor of the house before you move in. Although plastering, painting, plumbing, etc. all of the rooms in the house at one time may be more efficient (and cheaper if you are hiring a contractor), this creates chaos if you are living in the house. If you work room by room you can avoid tearing up the entire house at one time.

Also, since construction creates a plethora of dirt and debris, and things can easily get damaged or broken, you shouldn't unpack your good decorations, furniture, china, etc.

MAKING PLANS

First, get acquainted with your house and let your ideas crystallize. You will have an easier time judging where a certain fixture—or a certain room—belongs after you have become familiar with your house.

One of the first projects you should undertake is drawing a set of scale plans of your house. Even if you do not plan any major remodeling, these can be invaluable for estimating the amounts of materials you will need and for planning your rehabilitation activities.

A good book to aid you in planning is *Designing Houses: An Illustrated Guide to Building Your Own Home* by Les Walker and Jeff Milstein (New York: Overlook Press, 1976). Although it is intended for those who are starting from scratch, it has much valuable information and gives directions for drawing plans.

START AT A LOGICAL PLACE

Obviously, you won't choose wallpapering as a first task if you are subsequently going to tear up the wall to work on the electrical system. Those jobs that necessitate removing walls, floors, or ceilings should be done first. This includes structural work, heating, gas pipes, dealing with dry rot, and re-plumbing. Also, while any floors, walls, or ceilings are torn out, you should check and replace or repair the wiring.

Bathrooms and kitchens are the most complicated rooms in the house. I prefer to do these first, to "get the hard part out of the way." Others would rather wait to tackle these rooms until the rest of the house has been done. Whatever you choose, give these rooms plenty of thought. For assistance, consult the Sunset paperbacks: *Kitchens* and *Bathrooms*.

PRIORITY TASKS
- Dry rot and termites will continue to damage the house if not eradicated.
- Broken windows should be replaced, for security and to keep out the elements.
- If the exterior paint has flaked off, a coat of primer can protect bare wood from sun damage.
- Roof repair.

PREVENTIVE MAINTENANCE TASKS
- Replace the washers in the supply lines feeding sinks, bathtubs, and toilets. These can disintegrate and cause minor flooding.
- Check your electrical system for shorts, damaged receptacles, etc. that, if undetected, can cause fires.

CHAPTER 5

The Renovation Workshop

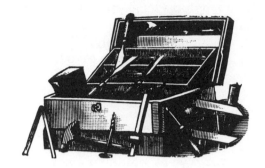

The type and quantity of hand and power tools you buy depend on both your pocketbook and perspective. Everyone has his or her favorite tools, and you, too, will develop personal preferences with time and use.

If you have scant experience using tools, take some time to familiarize yourself with them before you attack your precious old home. Many college extension and community adult education programs offer building classes that will, among other things, teach you to use the tools of the construction trade. Books, such as *Everyone's Book of Hand and Small Power Tools* by George R. Drake (Reston, Virginia: Reward Publishing Company, 1974), are helpful, but textbooks are not a substitute for experience. Practice by building yourself some freestanding shelves or wooden bins to hold tools and materials, or build yourself a workbench.

Weigh the following considerations when purchasing tools:

● *How much of a particular job are you planning to do?* If you intend to do a lot of plumbing, by all means purchase a complete, good set of plumbing tools. If you are only going to do minor repair work, borrow or rent the tools for the little use you will give them (nearly every type of tool can be rented at a good-sized rental yard).

● *How much money are you willing to spend?* Tools cost a fair amount. One way to circumvent this expense is to form a "tool pool" with other renovators, purchasing a community set of tools that you can all use. Although this can work well for tools that are not used very often, problems within tool pools arise when everyone wants to use the same tool at the same time. Also, make sure the people in your pool, if you form one, will take good care of the tools.

● *If you are the recipient of a renovation loan or grant* the government program will probably not pay for tool purchase, which is considered a capital expenditure, but will usually foot the bill for tool rental. You might, therefore, consider renting the tools rather than buying them.

● *Buy good quality, forged-steel hand tools.* Virtually any tool manufactured ten to twenty years ago was of good quality; this, unfortunately, is no longer true. Today, even the supermarkets carry discount tools. Stay away from these "bargains." Cheap tools do not last, and the few dollars you think you've saved will be lost when the tool breaks—right when you are using it. Also, you will probably spend more money to buy and then replace a cheap tool than you would have spent purchasing a good-quality tool in the first place.

Check the warranties on the tools you buy; Sears Craftsman-brand hand tools, for example, are guaranteed for life.

● *Buy heavy-duty, high-horsepower power tools.* When comparing different models of power tools, choose the one with the higher horsepower. This will be a heavier-duty tool that can stand up to more use than a light model.

● *Buy the right tool for the job.* A drill, for example, is not made to be a grinder and will break down under heavy use with a grinding attachment. If you need to grind something, use a grinder! Also, stay away from multiple-use tools—those "miracle-three-in-one" tools are designed for light-duty, hobby work only: they may do three different types of jobs, but they will probably not do any of them adequately for renovation work.

● *Buy tools that fit you.* If you are small you will probably be unable to control industrial-strength power tools; instead, look for hand tools that enhance your strength and your leverage.

● *Pros and cons of used tools* Used tools are usually prolifically available through private newspaper advertisements, flea markets, used tool stores, and rental yards.

Used high-quality hand tools can be purchased for a fraction of their cost new, and this can be a real boon if the tools are in good condition. Blades on screwdrivers and edges on chisels should be free of nicks; pliers and wrench jaws should not be loose. Avoid tools that show considerable wear.

(Since flea markets have developed the reputation as marketplaces for stolen tools, used-tool stores, rental yards, and classified advertisements are probably the best sources.)

In general, avoid purchasing used power tools. You don't know what sort of wear they've received. This is especially true for rental yard tools, which have received rough use from many different hands. The one exception to this rule is reconditioned power tools—returned on warranty and offered for sale by local manufacturers' service centers. These tools generally have less than one year's wear on them, are completely reconditioned, and usually carry new warranties.

SAWS

If you do any volume of carpentry, from rough to finish work, you will need a saw capable of cutting both sheet goods and making accurate miters.

● A *table saw* is probably the most accurate, especially for cutting sheet goods and ripping (cutting with the grain) lumber. It is also expensive—at least $250 for a decent model—and it cannot cut compound miters and is not portable.

● A *radial arm saw*, which is essentially a circular saw mounted on a movable arm, is the most versatile and is capable of making nearly any type of cut. Attachments are available with which you can construct moldings and dovetail joints for cabinets. Radial arm saws are expensive, however, and cost more than $350 for a decent model.

● A *circular (hand power) saw* is a good investment, even if you purchase a table or radial arm saw, since you will occasionally have to cut studs or other lumber that is already in place.

There are several different types of circular saws. The *worm-drive saw* (of which the Skilsaw is

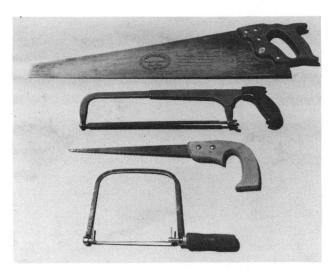

Hand saws, from top to bottom: wood hand saw, hacksaw (for metals, plastics, etc.), keyhole saw (for plunge cutting and cutting some curves or holes), coping saw (for moldings and other small items).

Circular saws: a worm-drive circular saw (top) has its motor in line with the handle for better control and accuracy; note how the motor on the sidewinder saw (bottom) is at right angles to the handle.

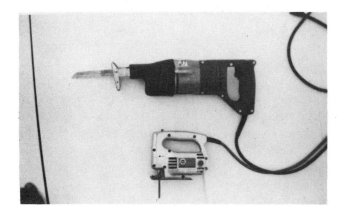

Reciprocating saw (top), jigsaw (bottom).

the best known) is the professional model—the Cadillac of the line. The beauty of the worm-drive saw is that, because the motor is mounted in line with the blade, the blade flexes hardly at all. This gives you an extremely accurate cut, and the blades stay sharper.

A professional who is practiced with a worm-drive saw will probably have no need for either a radial arm or a table saw. Unfortunately, however, worm-drive saws are expensive ($150 or more) and are heavy and difficult for the neophyte or small person to use, thus negating their accuracy.

Circular saws that are not worm driven have motors mounted at right angles to the blades. This creates sideways torque, which impairs the accuracy of the cuts and tends to be much lighter in weight and also cost less: you can purchase a decent model for about $50.

If you do not have the money to purchase a radial arm or table saw and must rely on a circular saw, there are tricks that can enhance your accuracy. One of these is to use a guide to ensure straight cuts on sheet goods. The factory edge on a sheet of plywood is extremely true. Cut a 4- to 6-inch strip of plywood and tack-nail it (nail it in just far enough to affix the board; leave the nail heads protruding so you can pull them after you cut) parallel to the cutting line of the material you wish to cut, so that the factory edge is flush against the edge of the saw guide.

A radial arm or table saw can cut accurate miters, but if you are relying on a circular saw, you will need a *miter box*. Power miter boxes are designed specifically for use with circular saws; however, an inexpensive ($45) hand miter box with a small, fine-toothed, sharp handsaw is perfect for moldings.

● A *reciprocating saw* is a great investment for renovation work. The blade travels in and out ("reciprocating") of the housing, allowing you to cut flush to a surface and in tight spaces. Slip the blade behind a molding, and you can cut nails and remove the wood without damage. The reciprocating saw can also be equipped with special blades for cutting metals, plastic, clay, wallboard—even galvanized or cast-iron pipe. A reciprocating saw eliminates the necessity of a hacksaw.

The Milwaukee-brand Saws-all is the preferred professional model. This, like the worm-driven

Skilsaw, is durable and accurate but also expensive (upwards of $125) and heavy. Several companies manufacture smaller, light-duty reciprocating saws that will suffice for home renovation use.

● *Band saws, jigsaws, and saber saws* are specialized power saws capable of cutting curves in wood. Unless you plan to do decorative cutting, you probably do not *need* any of these tools, since a hand *coping saw* (which only costs a few dollars) can cut curves and moldings.

If, on the other hand, you plan to saw wood ornamentation, you will need a power saw. The band saw is great and accurate, but will cost you over $150. A jigsaw or saber saw can be purchased for as little as $20. The scroll model—one with a big knob on the front—gives you better control for precision. A jigsaw or saber saw is also useful for cutting holes in walls (such as for electrical receptacles) and for demolition work.

SAW BLADES For jigsaws and reciprocating saws, use a blade specifically designed for the type of material you are going to cut: natural wood, Masonite or fiberboard, ferrous or nonferrous metal, ceramics, stone, plastics, etc. If the blade becomes damaged or dulled, replace it.

There are literally hundreds of different types of blades for radial, table, and circular saws. Different blades are designed for *ripping* (cutting with the grain of the wood) and *cross-cutting* (cutting across the grain). *Combination* blades will perform both tasks.

Generally, for wood, the more teeth a blade has, the finer the cut will be. A blade with two or three teeth per inch will usually suffice for most types of wood; for cutting veneer, you'll need a blade with five teeth per inch.

Another factor in the type of cut a blade will make is the configuration of the teeth. There are various different types; for wood, two are common: *set* (where the ends of the teeth bend alternately to the left and to the right—this creates a rough cut), and *hollow ground no-set* (where the teeth are in line with the rest of the blade, producing a very fine cut).

Perhaps the most important factor in the quality of the cut is the sharpness of the blade. A dull blade requires more power to cut through an object, and therefore makes a poorer cut. Blades may be dulled by cutting hardwood, improper blade sharpening, cutting through nails or other metals, cutting wood that has been treated (fireproofed, glued, reinforced with resins or binders), or just from long use.

Blades tipped with teeth of tungsten carbide will stay sharp up to one hundred times as long as plain steel blades, but these may cost as much as three times the price of a conventional blade. Do not buy a cheap carbide blade. These will not stay sharp, and the teeth can come off while the saw is being used, creating hazards. Unless you really know what you are doing, leave saw blade sharpening to a professional company. These can be found in the telephone book.

SANDERS

I find that, with one notable exception, *finishing sanders* are not worth the money they cost ($25 and up). Most do not deliver enough torque to sand any better than you can by hand, and those few that do invariably leave marks on the wood.

The one exception to this is the Rockwell Bloc Sander, a small, high-frequency orbital (moves in a circular direction) sander that is well worth the $70 it costs. It sands efficiently without gouging the wood, fits in tight corners, and, with a heavy pad attachment, even sands moldings and other curved surfaces.

A *belt sander* is the perfect tool for heavy-duty sanding on flat surfaces, such as removing paint from the edges of old floors or S4S molding (a flat, plain piece of wood surfaced on four sides). Most brands are comparable; choose the model that feels comfortable to use and that has at least a 1/2 horsepower motor.

Because of the extreme high torque, a belt sander can easily damage wood, so practice first with several different grit belts. Also, a good belt sander costs upwards of $75, and belts cost a dollar or more apiece.

DRILLS

A good drill is a must. Buy one with a strong (at least 1/2 horsepower) motor and a 1/2-inch chuck (the clamping device that holds the bit in place).

Smaller (1/4- and 3/8-inch chuck) drills won't adapt for many of the attachments or larger drill bits and will wear out quickly with heavy-duty use. A decent drill should cost around $50. Plan also to spend as much for a set of drill bits as you do for the drill, and make sure the bits stay sharp. Bits can be sharpened on a grinding stone or electric grinder; hold each side of the bit at a 45-degree angle.

Myriad attachments are available for the drill: grinding stone, sanding disk, wire brushes, polishing disks, countersinking heads (for setting wood screws so they sit flush or below the surface of the wood), holesaws, large auger bits, masonry bits, screwdrivers, etc. Purchase these attachments as you need them.

Don't be tempted to make your drill into another tool. Attachments are designed for light-duty use only. If you have a lot of sanding to do, use a sander; use a grinder for grinding large areas.

HAMMERS

Hammers are manufactured in different weights, with different handles, claws, and faces.

Hammer handles are made of wood (usually ash), fiberglass, or rubber. A good-quality hammer will have a handle that is securely affixed to the head—so that the head will not fly off the hammer while you are swinging it.

The face of a hammer is either smooth, convex, or waffled (cut in a crisscross pattern). A smooth-faced hammer is used for finish work. A convex face is used for drywall: the dimple it leaves in the wallboard provides a good surface to which joint

From left to right: framing hammer (waffle-faced with straight claw); smooth-faced hammer with straight claw; and finish hammer (smaller, smooth-faced, curved claw).

compound can adhere. A waffle-faced hammer grips the nail head and won't glance off it when the hammer strikes hard; this hammer is used for framing and other rough carpentry, where the marks it leaves on the surface of the wood are inconsequential.

A curved claw on the end of the hammer is best for extracting short (often finishing) nails without damaging the wood. The wood is protected with a block, the nail is gripped between the hammer claws, and the hammer is then jerked straight back. A straight claw is best for removing large nails quickly, when marking the wood is inconsequential, such as for framing or other rough carpentry. The nail is grasped between the claws, and the hammer is pulled with a sideways motion to remove the nail.

The heavier the hammer, the more force it will hit the nail head with when swung, and, consequently, the quicker it can drive the nail. Hammers used for framing tend to be heavier; those for finish carpentry are lightweight. A person who can swing a 22-ounce hammer for framing might use a 16-ounce hammer for finish work, since weight is not as important when driving small nails—the objective is to avoid damaging the wood. When considering the weight of a hammer, purchase one that fits your hand and that you can swing accurately in a wide arc.

SCREWDRIVERS

A complete set of screwdrivers is a must for any renovation project. There are two different types of screwdrivers: those with flat, or *slothead,* blades (for slothead screws) and those with *Phillips* or *crosshead* blades (for Phillips screws). Screwdrivers also come with different-sized length shafts and different-sized heads.

Heads of slothead screwdrivers are sized by fractions of an inch; those of Phillips- head screwdrivers are numbered, with size "1" being the smallest. Always use a screwdriver with a head size that will easily yet snugly fit into the slot in the screw. If it is too big or too small, it can easily damage screw heads, especially those of brass screws, which are soft.

The longer the screwdriver shaft, the more torque it will provide and therefore the easier a screw will be to loosen or tighten. Short-shafted, or *stubby,* screwdrivers (those with 1-1/2-inch-long shafts) are indispensable for reaching in small places, although they do not offer much leverage. An *offset* screwdriver (where the handle is set at a 90-degree angle from the head—usually these offer Phillips and slothead combinations) can reach in even tighter places; these most often come with 3/8-inch blades.

For renovation work, the following screwdrivers make a good set:

SLOTHEAD
stubby (1-1/2-inch) with 5/16-inch blade
4-inch shaft with 3/16-inch blade
6-inch shaft with 5/16-inch blade
8-inch shaft with 3/16-inch blade
8-inch shaft with 5/16-inch blade

PHILLIPS HEAD
stubby with No. 3 tip
4-inch shaft with No. 1 tip
6-inch shaft with No. 3 tip
8-inch shaft with No. 1 tip
8-inch shaft with No. 3 tip

OFFSET SCREWDRIVER

If you cannot unscrew a screw, try first to apply direct downward pressure while turning the handle, to achieve maximum torque. If this does not work, apply some Liquid Wrench (page 37), unless the surface is wood, which would be damaged by application of this petroleum oil. If all else fails, you can drill out the screw, using a drill bit just slightly smaller than the shaft of the screw.

Don't use your screwdrivers for anything other than screws, although this is tempting, since screwdrivers are great for removing delicate moldings and for opening paint cans. I usually buy a couple of 99-cent slothead screwdrivers to use for these jobs.

EQUIPPING YOUR WORKSHOP

Following is a list of tools for the basic home renovation workshop. Tools required for specific tasks only, such as plumbing or wiring, are not listed here but instead are discussed in those particular chapters.

The list of tools is divided into three categories: *essential*—absolutely required for renovation work; *important*—you can work without these, but they make the job easier; buy as soon as you are able; *desirable*—buy only if you have the interest and the money.

ESSENTIAL TOOLS

- *Complete set of screwdrivers*
- *Hammer*
- *Saw* that will cut miters.
- *One-half-inch drill* with a good set of bits.
- *Ten-inch adjustable wrench* This is a good medium size for use on all sorts of nuts and bolts and fittings.
- *Medium-sized multiple joint pliers* These are good for gripping all sorts of items and are especially useful for large-sized nuts. Purchase a pair with jaws that will open farther than those of the adjustable wrench. Also known as *channel locks.*
- *Locking-grip pliers* The Vise-Grip brand is perhaps best known for quality. These can be used to pull small nails, to hold a pipe in place while you unscrew a nut, and even to substitute for a small clamp.
- *Two-pound sledgehammer* You will need this for any demolition, and for driving heavy nails or stakes.
- *Flexible putty knives* Purchase one with a 1-1/2-inch blade and one with a 4-inch blade. Since you do not want to mar the blades, avoid using these knives for wood stripping or scraping.
- *Wood chisels* One with a 1/2-inch blade and one with a 1-inch blade will provide versatility. Use them only for wood, keep the blades sharp, and avoid cutting across the grain.
- *Combination square with angle finder* This versatile tool includes a 12-inch steel ruler attached to a movable head, which locks in place with a screw nut. It measures 90 and 45-degree angles, and has a built-in level and a tip that is a scribe.
- *Carpenter's 2-foot level*
- *Ladder* Purchase one that will enable you to reach the ceiling easily. Use a stepladder, which can stand by itself in the middle of the room. An extension ladder must be leaned against a wall.
- *Flat pry bar* This is necessary for removing moldings, paneling, casings, etc. Buy one with a long handle, which provides more leverage.
- *Nail punch set* For driving the heads of finishing nails below the surface of the wood.
- *Electrical circuit/continuity/voltage tester* See page 91 for instructions on use.
- *Workbench with vise* The simplest solution (and also portable) is a set of sawhorses with a plank and a vise. If you are going to be working on many doors and windows, you should consider purchasing a portable workbench/vise combination, such as the Black and Decker Workmate ($50 and up), which can hold a door or window while you work on it.
- *Ten-foot steel measuring tape*
- *Fire extinguisher* Buy a small one, so that you *will* carry it from room to room. One with a rating of "ABC" can be used on all types of fires.
- *Heavy-duty extension cord*
- *Safety goggles* For use with all power tools.

IMPORTANT TOOLS

- *Circular or radial arm or table saw* A well-equipped workshop should include a circular saw and either a radial arm or table saw.
- *Jigsaw or saber saw*
- *Belt sander*
- *Portable trouble light* For working in dark areas, such as plumbing underneath sinks or wiring in attics. Purchase one with an electrical receptacle that can also serve as an extension cord.
- *Rockwell Bloc Sander*
- *Large framing square* For measuring right angles and for marking walls and sheet goods.
- *Large adjustable wrench, small adjustable wrench*
- *Set of box and open-end wrenches, socket set* Good for use in tight places; provides more leverage than does an adjustable wrench; loosens nuts without damaging the edges (as adjustable wrenches sometimes do). If you are going to purchase a socket set, buy one with a 3/8- or 1/2-inch drive and a reversible handle.
- *Needle-nosed pliers* Good for bending wires and for gripping in small spaces.
- *Bull-nosed pliers* Stronger than slip-joint pliers.

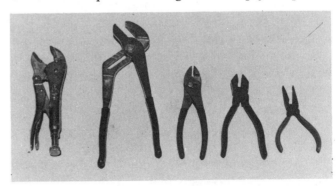

Different types of pliers. From left to right: locking-grip pliers (Vise-Grip brand), channel-lock pliers, adjustable (slip-joint) pliers, bull-nosed pliers, and needle-nosed pliers.

- *Attachments for drill* Wire cup brush, hole saws, countersink, wood boring bits.
- *Propane torch* This is not an expensive tool (under $20) and is good for some paint stripping (especially metal), softening window putty to remove old glass, softening old vinyl flooring so it can be removed.
- *Complete set of pry bars* In addition to the long-handled flat bar, a small flat pry bar (for tight spaces), a large wrecking bar (for maximum leverage; the curved claw is great for removing large nails), and a screwdriver-handled mini-pry bar (for removing small hardware, nails).
- *Complete set of wood chisels* A 1/4-inch, a 3/4-inch, and a 1-1/2-inch chisel to add to the 1/2- and 1-inch ones.
- *Cold chisel* Use with a hammer for loosening "impossible" nuts and fittings.
- *Complete set of hammers*
- *Sharpening stone* For maintaining the edges on chisels and knives. (You should also have chisels professionally sharpened about once a year.)
- *Staple tacker* For affixing thin materials, such as insulation, tarpaper for roofs, plastic to seal off windows, etc.
- *Utility/razor/mat knife* This has a razor edge that retracts into a metal handle. Handy for opening boxes, cutting drywall, etc.
- *Flat bastard/rattail file* To remove burrs from pipe or hardware.
- *Small stepladder or stool* Easier to move around a full-sized ladder.
- *Plumb line* Measures true vertical drop.
- *Chalk line* For marking floors, walls, etc.
- *One-hundred-foot steel measuring tape*
- *Block plane* This is essential for rehanging or adjusting the sizes of doors and windows.
- *Nail pouch or tool belt* These save steps, especially when you are working on a ladder.
- *Heavy work gloves*

DESIRABLE TOOLS

- *Nail puller* Punch this into the head of a nail, and it extracts the nail from a piece of wood without damaging the wood. This is especially good for square nails, which usually damage the wood when they are pulled with a pry bar or claw.
- *Bolt cutters* Good for cutting bolts to proper size and for cutting nails when removing moldings.

- *Air compressor* A good model (at least 2 horsepower, 240 volts) costs between $300 and $500, but it can save you much time and money. Scores of attachments are available for use with a compressor: pneumatic nail guns in all sizes and types—from finish nailers to "T-nailers" for shingles (these rent for about $15 per day); a paint pot, for spraying, costs about $25 to $50; a sandblasting gun and sand hopper (about $60 for a heavy-duty model) will enable you to make your own etched windows. A blast of air from a compressor is also good for cleaning tools and fittings.

  Since a compressor costs about $100 per day to rent, buying one is cost-effective if you plan to do a lot of nailing or painting.
- *Airless paint sprayer* A small commercial-duty airless sprayer costs about $400 and can be used for interior and exterior painting. This might be a worthwhile investment if you have a lot of painting to do. Although you can rent airless sprayers, most of these are heavy-duty models that apply the paint too fast for interior use; and they cost as much as $100 per day to rent.
- *Mini side grinder* A mini side grinder, which costs $100 to $150, can save you hours of wire brushing and scraping and is especially useful on cast-iron bathtubs. The Bosch Company manufactures one little model that will also adapt for a wire cup brush and sanding and polishing disks. (If you are unable to locate this in hardware stores, try a welding supply store.)
- *Attachments for drill* Grinding stone, angle head (which allows you to drill in tight places), screwdriver.
- *Yankee drill* This is a hand-punch drill that operates by pushing on the wooden handle. It is good for tight spaces that won't accommodate a power drill, and for areas where electrical power is unailable.
- *Additional fire extinguishers*

THINGS TO SAVE

- *Rags, cloth scraps* Necessary for nearly every project. Cotton is most absorbent and therefore best.
- *Coffee cans* Good for wood stripping, parts, and tools.
- *Frozen juice cans* For storing nuts and bolts or for mixing small batches of stain or glue or plaster.

● *Newspapers*
● *Old toothbrushes* Good for cleaning tools, removing paint from intricate moldings and hardware.
● *Tin cans* For storing nuts, bolts, etc. Cans with plastic lids are good for small dabs of leftover paint or stain mixtures, and for soaking fittings in lacquer thinner. The plastic lids make great palettes for mixing two-part epoxy, mixing stain with putty, etc.
● *Jars* For mixing non-flammable liquids or storing things. Some restaurants give away or sell used gallon-sized jars.
● *Old paint brushes, flatware, bowls, sponges* Use your imagination; these have hundreds of uses. You can often find them for pennies at garage sales and thrift stores.
● *Cardboard boxes* For storing wood scraps, electrical and plumbing parts, etc.
● *Blocks and scraps of wood* Blocks of wood provide leverage for use with pry bars and protect wood when using a sledgehammer. Small bits of wood can be used for shimming door casings, fixtures, and cabinets.
● *Old sheets* For use as drop cloths.

MATERIALS

Following are small items, costing not more than a few dollars apiece, that are handy to have:
● *Single-edged razor blades, razor scrapers* For cleaning paint from windows, crud from porcelain fixtures, cutting cardboard, etc.
● *Cheap putty knives* For paint scraping, wood stripping, applying adhesives and caulking.
● *Cheap paint brushes* For applying paint stripper, lacquer thinner, oil, etc.
● *Wire brushes* You will need a large one for cleaning metals. The tiny ones (they resemble toothbrushes) are good for cleaning hardware, pipe threads, etc.
● *Caulking compound* For bathroom fixtures, weatherproofing, filling cracks in floors and walls. A good brand is Polyseamseal (by the Darworth Corporation), which hardens, will not peel or crack, and is available in various colors.
● *Silver duct tape*
● *Pencils and paper*
● *Sheet plastic* For covering valuable fixtures, sealing off holes in windows.
● *Lacquer thinner* For removing oil, crud, grease, glue, etc., etc., etc.

● *Penetrating oil* Known best by the trade name *Liquid Wrench,* this is a solvent that is brushed or sprayed onto—and subsequently loosens—a frozen (stuck) joint or part (sometimes several applications are necessary).

LOCATION

Ideally, you should have a central location for a workshop—an area where you can store all your materials and keep your tools. A garage is a logical choice, but if it is too far from the main house, you'll lose precious time running back and forth to find a tool or to saw a board. A basement is also a good workshop site, as are one or more unused rooms in your house.

Whatever location you choose should have adequate wiring, lighting, and ventilation and should have shelves, a pegboard, chests, or some other means of organizing and storing tools.

If you are planning to work on the entire house at one time, you will probably prefer a central location for tools and materials. If you are working room by room, you may prefer to keep your tools where you are working, moving them to different locations as the renovation progresses. Larger tools can be kept in a chest equipped with large castors. Small plastic utility trays with handles are good for small power and hand tools.

If you prefer to have a portable workshop, this will also influence the type of tools you buy. Large power tools—such as a radial arm or table saw or band saw—tend to be less practical than small portable tools. Also, a small portable workbench or sawhorses and clamps would be more immediately useful than a large nonportable workbench.

Even with a portable workshop, you will need a place to store materials and additional tools. A storage area should provide you with sufficient space to segregate wood by type and size and to store salvage items, fixtures, fittings, cans and rags, etc. Make sure you store paints, solvents, varnishes, wood stripper, and anything else that is flammable away from electrical outlets, power tools, propane torches, and any other items that might pose a fire hazard. *Don't* store dirty, oily, or paint-soaked rags; wash or dispose of them immediately.

CHAPTER 6

Contractors & Building Codes

DO THE WORK YOURSELF OR HIRE A PRO?

Different people have different ideas about their personal involvement in rehabilitating an old house. One fellow, whose big interest is running, not remodeling, wanted someone else to do all the work. "I want to walk into the house after it is all finished," he proclaimed, "when it's completed and ready to live in." Another friend of mine—and a licensed contractor—insisted on doing everything in her old house herself: "When it's done," she said, "I want to say 'I did this all myself, with my own hands. Nobody else even touched it.'"

These, of course, are the extremes. Most old-home rehabilitators have more of a desire to be involved in their projects than does the running fanatic; and, whereas doing *all* the work yourself might be feasible if you have unlimited time and expertise, most people have neither and should consider hiring professionals for at least part of the rehabilitation.

Weigh the following considerations when deciding whether to hire someone to work on your house:

● *Which tasks do you like to do?* Unless precluded by financial limitations, hiring someone to do those jobs you don't like—perhaps plumbing, wood stripping, clean-up, or whatever—will free you to concentrate on projects you will enjoy.

● *What do you know how to do?* If you don't know how to do a certain job, you might not want to make your debut attempt on your house. Hire a pro the first time and watch to determine how the task is done and whether you would like to do it the next time. I did this with both floor sanding and replacing windows. I not only saw firsthand how to work a large floor drum sander and how to putty wood

sash windows, but also, in each case the professional I hired offered tips of the trade to an eager disciple.

● *How much time do you have?* Rehabilitating an old house can be more than a full-time job. If you can only give a few hours on the weekends to your house, you should either expect the project to progress slowly or hire some help. Not only do more hands do the job quicker (a crew of professionals can work amazingly fast), but many times contractors own specialized equipment that do-it-yourselfers can't afford and don't need—but that can reduce to a fraction the time required for a job. A "bazooka" Sheetrock taper system, for example, which costs thousands of dollars and is unavailable on the retail market, can enable a professional Sheetrock person to tape and texture an entire house in a single day.

● *How much money do you have?* Remodeling can cost up to $100 per square foot, and most of us have limited funds with which to hire someone to work on our houses. On the other side of the coin, when the construction industry is slow (as it has been for the past year), bidding is extremely competitive and you may be able to hire someone for much less than you'd thought.

● *Are you getting mired in the project?* Are you, in the midst of the rehabilitation, discovering that it is not going as quickly as planned? Does a particular task continue to frustrate you? Hiring someone to do some of the work and seeing an entire segment of the project accomplished quickly—and by someone else, for a change—may provide a shot in the arm and the impetus to continue.

● *Will hiring a professional be cost beneficial?* Many times, hiring a pro to do a large project will pay, but employing one for small tasks will not. If you employ an electrician ten times—each time to rewire a single circuit, for example—you'll pay dearly, for most professionals charge a minimum flat rate for a small service call. If, however, you can save all your electrical work for one visit from the electrician, you can significantly reduce the total cost.

CHOOSING THE RIGHT PROFESSIONAL

Many contractors have had virtually no experience with remodeling work; fewer still are conversant with old houses. When the building industry enjoyed better economic days, many contractors would not touch a renovation project; now, the depressed new-housing market has enhanced their willingness to tackle remodeling work. This has brought to the renovation field many "professionals" who have never worked on old houses.

Make sure whomever you hire knows old homes, for they have peculiarities that new construction and modern house remodelings do not pose: walls, ceilings, and floors might not be square or level; old materials—dimensional lumber, warped or brittle moldings, etc.—may be difficult to work with. Many of your old house parts are irreplaceable; don't trust them to just anyone.

There are several ways to locate a contractor who knows old houses:
● Ask friends, architects, realtors, etc. for recommendations.
● Visit renovation projects in progress in your area. If you see some particularly good work, talk with the people on the job, who might lead you to a valuable source.
● Contact the local branch of the contractors' union or professional group in your area. They might be able to provide the names of contractors in your area who specialize in old-house renovation.

To choose the right contractor for the job, get several different bids. Even in a highly competitive market, bids will vary widely. And don't necessarily choose the lowest bidder, either. Ask each for references, and take a look at old-house projects that each has completed recently. Remember that a prospective contractor will probably send you to view his/her best projects, so what you see probably will be the best you can expect. Also, don't automatically assume that the prospective contractor has actually done the work s/he sends you to view until you have actually verified this.

Other tips:
● Obtain the license number of the prospective contractor and check it with the contractor's licensing authority in your area, to verify the licensure and to ensure that no complaints have been filed against the contractor.
● If you are working with an architect, introduce him or her to the prospective contractor to ensure they are compatible, since they will be working closely together.
● Choose someone with whom you are comfortable, since that person will be working on *your* house. Ideally, the contractor you pick should share your renovation philosophy and reverence for old houses.

If you do not want to employ a contractor, consider hiring a journeyman (hired by the day, not by the job) to work with you, or even just a helper. You will be surprised how much quicker two—even you and a friend—can finish a task. Don't forget that unless the person you hire has a professional license, most states will require you to carry special workers' liability insurance in case of an on-the-job accident.

Another option to consider is hiring several specialists—plumber, electrician, carpenter—instead of one general contractor. Although hiring a single company to do the entire job has the advantage of centralized responsibility (*you* only have to deal with one person), you can save money by eliminating the middleman and hiring your own specialists. Also, when you pick the subcontractors you want, you may get a superior result.

SETTING THE PRICE.

This may pose a dilemma: you, as the owner, are probably better off with the certainty of a set bid—so you'll know exactly what the project will cost. Many contractors, however, insist upon being paid on an actual *time and materials* basis.

"Its hard to tell what a project on an old house will entail before you get into it," one contractor comments. "Estimating the number of hours can be virtually impossible. Material costs may be more than I thought too—especially if parts have to be custom made."

A compromise is to set a ceiling price for the job, with several flexible components, based on a tentative bid from the contractor. If the job justifiably takes the contractor longer than estimated—or costs more in terms of materials—you can then reduce the number of things the contractor must do for the price. If the job takes less time, the contractor agrees to do a few extra tasks for the same price.

KEYS FOR A SUCCESSFUL PROJECT

Once you've found the right contractor, clarify your expectations before construction begins. Many people, believe it or not, do not know what they want the contractor to do. Have your renovation plans formulated before you begin. As with any contract, spell the terms out formally and succinctly before you begin to avoid misunderstandings and possible lawsuits later on.

Among the aspects of the renovation contract that should be delineated are:

● *Tentative completion date* You should retain some flexibility on this aspect, since unforeseen delays (such as extra time required to mill lumber) often occur over which the contractor has no control.

● *When payments are expected* Contrary to what some of them may tell you, you are not required to advance any money to a contractor.

● *Type of materials to be used* Some contractors automatically use economy or builder's grade materials on a project. Let the contractor know if you want to go first class with your house.

● *What in the house is to be saved* Some contractors may not recognize the value of old moldings, wainscoting, etc.

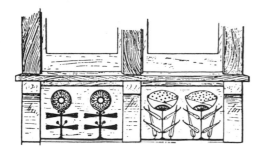

More tips:

● As work progresses, don't continually change your mind. This can be avoided by knowing what you want done ahead of time. Constant alterations delay a project and build enmity.

● Have weekly or biweekly progress checks. Keep abreast of the construction. If something is wrong, let the contractor know about it immediately, and don't be afraid to stop the project if it is not progressing to your satisfaction.

● Give the contractor some room. You may be tempted to work alongside him or her; however, this usually only impedes progress.

● Don't hold the contractor up because you have not purchased needed materials or completed a part of the project that you are doing yourself.

● Lastly, be prompt with your payments. If you fail to meet your obligations, you not only cause problems for the contractor, you often create a hardship for those persons working for him or her. Frequently these persons have no other income and rely on *your* payments for subsistence.

BUILDING CODES

How you do the work on your house—including specific construction techniques and grades and types of materials (even down to the kind and size of nails)—is regulated by your local government's building code.

Local codes are based upon one of four sets of requirements: the National Building Code (NBC) of the National Board of Fire Underwriters, the Basic Building Code (BBC) of the Building Officials and Code Administrators International, the Standard Building Code (SBC) of the Southern Building Code Congress, and the Uniform Building Code (UBC) of the International Conference of Building Officials. These codes differ to account for variances in custom, climate, and even politics across the country. Different materials, for example, will be required to withstand temperature extremes. Certain materials will be more common or more accepted in different areas. Some code requirements reflect the strength of labor unions; others of building inspection administration. In addition, local governments frequently impose supplemental or more stringent requirements, so that even though there is a basic standardization, codes vary widely from area to area.

The people at the building department can help you with specific questions about building codes, but you should research the code requirements before you bother them: you can obtain from a bookstore a copy of the general code (NBC, BBC, SBC, or UBC) that governs building in your area. Also obtain a copy of specific local requirements, which is usually available from the building department. If you have questions after you have studied the codes, then approach the experts at the building department.

CODE EXEMPTIONS AND VARIANCES

Unfortunately, some old buildings cannot be modified to meet code requirements without destroying significant architectural features. One common problem, for example, is that stairway or balcony balusters may not be high enough. Another is the requirement that there be a certain amount of room around a toilet. To cope with such dilemmas, most building codes have a variance process, whereby, after a lengthy bureaucratic process, you *might* be granted an exemption from certain code requirements.

In addition, some states have initiated historic-building codes that provide special exemptions from code requirements for certain old houses. These may either provide special modifications of the basic local code, or they may consist of a special alternative code. These codes are designed to promote the retention of a historic building's integrity. Some impose special requirements on an old house, such as prohibiting removing certain decorative or architectural features.

The building department may not be the best place to go for information about historic-building codes. Most alternative codes were initiated by preservation departments, not building departments. In some areas there are differences of opinion between these two agencies. Therefore, know the political climate in your area; many building department officials are friendly, some are not. It's usually a good idea to consult the preservation agency in your area, as well as the building department.

OBTAINING PERMITS

Anytime you remodel any part of your house, you are required to obtain a permit from the local building department and have the work pass inspection by one of their representatives to make sure it meets building code requirements.

Many people do not obtain permits for minor jobs, although technically they should. If you are undertaking a major remodeling, virtually everything you do—roofing, siding, adding fixtures, cabinetry, electrical, plumbing, carpentry, etc.—will require approval.

To apply for a building permit, take scale drawings of what you are remodeling, noting planned changes, to the building department. (Different areas require different types of plans; check before you go.) Permits can usually be issued either to a licensed contractor or to an owner/builder; but there may be restrictions on owner/builder permits, such as requiring proof of workers' compensation insurance for anyone hired. The building department will charge you a fee for the permit, based usually upon the value of the work to be performed.

INSPECTIONS

Your work must also be inspected, as specified by the building department, at various stages of completion, to ensure that it meets code requirements. Although specific rules will vary in different locales, generally inspection and approval must be made of all rough work before it is covered. If you neglect to call for progress inspections, as these are known, the inspector may insist that you remove any finish work so s/he can see and inspect the rough work.

If the inspector finds any work that does not meet code requirements, s/he will list the specific violations. You will be required to correct these, to perhaps pay a reinspection fee, and to have the work approved.

A final inspection is required after all finish work is complete.

APPEASING THE INSPECTOR

Inspectors usually have leeway concerning what they approve or reject in a project. An inspector's decision will be based, at least in part, upon his/her subjective impression of you and your work. Some inspectors are especially stringent with do-it-yourselfers. Although this may seem unfair, consider the inspector's point of view: s/he probably knows the contractors in the area well enough to trust the competency of their work, and probably does *not* know you yet, so you will therefore have to prove that you know what you are doing and that you did the job correctly.

You stand a better chance of having your work pass inspection if you:
● know the code requirements and make sure your work meets them.
● do neat work; sloppy work suggests slipshod construction techniques.
● call for inspections only when the work is ready to be inspected.
● clean the work area before inspection.
● are always present for an inspection. Sometimes the inspector may be unable to find what you have done and will not pass the work. If you are there, you can point out what s/he is looking for and perhaps save yourself a reinspection fee. Also, if you are present when and if the inspector finds violations, you can find out from the inspector exactly how they should be corrected.

Unfortunately, no matter how hard you try, you may encounter an inspector who you believe is hostile towards you: maybe because you are a do-it-yourselfer (or a woman do-it-yourselfer), or maybe because the inspector does not like old houses. Inspectors are, after all, human. Fortunately, for every hostile one I've encountered, there have been several who are sincerely pleasant and helpful.

WORKING WITHOUT A PERMIT

Although many people remodel their houses without obtaining permits, this is inadvisable. If you are hiring a contractor, the building permit and inspection process is your insurance that the job will be done correctly. A contractor who is not willing to do the job by the book and submit to inspection could very well do a poor job or leave the job unfinished. If this occurs and there is no permit on a job, you probably have little or no recourse against the contractor.

Also, if you work without a permit, you stand a good chance of getting caught. Each inspector usually has jurisdiction over a particular territory and knows what projects are in progress in his/her area. If the inspector in your area notices people working on your house and a dumpster sitting in front of it, s/he may wonder why a progress inspection has not been requested and will probably check to see if you have a permit.

When you're caught, you will probably have to pay penalties and extra permit fees. You may have to remove finish work so progress inspections can be made. And the inspector may very well be especially stringent on the inspections.

Materials

The types of materials that were used in constructing your house depend partly on the tastes of the person who built it, but were largely determined by the geographical location of the house. Certain materials were plentiful in certain areas (wood on the West Coast, fieldstones in the Midwest); manufacturing produced more materials in some areas than in others (brick foundaries, for example, were prevalent in the East; ornamental ironwork in the North and antebellum South).

The type of hardware—door hinges and knobs, window locks, nails, etc.—used in your house is at least partially a result of the actual time period that progress (including the railroad) reached your area. Machine-made nails, for example, were manufactured and used for construction in the East in the 1860s. In the West and in many rural areas not served by the railroad, however, handmade square nails sufficed for years past this date.

LUMBER

Seventy-five to one hundred years ago, wood was cut from trees that were at least a hundred years old, and it was hard and strong. (Joists in one of my houses were so hard that I could not hammer a nail into them.) Today, the supply of hundred-year-old trees is exhausted. Lumber companies have replenished cut forests with fast-growing species of trees. Although this practice provides abundant supplies of wood in a short length of time, that wood is nowhere near as strong as wood from the old giants.

In addition, to increase the number of board feet produced by each tree, lumber companies have decreased the dimensions of lumber. Two-by-fours in an old house, for example, are actually 2 inches by 4 inches—these are also known as *dimensional lumber.* Modern two-by-fours, on the other hand, are only 1-1/2 inches by 3-1/2 inches. Dimensional lumber is no longer made; if you have to replace a structural member in your house with one of equal size, you'll probably have to have it custom milled.

Because new lumber is not as strong or as large as old, building codes have been modified to require a smaller span between structural members in new construction than was common in older houses.

LUMBER CLASSIFICATIONS During the nineteenth century, lumber was divided into two categories: *clear* (without knotholes) and *common.* Over the years, other distinctions were drawn, and today there are more than two thousand different types and grades of lumber, based upon variances in quality, strength, milling and seasoning techniques, and finish. For more information on wood types, consult the U.S. Department of Agriculture's pamphlet, *Selection and Use of Wood Products for Home and Farm Building,* available from the Superintendent of Documents, U.S. Government Printing Office, Washington, D.C.

LUMBER SEASONING Between 25 and 30 percent of the total weight of a piece of green wood is water. Wood will shrink considerably across its grain but shrinks very little longitudinally—its length remains virtually constant.

Wood should be *seasoned*—shrunk to its final size—before it is used for building, and the way this is done is important. Poorly seasoned wood will warp and change size when exposed to rapid changes in humidity, and it will *check:* crack parallel to the grain.

If wood is seasoned carefully, it will be stronger and better able to support heavy loads without bending or being crushed. It will also be harder and more difficult to nail.

A new method, known as *kiln drying,* has been developed to speed the seasoning of wood. The wood is heated to reduce its moisture content; this process also kills insects and fungi.

IDENTIFYING AND MATCHING OLD WOOD Over the years, wood may loose many of its identifying properties, including color and strength, and may therefore be difficult to identify. To match old wood, choose wood with a compatible appearance, even if it is a different kind.

SALVAGE

Virtually everything—from the siding to the faucets, light fixtures to nails—is saved when a Victorian house is torn down. Old-house salvage has become such a booming business that salvage companies carrying nothing except old-house parts have sprung up. Many of these companies do a mail order business as well.

Although salvage yards are a good source for items you cannot locate elsewhere (some companies will look for items for you), prices at these companies tend to be high to support their overhead.

You can save money by dealing directly with the demolition companies. Look for them at work in areas where buildings are being torn down; the bulk of the materials are sold on site.

When dealing with a demolition company, don't appear too anxious to buy something, or the demolition company will realize it has what you want and will demand a high price.

Also, if possible, wait to purchase the materials until they have been removed from the building. The demolition company will probably not want to do this, since it wants to sell you everything—junk included. Some items, particularly siding and moldings, can be easily damaged when they are removed, and you don't want to have to pay for something that is ruined. And the demolition company might not take as much care in removing an item if it knows that it is sold.

Purchasing salvage items may not always be worthwhile. Some salvage items cost more than even custom-made reproductions. Others require so much work (stripping, filling, and sanding) that they will ultimately cost more in time and labor than you save in money.

PART III

The Shell

Victorian-Era House Construction

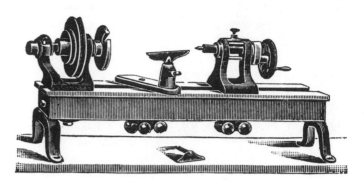

Until the middle of the nineteenth century, houses were constructed in basically the same manner as they had been since the Middle Ages. *Braced construction,* as the popular method was known (it is also called *eastern* or *combination framing*) was predicated on several factors: first, power saws had not yet been developed, so large-sized timbers were used in construction, because this was less expensive than milling smaller boards. Nails, too, had to be handmade (usually by convict labor), so structural members were joined by notching them and fitting them together in a manner known as *mortise and tenon.* Since labor was plentiful during the first half of the century, and the demand for housing was slight, the construction industry could afford to utilize this slow, labor-intensive method.

Braced construction is so named because of the heavy, diagonal braces that are *let in* (mortised into) the supporting posts of the house. This, along with the massive timbers and hand-crafted joints, creates an extremely sturdy house—as evidenced by the number of braced-frame dwellings that are still standing centuries after they were built.

During the 1860s, mechanization and mass production (including the development of the power saw) made ready-milled lumber and machined nails inexpensive and abundant. At first, traditional methods of braced-frame construction were adapted to accommodate these new developments: smaller timbers were used for construction and were nailed, not mortised, together.

Erecting a braced-frame house, however, still required a lot of time and labor, and this method was much too slow to keep pace with the tremendous housing demand that had developed in America by the late 1860s. Labor, also, had grown scarce and expensive, especially in the West.

Consequently, a new form of construction evolved. Known as *balloon framing,* it made use of readily available milled lumber and machined nails. Only a handful of workers were required to build a balloon-frame house, and they could erect one in a matter of hours.

The distinguishing characteristic of balloon-frame construction is that the studs run continuously from the foundation to the top plate and they may therefore be as long as 40 feet. Standard 2-by-4-inch lumber is employed for studs; where additional load-bearing capacity is required, several two-by-fours are often nailed together to form a larger piece.

Balloon-frame construction is much lighter than braced framing. A diagonal brace and/or sheathing should always be applied over the studs to prevent them from *raking* (falling on a slant). After this sheathing is applied, a balloon-frame house is as structurally sound as any other type of construction.

Because there is no interruption between the studs at different levels, pipes and wires can be run between stories without compromising a balloon-frame building's strength. Lumber shrinkage is also not a problem in balloon-frame houses, because lumber usually shrinks across the width—not the length—of the grain; and a balloon-frame house has few cross-sectional members.

The spaces between the studs in a balloon-frame house, however, must be closed with boards called *firestops,* otherwise the continuous run between floors creates a flue effect, and (as many unfortunate owners of early balloon-frame houses discovered) a fire originating in the basement of a house can sweep to the roof in merely minutes. These firestops also add extra support to the structure.

By the end of the nineteenth century, the supply of large trees, which had appeared nearly inexhaustible a few decades earlier, was seriously depleted; and the construction industry was forced to find a new framing method that could utilize shorter lengths of lumber.

Subsequently, *western platform framing* was introduced. In this method, now used almost exclusively, each floor of the house is framed as a separate platform, independently of the other floors. The first floor is erected and covered by a subfloor, which becomes the platform for the second story. Western platform framing is structurally sound—if the floors are nailed together adequately.

Platform framing proved even more compatible with mass production than balloon framing. Structural members (trusses, headers, etc.) can be cut and assembled before the studs are erected and many times are mass produced at a different location, then shipped to the construction site.

Wood shrinkage is an important consideration in platform construction, because it incorporates many cross members as structural components. To compensate for this, calculations are made to ensure that shrinkage is uniform throughout the structure. Platform construction is not recommended for masonry veneer and stucco houses, since the wood will shrink and the stucco or masonry will not, causing severe cracking.

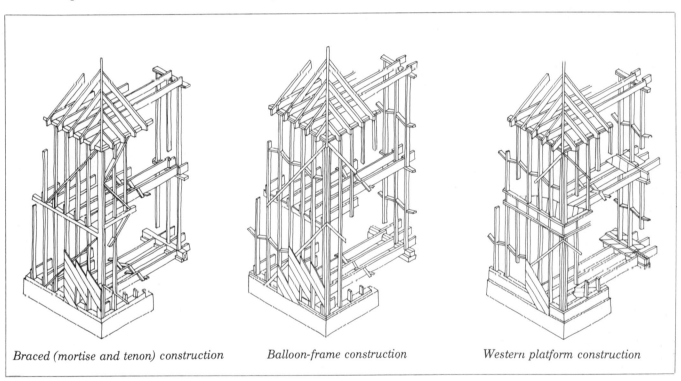

Braced (mortise and tenon) construction   *Balloon-frame construction*   *Western platform construction*

CHAPTER 9

Structural Integrity

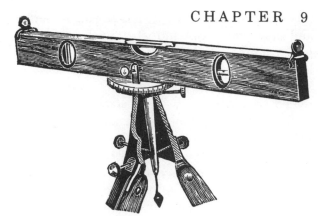

Fixing structural defects can be a serious problem, and, if you suspect a house has structural problems, you should always consult an engineer—ideally before you buy the house. The problem may be even more complicated than it appears, for a house could have settled in several different directions at once. Also, any structural renovation most likely will be costly.

Serious structural defects can usually be seen just by looking at the house. Site along the ridge line of the roof and down the exterior walls, comparing the lines of the walls and roof with neighboring buildings. Other indications that the house may have structural defects include door and window casings that have sagged so that doors and windows do not operate, gaps or buckling in exterior siding, latch sets that are misaligned.

A good frame house has a lot of give and take. You can raise a corner, lift it up for a new foundation, or even elevate it permanently 12 to 15 feet in the air to accommodate a new first story. If the entire house is leaning sideways, it can literally be pulled into line.

Most of these tasks, however, should not be attempted by someone who has never done them before. Any pro you hire should be knowledgeable about old houses, particularly if yours is balloon-frame or mortise and tenon construction.

Someone who does not know what s/he is doing can cause a lot of damage in a very short time attempting structural realignment. The house has sagged slowly and gently for three quarters of a century or more, and extensive care must be taken if that is going to be undone in the space of a few weeks.

What might appear as an obvious solution to a structural problem—such as raising one corner of the house—may actually worsen other structural problems. If one corner of the house has sagged, the opposite corner might have risen at the same time. If you jack up the lower corner this will not lower the opposite corner, but will instead compress the house against it. This can cause a host of problems, including buckling floorboards and siding, doors and windows that won't work, and paint that is rippled and ruined.

Obviously, whether or not you can do a particular structural task depends upon the scope and nature of the problem and upon your personal experience. Always consult a structural engineer first to make sure you are correcting—not intensifying—the problem.

Any lifting of the outside shell of the house, such as jacking up one corner, lifting the house for a new foundation, etc., should be left to a pro. Tasks that a do-it-yourselfer can tackle include:

- Lifting or straightening small outbuildings, additions, porches, etc., that are *not* an integral part of the house.
- Jacking up sagging girders and joists.
- Correcting some roof sags.
- Adding structural bracing.

ADDITIONS

Structural problems often occur in additions to original structures. The addition may not have been intended to support the weight it now bears—a common occurrence where a porch is framed in to accommodate an added bathroom or service area. Or, the addition just may not have been well built in the first place.

A key consideration in determining whether to remove, raise a sagging corner of, or otherwise alter an addition is how any such action will effect the rest of the home. Are the structural members of the addition also structural members of the original house? If so, any change might create structural problems elsewhere in the house.

Generally, if an addition is a totally separate entity from (i.e., shares no structural members with) the main structure, you can do almost anything to it, including cutting it off the main house with a chainsaw. Avoid jacking up an addition so it leans against and exerts pressure on the main house, however, since this will probably create further problems.

As with other structural problems, the best first step in dealing with problem additions is to consult a structural engineer.

USING A JACK

Whether foundations, sagging corners, joists, or girders are the problem—or whether you need to support the house while you work on the foundation—the tool to use to straighten them or to hold girders in place while you replace rotted posts is a *jack screw*. Both *hydraulic* (temporary) and *jack post* (permanent) models are available.

Jack posts are best when you're planning to add some bracing to the house. You can install a jack post and leave it in place permanently, and thus do not have to construct a permanent support post. One permanent model, offered through the Sears, Roebuck and Company catalog, is available

in three sizes: short (for spaces 20-3/4 inches to 36 inches), intermediate (36 to 56 inches), and long (56 to 93 inches).

Temporary hydraulic jacks are readily available at rental yards. You will need one capable of lifting twelve to twenty tons. A hydraulic jack is not designed to sustain a heavy load for prolonged periods of time. As you lift with a hydraulic jack, you must support what you are lifting with large beams of wood, shimming tightly every time you raise the jack even a fraction of an inch. If you do not, the jack could slip or blow a seal—and there goes your house.

If your cellar or crawl space has a concrete floor at least 4 inches thick, you can set the jack posts or jack directly on the floor. If the cellar is dirt or the concrete is less than 4 inches, you will have to use a redwood pad or pour a concrete footing for the jack screw. This can be a 24-inch-square pad that is at least 6 inches thick, poured or placed directly upon the existing floor. An even stronger footing can be obtained by digging an 18- by-18-by-18-inch hole and filling it with concrete.

Be patient when using the jack screw: don't try to raise the joist or girder more than a quarter of an inch every few days. It may take several weeks before the floor is level, but this is necessary to avoid undue stress upon the house—which could create even more serious problems.

When you raise a jack against the house and begin to lift, you will hear a loud "popping" noise. This is normal. Remember that you are lifting an

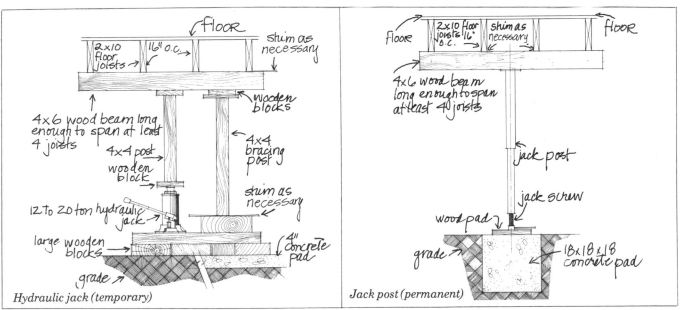

Hydraulic jack (temporary)

Jack post (permanent)

incredible amount of weight. Beware, however, if you hear a loud popping sound *after* you have finished raising the house an increment—this is a sure sign that something has given. Other indications of movement within the house include paint rippling, doors that will not shut or that begin to move freely. This movement may or may not be desired; just make sure that you are aware of how the house is moving. If it is not moving in the direction you want, stop immediately—do not raise the house any more—and contact a structural engineer.

THE FOUNDATION

Walter learned about the earthquake from his car radio. "Minor damage," the newscaster reported. Not much to worry about, Walter thought, for he owned few breakable items. As Walter approached his house, though, he saw a crowd. He didn't, however, see his home, for the foundation had crumbled in the quake, and the house had slid down to the bottom of a hill.

It sounds farfetched, but this nightmare was a reality for one California man. Although few areas of the country are as susceptible to earthquakes as California, natural disasters such as floods and landslides can happen in any area, and a poor foundation just might cost you your house. Defects in the foundation will also exacerbate other problems within the house, such as cracking plaster, buckling porches, sticking windows and doors.

Victorian homes were often built without foundations, or with brick foundations that don't support the house. Until recently, few lending institutions would loan money on homes with inadequate foundations or foundations made of brick.

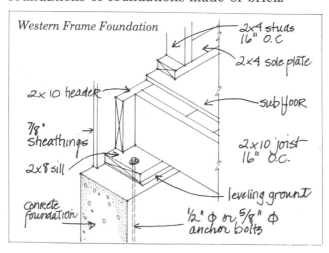

Western Frame Foundation

2x4 studs 16" O.C
2x4 sole plate
2x10 header
subfloor
7/8" sheathings
2x8 sill
2x10 joist 16" O.C.
leveling grount
concrete foundation
1/2" ⌀ or 5/8" ⌀ anchor bolts

If the foundation *is* brick, check both bricks and mortar carefully for the types of deterioration described in Chapter 11. If you note any problems, consult your local building inspector or a licensed contractor for a professional opinion on whether you should replace the whole foundation.

Your house might have an original concrete foundation, since concrete has been used as a building material since 1840 (although it was not popular during its early days). Minor cracks in concrete are common, but beware of large, open vertical or horizontal fissures. Vertical cracks usually indicate uneven settling, which is probably the most common structural fault in a house. Horizontal cracks might indicate there is excessively heavy pressure on the foundation from dirt pressing against the outside walls.

If your home is built on a wooden foundation, examine carefully all places where the wood comes in contact with the earth and look for dry rot or insect damage. You might have to dig down the side of the house to unearth the foundation, since years of silting might have covered it.

Although you can probably rebuild a foundation yourself, seek at least a consultation from a structural engineer or a licensed contractor before you begin.

THE SILL

The *sill* (a horizontal board that sits on the foundation and to which the house studs are affixed) is an especially vulnerable part of the foundation, since water can rise up through the foundation to the sill via capillary action or can run off the walls of the house and sit on the sill. If this piece rots, the whole house could literally slide.

Check to make sure the sill is affixed to the foundation, for sill bolts, as poor Walter discovered, are a vital structural component. If your house lacks these, you can screw large (5- or 6-inch, at least) lag screws through the sill and foundation; or you can secure the sill to the foundation with metal angle irons.

You can probably replace a rotted sill, even if you have never before attempted structural renovation. The technique for the do-it-yourselfer involves working on one small (6- to 8-foot) area at a time, using a jack to support the house while you cut away and replace the sill and any rotted studs. (Note: This method can be used for replacing a small section of the foundation, but only if the house has not sagged. Seek professional consultation first!) A professional, using a steel I beam and several jacks, can support half the house at one time and can therefore finish this job much quicker.

Know what you are going to do before you begin, since the house should be supported by the jack for as short a period as possible. How much of the sill is rotted? Have the studs affixed to the sill deteriorated? To what extent? Also, consult a structural engineer before you begin. You will need the following materials and tools to support the house:

● A 4-by-6-inch beam long enough to span at least four joists.
● A 4-inch-square post a foot or so shorter than the height of the basement or crawl space.
● A 12- to 20-ton hydraulic jack.
● A 4-inch-square post several feet long to place on top of the jack.
● Large wooden blocks and wooden shims for supports.

Placing the four-by-six and four-by-four as shown on page 49, lift it with the jack until the weight is transferred off the studs and onto the jack, shimming as necessary so that the four-by-six is tight against all girders and joists.

Remove the rotted sill plate and any concrete or mortar it is set in until you have reached the foundation material. Also, cut away the bottoms of any studs that have rotted. Don't cut away any more than you have to, since these studs are holding the exterior siding.

Set a new piece of sill plate in place, using a two-by-four (treated to resist rot), anchoring it to the foundation with large (at least 5/8 of an inch) high-quality lag screws. Install one lag screw at each end of the new sill plate and two more, evenly spaced, in the center of the board. Although exceeding virtually all code requirements, this number of lag screws is necessary to properly anchor a short piece of sill.

Because new two-by-fours are smaller than old dimensional lumber, and because the old sill may have been set up on a bed of concrete, there will probably be a gap of at least 2 inches between the new sill and the studs—more if the studs were cut back. How you bridge this depends upon how your house is constructed and how large the gap is.

Whatever method you use, make sure the studs fit tightly against the sill, and shim if necessary.

If the house is platform construction, the optimum method is to bolt and glue new studs to the old ones, running the new boards the entire length from the sill plate to the next-story platform. This method will not work, however, for balloon-frame construction, since the studs have a tendency to *rake* (slant to one side) and therefore must be braced to prevent this.

On a balloon-frame house, first place a block under each cut stud (if all the studs have been cut off at the same height, one length of wood can be used instead of blocks). Then, *cripple* (brace on either side with blocks of wood) both sides of the stud. If you've only used short blocks under the studs, you can cripple them with running boards on top of the sill. If, on the other hand, a large part of the stud has been cut away, bolt larger boards flush on either side of the stud.

Also, exterior and bearing walls in balloon-frame construction have braces known as *let-ins* running diagonally from top to bottom to help prevent raking. These were 1-by-2-inch boards that were either cut into blocks and nailed between or mortised into ("let" into) the studs. If you remove any of these let-ins, make sure you replace them.

A new section of the sill should now be complete. Make sure all studs and other bracing are nailed tightly before you release the jack and start the process again on a different length of sill.

THAT SINKING FEELING

You know the feeling: a nagging sense, when you walk across the floor of your house, that something is wrong. There's that squeak again, or a sponginess in the floor.

If you believe the floor of your house has structural problems, don't wait until you fall through to the cellar to investigate. If you procrastinate, the problems will only worsen.

The situation could merely be that the nails holding the flooring have loosened. If you suspect this, you will have to renail the floor; simply rehammering the nails won't last. Rehammer the old nails and add additional nails, using either screw or ring-shank nails or flat-headed wood

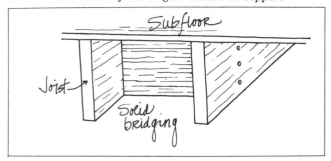

Above: *Wooden cross-bridging between joists.* Below: *Solid bridging, commonly a piece of 2-inch lumber, can also be inserted between the joists to give additional support.*

screws (countersink the heads and fill or plug the holes).

If this does not solve the problem, or if the floor visibly sags, the culprit is either the joists beneath the floor, the girders that support the joists, or the posts that support the girders. (Rule out foundation problems first, of course.)

Specific structural failures on the first floor can usually be spied by checking underneath the house. Especially vulnerable areas are beneath those rooms that carry large loads: bathrooms (especially near the tub), living rooms (around fireplaces), or where joists are affixed to the foundation.

Also, don't forget to examine areas likely to collect water, including outside steps and drainpipes, for dry rot or insect damage.

Many times, a floor will sag a fraction of an inch if the supporting joists have shrunk. This problem is minor and is easily corrected by inserting wooden shims between the floor and the joists. If the gap between the subfloor and the joists is greater than 1/2 inch, brace the joist with a 2-by-6-inch board. (Rather than nailing this board in place, use a combination of tight-bonding glue, such as Resorcinal, and lag screws.)

If the floor bounces and vibrates when walked on (but does not necessarily sag), the joists may be insufficient to carry the load. Some floors have "bridging": two-by-twos or larger boards nailed in

an X pattern between the joists to stiffen the floor. If the floor lacks bridging, try nailing or screwing boards between the joists. Some hardware stores sell expandable metal bridging that is expensive but might do a better job. Another alternative is to affix pieces of 2-by-6-inch board between the joists.

If the joists appear to be sound, the problem may be in the underlying girders. If the girder has shrunk or sagged only a fraction of an inch, wooden shims inserted between girder and joist or between girder and supporting post could solve the problem.

Sometimes, there are no girders supporting the joists. These can be added, but, again, consult a professional first.

If the girder has sagged considerably, this could be the result of failure or inadequacy of the supporting posts, which can deteriorate with age or from infestations of dry rot or termites.

Sagging floors can also occur when supporting joists are notched or otherwise cut. This is common in older homes where plumbing and electricity were frequently added many years after the house was built.

If there are wires, pipes, etc. running through your joists, you can support the joist by placing a permanent jack screw underneath it. Another solution is to bolt 1/8-inch steel plating underneath the cut on either side of the joist, or to glue and screw a 2-by-12-inch board directly to the existing joist.

You can also "head off" the joist, building a box around the area that has been cut, to transfer the weight to neighboring joists. Make sure, however, that those joists can carry additional weight.

Another common cause of sagging floors is dry rot or termite damage to joists, girders, or posts, so check it out (see Chapter 14).

UPPER FLOORS

Generally the methods for detecting and dealing with upper-floor structural problems are similar to those for ailing ground levels.

Since the underside of an upper floor is visible from beneath, structural problems might have been corrected on a timely basis over the years, simply because they were visible and appeared unsightly from below. Specific signs that may indicate problems on an upper floor include bulging in the ceiling on the floor beneath, large cracks in the plaster, or separation of the plaster from the corners of the room. If you notice any of these conditions, chip away some of the ceiling plaster to examine conditions underneath.

Check carefully around bathroom fixtures and areas where water and waste pipes enter the floors or walls. If you notice visible dry rot, examine underneath to determine the extent of the decay. Even if the wood surrounding a fixture or pipe is still sound, the joists underneath could have deteriorated from, for example, a slow leak.

If you suspect any structural problems in an upper-story floor, you will probably have to remove a substantial portion of the ceiling beneath it to reach the problem.

If you have to add visible structural suppport to an upper story, try to be creative. If you're adding girders to brace a floor, you might want to box them in to resemble exposed ceiling beams. If you absolutely must add a post to bolster an upper-story floor, try disguising it as a column, trimmed with decorative moldings. Again, seek professional assistance before you take action.

A sagging roof ridge indicates that the top of the walls have probably bowed outwards. This can be corrected by running a cable (at least 3/4 inch thick) around the perimeter of the house just under the roofline, attaching it to a *turnbuckle* (a metal connector that holds both ends of the cable, each end on a threaded bolt that can be turned to tighten the cable). Turn the screws approximately 1/4 inch each day until the walls are true.

If you are adding wiring or plumbing to your house or are removing walls, don't forget to consider the structural ramifications.

● If possible, avoid cutting through the joists. Perhaps you could raise the floor of that new bathroom and let the pipes run on top of the existing floorboards.

● If you want to cut through a joist, head it off first, if possible (see page 52).

● If you must cut a hole through a joist, try not to notch the top or bottom. The least destructive alternative is to drill a hole into the center of the joist one quarter of the way across the width of the joist.

● If you must notch the joist, try to do so at the very end of the span; notching the middle of the joist seriously reduces its strength. You can also reinforce any notches or cuts with 1/8-inch-thick steel plates.

● When remodeling, locate heavy fixtures (bathtubs, stoves, freestanding fireplaces) directly over a junction between a joist and a bearing wall or a joist and girders.

● To provide additional support to joists, you can bolster them by nailing two-by-fours to each side of the bottom of each joist. This additional width will increase the load-carrying capacity of a joist.

● You can also locate pipes and wires on the outside of walls and box them in with decorative moldings.

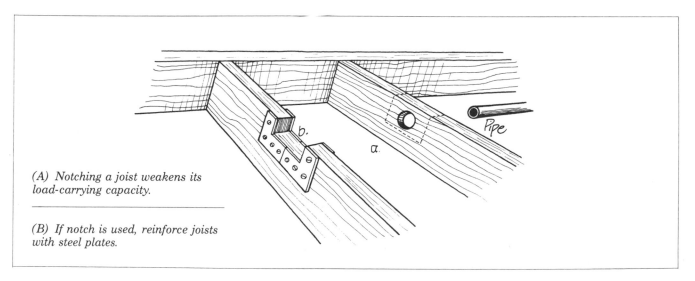

(A) Notching a joist weakens its load-carrying capacity.

(B) If notch is used, reinforce joists with steel plates.

CHAPTER 10

Moving Houses

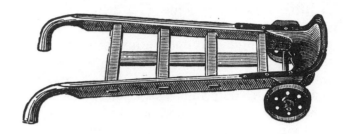

House moving was a thriving business during the Victorian era; in some cities it was even a fad. As new neighborhoods developed, people chose to relocate. And the best way to do that was to pack up everything—house included—and move.

Homes were even prefabricated in sections, then moved to their sites and assembled. Some houses were partially assembled on the East Coast and traveled clear around Cape Horn to their destinations in the West.

The booming cost of urban land during the late nineteenth century also bolstered the house-moving industry. In large cities, many of the early houses were built in the center of large lots. When land prices soared, these old homes were often moved to the corners of their original lots, and the lots were split to accommodate three or four additional houses.

Before a house is moved, it is jacked up and placed on a wooden "crib" supported by steel or wooden I beams. Wiring, plumbing, and gas lines are unhooked and removed from the house. All outside and most inside fireplaces are removed, as are most fixtures.

If you've ever seen a house waltzing down the street (actually, they're pulled by large truck and trailer rigs), you've probably wondered how it could withstand the move without being seriously damaged. Actually, virtually any structure in almost any condition can be moved, and damage should be minimal or none at all, even to an older home, as long as the move is conducted by a reputable house mover who sufficiently bridges the house before the move. (Note: Special bridging is necessary to support Victorian-era balloon-frame construction.)

Even lath and plaster walls should suffer no major damage. Plaster *may* receive damage if the roof has leaked over the years, wetting the plaster,

which will become brittle and crumble easily after it has dried. Also, areas of the house where structural cracks (caused by uneven settling of the house) have been patched may give when the house is set on a new, straight foundation.

In some areas, historic structures are preserved by law from demolition, and developers literally give away old houses to anyone who will move them to new sites. Despite this manna, the cost of moving (as much as tens of thousands of dollars) may be prohibitive. And this cost, contrary to popular belief, is based less on the distance the house will travel than on other factors that will lengthen the time the move will take: trees that have to be trimmed, telephone and power lines that have to be taken out of the way, corners that have to be negotiated.

Another prohibitive aspect may be the amount of work—especially bringing the structure up to code—that will be required after the house is moved. In some areas, a building that is moved will have to be completely brought up to code, and the enterprising renovator may have to totally gut the house to redo everything. Also, it may cost even more to dig a new foundation and rewire and replumb the house than it did to move it.

Red tape is another obstacle in the path of house moving. Many different city permits, usually necessitating different signatures, are required before a house can be moved. If you are lucky, the move will take place within one city's limits. Even then, one municipal department usually governs the permit for the move; another has jurisdiction over the streets; yet another has responsibility for the trees in the path of the move.

If you're unlucky, you could be up against several different city officials, county functionaries, and even state bureaucrats. In addition, removing low-hanging power and/or telephone lines must be coordinated with the utility companies (and paid for, too!).

If you are contemplating moving an old house, make sure all your homework is complete before you approach the bureaucrats. First, determine the site where you want to move the house. Next, take pictures of the house, the proposed site, and the path it will travel from its old home to its new one. Contact a reputable moving company—preferably one with experience moving old houses—and discuss the project and how much it will cost.

Also, remember that the final foundation work is done *after* the house is moved, not before. House movers cannot set a house absolutely accurately in a particular spot—such as on a foundation that has already been built—and cannot adjust the building after it has been set in place. You can't say to the movers: "Turn it, please—a little to the right."

A house set into its new location on a crib made of wooden beams and cross members.

Virtually any building can be moved. The picture, below, from the May 1886 edition of the Scientific American, *depicts the moving of the Brighton Beach Hotel on Coney Island. The hotel, which was moved in 1888, required 112 railroad cars, one 90-ton, three 60-ton, and four 10-ton hydraulic jacks.*

Bricks

During the Victorian era, bricks were valued as a building material because of their strength and permanence.

Bricks vary widely in strength, color, and texture, depending on the materials from which they are made, the firing temperature, and the length of firing time. You can determine the basic composition of a brick from its texture. Shale bricks are smooth and may have markings resembling crow's feet. Clay brick is more porous than shale, while brick made from silt materials is more porous yet and feels sandy.

Sun-dried bricks (usually adobe or homemade) or those fired at temperatures under 500 degrees F. are the least durable and may totally disintegrate if soaked in water. Bricks fired between 500 and 900 degrees F. will hold together but are susceptible to damage from moisture and temperature extremes. Their absorption rate is high and their tensile strength is low. When exposed to significant temperature changes, they will spall and crumble, and their faces will pop off. Bricks that are fired above 900 degrees undergo a change in their crystal structure during the firing, which makes them considerably stronger and impervious to moisture. Vitrification—when the components of the brick actually melt together—occurs between 1,500 and 1,850 degrees F. and produces the strongest, least porous bricks. Modern brick manufacturers fire bricks at temperatures exceeding 23,000 degrees F.

Old brick houses, especially those outside of metropolitan areas, were often fabricated of bricks made at the construction site using materials found there. If this was the case with your house, the surrounding soil is probably a similar color to the bricks. These bricks were fired in "field kilns," which were usually constructed of bricks themselves and were stoked with manure and wood. There was little or no way of controlling firing temperature, which usually ranged from 900 to 1,500 degrees F., and the resultant bricks varied widely. The strongest of these field kiln bricks were usually used to build the house's chimneys and foundation; the most uniform were placed on the face of the house.

BRICK DETERIORATION

There are several deteriorations that occur in very old or field kiln bricks as a result of age and exposure to the elements.

● *Efflorescence,* a powdery salt deposit on the bricks, is caused by a chemical change within the masonry. This condition is often due to chemicals that have come in contact with the bricks, but it may be the result of excess moisture.

● *Cryptoflorescence,* similar to efflorescence, occurs within a masonry wall and may not even be visible.

● *Spalling* is the actual disintegration of the bricks. This may be caused by exposure to excessive moisture, intense heat, or rapid freezing and thawing fluctuations over a period of years. Spalling bricks actually crumble, become soft, and break into pieces. If the bricks are exposed to years of extreme daily temperature fluctuations, their faces usually pop off.

● Bricks may also crack or crumble from uneven settling of the house or from trauma.

Before you treat damaged bricks, remove the source of chemical deterioration or excess moisture. Check the gutters, windowsills, and other places where water might collect. To determine if there is unseen moisture within masonry walls, drill into the wall with a 1/4-inch masonry bit and examine the material ejected by the drill for any signs of wetness.

The most important thing to remember about replacing old bricks is *don't*—if you can help it. The process of removing deteriorated bricks can easily damage those nearby. Also, if you must replace some bricks you'll probably discover that they're virtually impossible to match. During the Victorian era, there were thousands of brick makers, and each one used a slightly different mix of materials and slightly different firing technique.

Also, bricks age and weather uniquely, depending on such factors as climate, heat inside the house, proximity to smoke and factories, and how or whether they were cleaned.

To find the best match, look for used bricks, preferably near your house. Sometimes a brick manufacturer will stamp his name into some of the bricks; look for homes built nearby at the same time that might have utilized the same brand of bricks. If your house is built of field kiln bricks, search the area. There may be extra bricks buried on the property.

Do not replace old bricks with newly manufactured ones, since they will differ significantly in strength and composition. New bricks do not give or breathe like old bricks, and using them next to old bricks could accelerate the deterioration of the original masonry and also the mortar.

If you want to add a new brick structure, wall, planter box, etc. to your property and don't want to spend the high price for used bricks, brick companies are manufacturing processed "used" bricks. These are red *common bricks,* often intentionally under- and over-fired, which have been dipped in lime, coated with a water-based tar product, then tumbled in a machine that resembles a cement mixer. Some processed used bricks look more authentic than others, so shop around.

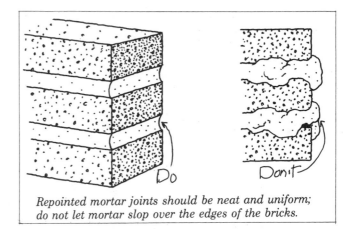

Repointed mortar joints should be neat and uniform; do not let mortar slop over the edges of the bricks.

REPOINTING MORTAR

One serious problem with old masonry walls is the deterioration of the mortar joints. Old, soft lime mortar crumbles with age. Although it may not have deteriorated to the point of weakening the house, damaged mortar is unsightly and creates pockets where water and dirt can collect and damage the masonry.

"Repointing" the masonry—redoing the mortar joints between the bricks—is not a difficult task, but don't just go to the local hardware store, buy mortar, and slap it into the grooves. You will need to determine the basic composition of your mortar, so that the new mortar will be compatible, both in strength and color, with the old. Also, proper surface preparation is important to ensure that the new mortar achieves a tight bond with the old.

Many old masonry houses were constructed with lime mortar, which is soft and expands and contracts with the elements, much as old bricks do. Portland cement, the major component of modern mortars, is hard and does not give. If you repoint lime mortar joints with cement-based mortar, in several years the surrounding mortar will deteriorate, and the nearby bricks may crumble and spall.

Have your mortar analyzed to determine the basic components. Take a piece of the mortar to a police crime laboratory or soils analysis lab, or try the local farm bureau or agriculture university. Tell

Spalling of filed kiln bricks, caused by age and exposure to the elements. Note that entire faces of some bricks have popped off; chunks of others are missing.

them you only need to know the basic ingredients and their proportions, since most laboratories are capable of extremely sophisticated analyses, which you don't need and which cost a fortune.

If you don't have access to such a laboratory or don't want to spend the time and money for the analysis, the Technical Preservation Services Division of the United States government suggests that a mixture of 1 bag of hydrated lime, 1/4 bag of white portland cement, and 3 cubic feet of sand will be compatible with most lime mortars. If your mortar originally contained cement, use 1-1/2 bags of hydrated lime, 1 bag of portland cement, and 5 to 6-1/2 cubic feet of sand.[5]

The next task is to match the sand. Place some crumbled mortar samples into a jar of dilute hydrochloric acid (1 to 8 ratio—always add acid to water). The sand will sift to the bottom. Strain it out and wash it. Check local quarries and gravel companies for a match.

The original color of your mortar was determined by mixing pigment with the lime or cement and sand. These pigments are usually available at a good-sized building-supply store or from a mason.

Matching the color of the mortar is basically a trial and error process. First, break open a chunk of the old mortar; the inside (unweathered) color is what you want to match. Mix a small amount (1/4 cup) of mortar, using a little pigment (keep track of the proportions). Make a patty from this mixture and either dry it in the sun or on a hot plate, but don't heat it higher than 200 to 250 degrees F., since higher temperatures will change the color of the mortar. Once the patty has dried completely, break it open and compare it to the old mortar. Then try again. And again.

Once you think you have arrived at a suitable color match, mix up a larger batch of mortar—at least several cups—and let it dry in the sun, just to make sure.

The next task is to prepare the joints for the new mortar. Rake out the old mortar to a depth of 1 inch, and remove any additional loose mortar. Use a cold chisel, small pry bar, pointing tool (available at supply stores), or small electric grinder (Bosch and Skil each manufacture a suitable miniature side grinder). Be careful not to damage any of the bricks. Make sure any loose mortar crumbs, dust, and dirt are removed: wipe the joints with a rag and (ideally) clean them with a blast of air.

Before you start to repoint, dampen (don't saturate) the old mortar and bricks by spraying with a hose. If you do not wet the area, the surrounding bricks and mortar will leach the water from the new mortar, reducing its strength. If the surrounding area is too wet, the mortar will dry too slowly.

You will need a medium- to large-sized mason's trowel (to hold the mortar while you work) and a small pointing trowel (to use in filling the joints). To shape the mortar joints, I use a small dowel the same diameter as the width of the joint.

Mix only a small batch of mortar at first, or it will set up (harden) on you while you are still working. Mix the dry ingredients first, then add them to the water. Small test batches can be mixed in a coffee can. Use a large bucket for a sizable batch.

Hold some of the mortar on the mason's trowel in one hand while you fill the joints with the other. Don't fill the joints too full, or they will appear thicker than the rest of the brickwork. If the edges of the bricks are worn, you may have to recess the mortar to achieve a compatible-looking joint. Using the dowel (sometimes your thumb or finger works best), finish the joint, trying to match the original brickwork.

When the new mortar is dry, it may be lighter in color than the old, since it has not yet weathered. Within one year, it should match; if you want to accelerate the "weathering" process, experiment by rubbing ashes or dirt on the new joints after they dry. New repointing may also effloresce slightly; this is common and should not recur.

If you desire more information about brick repointing, write to the Technical Preservation Services Division, Office of Archeology and Historic Preservation, National Park Service, Washington, D.C. 20402 and request Technical Preservation Brief No. 2: *Repointing Mortar Joints in Historic Brick Buildings.*

STRIPPING PAINT FROM MASONRY

Natural bricks are beautiful, and many times—especially on newer buildings—removing paint can be advantageous. Not only is paint on bricks often unsightly, it requires considerable maintenance, and the cost of removing the paint could easily be less than that of repainting.

On the other hand, consider the possible adverse effects that stripping could have on old, soft bricks. Were the bricks ever meant to be seen? Were they originally exposed or painted? Although paint was often an afterthought used to hide years of grime, some old homes were painted when they were built, to hide rough brickwork and reduce its permeability.

(Paint is not a foolproof moisture barrier, however, and should not be retained on masonry surfaces for that reason alone. It can actually trap moisture inside the bricks, especially from ground-seepage capillary action, increasing the possibility of spalling.)

There are two prevalent methods for removing paint from masonry: sandblasting and chemical stripping. While heat—propane, electric, or blow-torch—may be viable for small surfaces, it is really too time-consuming for large areas.

Many bricklayers and brick makers prefer sand-blasting. Sand or othr abrasive material is forced through a nozzle under high pressures exceeding 169 cubic feet per minute (cfm) onto the surface, and this process literally wears away the paint. Some commercial sandblasting operations use high-pressure water with the sand. This reduces the dust and the mess, but should not be used on brick, because the water may be forced into the masonry pores.

Sandblasting is a relatively inexpensive and easy method for the careful do-it-yourselfer. While small sandblasting units sold at hardware stores are inadequate (they deliver at most about 5 cfm and could require years to strip a house), larger ones, complete with a gas-driven compressor and sand, are available at most rental yards.

The type of sandblasting results you will achieve depends on the type of abrasive you use and the depth to which you blast. Generally, finer sand (00 grit) is best. It has less tendency to pit the bricks than does coarse sand, and, ironically, it also blasts faster and deeper, since it hits the wall with greater force than does coarse sand.

For most bricks, only minimal damage will result if the blasting is not done to too great a depth. Light blasting will not take off all the paint, however, which might not be what you expected. Oil-based paints are often impossible to sandblast off bricks without causing major damage, and you might have to combine sandblasting with chemical stripper for this type of paint.

Chemical stripping of paint from masonry is receiving much publicity, and many restorationists prefer this method to sandblasting. Be aware, however, that the use of any chemical on old, soft bricks may cause damage. Also, although what you see is what you get with sandblasting, you might not know for years the extent of damage done by chemical stripping agents.

Some sources suggest using household lye to strip paint from bricks. This is extremely inexpensive and therefore tempting, but it is much too caustic. Lye must also be neutralized with a strong acid, such as muriatic or hydrochloric, and old bricks and mortar are extremely vulnerable to acid damage.

American Building Restoration, Inc. (3309 West Acre Avenue, Franklin, WI 53132) manufactures a stripper designed especially for masonry, a special neutralizing spray to follow the caustic, and a sealer to finish the job. They also sell a test kit so you can try a small area.

Industrial Laboratories (429 Pine Street, Ripon, CA 95366) recommends its methylene chloride stripper for exterior masonry and suggests that, for

Sandblasting old bricks
can damage them, causing pitting.

deeper penetration into several layers of paint, it should be applied with a high-pressure airless sprayer.

If you do decide to remove the paint from your bricks or masonry, no matter what method or material you select, try a test patch first in an inconspicuous part of the house before you attack a whole wall. If you are planning to have the job commercially done, insist that the firm you choose test first. You might find that a combination of methods works best on your walls—or that the bricks underneath are too old and soft and should not be tampered with.

Once you have removed the paint from the bricks, if that is your decision, you face the additional dilemma of whether or not to seal the bricks. Proponents insist that this is a necessary step to preserve the bricks from damage from the elements, but sealer costs about $10 a gallon. Be sure that any sealer you use will breathe, otherwise you might be sealing the moisture *into* the bricks. Silicon sealer (such as Thompson's Masonry Sealer) is adequate, and an application lasts about four years.

If you can, strip the bricks in warm weather and let them dry thoroughly before sealing.

TIPS ON CLEANING OLD BRICKS

- Most dirt and grime can be removed from masonry with a good detergent and water. If you are considering chemical or abrasive (sandblasting) cleaning methods, first consult Technical Preservation Brief No. 1, *The Cleaning and Waterproof Coating of Masonry Buildings,* which is available at no charge from the U.S. Government Printing Office (request publication No. 024-005-00650-8).
- Never use a wire brush on masonry, since it may damage the surface and leave a metallic residue.
- To remove oil, grease, and many other stains from masonry, apply a poultice of talc mixed to a paste with a solvent such as paint thinner or toulene (all available at paint and large hardware stores). If the masonry is extremely porous, substitute shredded cotton rags for the talc.
- Efflorescence and lime deposits can usually be removed with soapy water.
- To remove rust stains from masonry, use muriatic acid or hydrochloric acid, mixed 1 part to 10 parts with water. Scrub carefully with a bristle brush,

and neutralize the acid with baking soda and plenty of water, since bricks are susceptible to acid burning.
- To clean old bricks before you lay them, soak them in water overnight, then brush well with a natural-bristle brush.
- Remove old mortar from bricks or stones either by scraping them carefully with a chisel or a putty knife or by burying them for several months in wet oak leaves.
- Black residue on fireplaces is caused by a buildup of resin. To remove it, use a very soapy detergent and a toothbrush. Older fireplaces may have been varnished or otherwise sealed. If the detergent does not remove the black resin, try a coat of acetone paint remover first.
- *Venation stains* are yellow and green and occur in bricks that contain a high nickel or cobalt content. The only antidote for these stains is a spray product known as IBCO, which is manufactured and sold by the Interstate Brick Company. This product is composed of several chemicals that neutralize the stain and render it transparent.
- A new brick job should be cleaned while the mortar is still damp and workable. Use a damp potato sack or a broom or a soft bristle brush and rub the brickwork to remove as much loose sand and cement as possible.

HOW TO FASTEN INTO MASONRY

Most hardware stores carry masonry nails. These are heavier than regular nails and are often ribbed to achieve greater purchase on the masonry. They work well in hard, fine concrete, but I have found them unsatisfactory in porous exposed aggregate concrete, and in bricks, which tend to crack or crumble around the nail.

Perhaps the best type of fasteners are masonry screws, which come with lead or plastic sleeves (I prefer the lead). Using a masonry bit, drill a hole the same diameter as the sleeve, then tap the sleeve into the hole with a hammer. Make sure the screws are large enough; they should just fit into the sleeves, which will expand and hold the screw tight against the masonry.

The best place to fasten into masonry is at a joint in the mortar between two bricks and two courses of bricks.

Roofs, Eaves & Gutters

Ensuring that the roof system functions properly should be one of your first renovation projects—obviously, problems should be corrected before the first seasonal rains. Not only is the roof the only protection you have from the weather, but problems with the roof, eaves, and gutters can lead to rot and structural problems in other areas of the house.

If you are planning to replace even one section of the roof, try to do this before you apply the exterior paint. Removing old roofing creates a terrible mess; just adding new roofing material leaves dust and debris. At the very least, you will have to clean the exterior of the house when you have finished roofing.

Also, before you repair or replace a roof, correct any problems with gutters, eaves, and downspouts. Many times, these are the causes of roof deterioration and, if not corrected, will cause further damage to the roof and possibly to the house structure.

ROOFS

Victorians who could afford them usually covered their roofs with slate shingles. These last virtually indefinitely unless broken. The majority of Victorian-era homes, however, originally had wood shingle roofs. Wood shingles and shakes (like shingles, only heavier) can last twenty to thirty years. They are manufactured, generally from cedar, in different weights and are most commonly sold in *squares*: bundles that will cover 100 square feet of roof surface.

Shingles yield a more uniform appearance than do shakes and are therefore better suited for most Victorian-era homes—except for the later styles (Craftsman, bungalow) that lend themselves to less formal treatment provided by shakes.

Asphalt roofing, manufactured in shingles and rolls, became available at the end of the nineteen century and is widely used today instead of wood shingles. It is made of roofing felt or fiberglass (the modern version), layered with asphalt, then covered with a fine, gravel-like material. Asphalt shingles are 12 inches by 36 inches, with slots cut into the sides so that, when laid on the roof, they resemble wooden shingles. Asphalt roofing lasts fifteen to thirty years, depending upon its weight and the conditions to which it is exposed. In addition, asphalt roofing offers some protection from fire.

Roofs can also be covered with tiles or clay (another long-lasting alternative) or with tin or (in rare cases) copper. Copper, also, will last almost forever, but tin is prone to rusting. Flat roofs are usually covered with hot tar and roofing felt, then recovered with a layer of sand or gravel.

ROOF PROBLEMS Roof deterioration may or may not show from the inside. Obviously, if you can see holes in the roof or if the water is dripping or pouring into your house, you have problems. Other conditions, however, might not be visible, especially if the attic in your house is finished or insulated.

Look first for pinholes of light entering a dark attic. These holes must definitely be patched. To locate them from the outside of the house, shove a wire through the hole from the inside to the roof to mark the spot to be patched.

Look also for water stains in the attic, both on the roof boards and on the floor. Stains may be from old leaks, however; current leaks should leave the inside of the roof wet after a heavy rain.

Examine also places where chimneys, plumbing soil stack vents, and other vents exit through the roof for signs of dampness.

Just because you find a water stain does not mean you have found the leak, either, because water may be entering the roof at one point, then running down the inside of the roof and dripping at another location. Trace the stain until you actually find a hole. You may have to remove attic insulation to do this.

Other indications of roof problems may be seen by examining the outside of the roof from the ground with a pair of binoculars. Don't tread on the roof if you can avoid it. Not only can walking on the roof be dangerous, it can damage the roofing material as well.

The following roof types may have these characteristic problems:

- *Wood shingle roofs* Look for split, missing, or rotted shingles, or shingles that are curled on the edges. If the roof has a greenish cast, it is growing fungus and should be replaced.
- *Asphalt roofs* Look for torn or missing shingles, bare spots where the gravel has worn away, fungal growth, or nails that have popped up and are no longer holding the roofing in place. Worn-out asphalt shingles often curl at the edges, giving them a cupped appearance. You may also notice granules of gravel that have come off the roof and are lying in the gutters or underneath downspouts. This is common when asphalt roofing is new; for an older roof, however, it indicates substantial deterioration.

- *Copper and tin roofs* Check for loose roofing. If the tin has rusted, it should be replaced.
- *Tile and slate roofs* As mentioned, tile and slate roofs last virtually forever, but you should inspect the roof periodically for damaged or missing tiles.
- *Hot-tar roofs* Examine the roof for places where the gravel has worn away, exposing the felt. Also, look for blisters or cracks in the tar, which might result in water leaks.

FLASHING Where something (vent, chimney, wall, etc.) protrudes from or abuts the roof—or where two slopes of the roof intersect to form an internal angle (known as a *valley*)—thin sheets of metal called *flashing* are applied to prevent water seepage. Flashing is usually applied to a surface in a continuous strip that wraps around the chimney or vent, covering the joint and extending 6 to 10 inches underneath the roofing material. Chimney flashing may also be mortared directly into brick chimney joints.

Aluminum flashing, most commonly used today, is quite durable. Copper, expensive and relatively rare, will last almost indefinitely. Galvanized metal, a common treatment, especially during the Victorian era, will rust after the protective coating has worn away. Lead flashing can also be found in many old homes. This is durable but easily distorted and may allow water seepage.

DO IT YOURSELF? Replacing a roof is actually not a difficult task. It is, however, a large and potentially dangerous job and is therefore most often best left

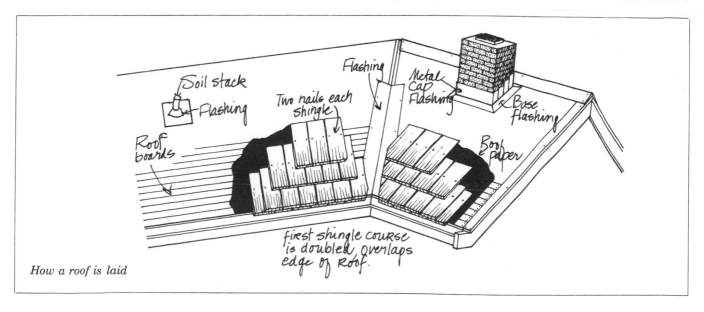

How a roof is laid

to a professional roofing company. Even a novice, however, can do minor roofing repairs. These include securing loose flashing; renailing, replacing, and patching loose shingles; patching cracks in hot-tar roofs; and resealing joints in tin and copper roofs. Even reroofing a small section of asphalt or wooden shingles is usually manageable.

Replacing flashing, however, should definitely be left to a pro. This is an extremely exacting process that, if done incorrectly, will cause leaks and may necessitate tearing out an entire section of roofing.

SAFETY TIPS FOR WORKING ON ROOFS
● Stay off the roof as much as possible, to minimize the possibility of falling and to help preserve the roof surface.
● Stay off the roof if the surface is wet or icy.
● Make sure the ladder you use is placed on a secure base. If possible, tie it in place.
● Wear soft-soled shoes that will grip the surface when you walk on the roof.
● Nail wooden cleats (strips of wood, 1 by 2 inches, will suffice) to the roof for footholds.
● If the roof pitch is especially steep, rent a belt harness and lifeline to attach to the chimney.
● Don't carry heavy materials up the ladder to the roof. Break squares of shingles into smaller bundles to carry them.
● Don't leave debris on the roof—you can easily trip over it.

ROOF REPAIRS The most common material used for roof patching is asphalt roofing cement, available at hardware stores for under $5 per gallon. The cement is applied cold, directly from the can, using an old putty knife. Caulking compound can also be used to patch roofs.

Although it's not always possible, try to make roof and flashing repairs inconspicuous; a mess of black gunk is unsightly.

FLASHING REPAIRS Lead flashing that has pulled away from the roofing material, chimney vent, or whatever can be tapped back into place, then sealed with roofing cement. Other than lead, where the flashing has pulled away, renail it, using nails made of the same metal as the flashing. (The use of dissimilar metals, such as galvanized nails on aluminum flashing, will cause galvanic action that can destroy both metals.) Cover the nail heads with roofing cement.

If the flashing is not mortared into the chimney joints but has pulled away from the chimney, seal it with two applications of roofing cement. Place the first between the chimney and the flashing; apply the second, after the first has hardened, directly over the seam between chimney and flashing, covering several inches of both chimney and flashing. You can also anchor flashing to the chimney with masonry screws.

If the flashing is mortared into brick chimney joints and the mortar has crumbled, carefully remove all the old mortar with a hammer and a cold chisel. Mix a new batch of mortar (see pages 57-58 for instructions on matching mortars) and carefully refill the joints. (Note: If the mortar in the chimney is crumbling, you should also assess the soundness of the chimney, see Chapter 17).

REPLACING DAMAGED WOOD SHINGLES If shingles are loose, you can renail them. Coat the bottom of the shingle first with a light application of roofing cement, and use sixpenny, hot-dipped galvanized roofing nails. Cover the nail heads with roofing cement.

If the shingle is split or rotted, you should replace it. Some professionals maintain that a split shingle can be repaired; however, I have found that the shingle will continue to split and eventually fall out.

Unless you take off an entire section, removing wooden shingles can be difficult, because the nails holding them down are covered by the course of shingles above them. Using a wood chisel, split the damaged shingle and remove it in pieces. Then, cut the nails off with a bolt cutter, reciprocating saw, or hacksaw. Cut a new shingle to fit into the opening, coat the bottom of the shingle with roofing cement, and nail it in place. Cover the nail heads with roofing cement.

ASPHALT SHINGLES Popped roofing nails are a common problem with asphalt roofing. Pound the nails back in and add an additional nail or two to hold the shingle in place. Cover all nail heads with roofing cement.

If an asphalt shingle is split, you can patch it with aluminum or copper sheeting. Cut the metal several inches larger than the crack, butter it with roofing cement, and slide it under the shingle. Nail it securely and cover the nail heads with roofing cement.

Removing a damaged portion of an asphalt shingle is easier than removing wooden shingles, for the upper course of shingles can be bent back carefully to expose the nails holding the damaged shingle. Use a nail prier to remove the nails, cut a new shingle to fit into place, butter the bottom of the shingle with roofing cement, and nail it in place. Cover the nail heads with roofing cement.

TIN AND COPPER Use roofing cement to seal joints and small holes. If the wind has lifted a corner of a section of the roofing, bend it back into place, coat the bottom of the roofing with asphalt cement, and renail. Cover joints and nail heads with roofing cement.

To fix a sizable hole, cut a patch several inches larger than the hole from the same material as the roof (use corrugated metal, if the roof is corrugated). Nail or rivet (if you have a rivet gun) it in place and seal with roofing cement.

TILE AND SLATE Cracks in tile and slate shingles can be patched with roofing cement. Try to work the cement deep into the crack so it seals it from both top and bottom.

Flat ceramic tiles are attached to *furring strips*: thin strips of wood also known as *roof boards* that are nailed to the rafters. Tiles can be removed by carefully lifting them until they pull away from the furring strips. Work a new tile into the opening, coating it first with roofing cement. Nail (use special nails especially for tile roofs) and seal.

Curved ceramic tiles are laid so they overlap both horizontally and vertically, with the underneath layer having its curved surface face up, and the layer on top facing down. Tiles on the bottom layer can be reached by first removing the upper ones covering them.

A special prying tool, available at most rental yards, is required for removing slate tiles. It slips underneath the tile and cuts the nails.

HOT TAR ROOFS Using a box knife, cut any blisters open, so the roofing felt will lie flat. Small cracks (less than 2 inches in diameter) can be sealed with roofing cement. For larger cracks and holes, first cut away the damaged section. Replace this with a piece of roofing felt (cut several inches larger than the hole) and nail securely. Cover this with a layer of roofing cement, sealing it several inches beyond the edges of the patch. Cover this with another piece of roofing felt, larger than the first. Nail the felt in place, and coat with a layer of roofing cement.

REPLACING THE ROOF A roof should be completely replaced, as a general rule, if more than 10 percent of the surface exhibits wear or rot.

You can add a new roof directly over the existing one, if the old surface is relatively sound. This avoids the considerable time and mess involved in removing the old roof. There are, however, contra-indications to over-roofing. These include:
● *Weight* Each new roof adds hundreds of pounds of weight and may place an undue burden on the rafters of the house.
● *Code requirements* Because of the added weight, building codes may restrict the number of over-roofings. Often, the maximum number of finished surfaces on a roof is limited by code to three.
● *Rot* If a roof is rotted (especially a wood shingle roof), don't over-roof. The rot can travel to other parts of the house, creating serious problems.
● *Aesthetics* Adding new material—especially asphalt—over an existing roof leaves the surface with a lumpy appearance.
● *Absence of sheathing* Underlying modern roofs is a layer of plywood sheathing, over which roofing felt, then the actual roofing, is applied. Old wood shingle roofs, however, often did not incorporate the sheathing layer. Instead, the shingles were nailed directly to furring strips laid perpendicular to the rafters.

Although a roof does not require sheathing to be watertight, nailing plywood sheathing with the grain perpendicular to the rafters can strengthen the roof and add protection against the rafters *raking* (falling on a slant to one side or the other).

If you choose to replace a section or all of a shingle roof, here are some guidelines.
● First, make sure eaves and gutters are in good shape (see below). Check local building code requirements; these may specify materials and construction techniques to be used, including installation of flashing and number of nails per shingle.

- If you are going to replace the roof completely, remove all the old roofing and the roofpaper (if any) underneath it. Install and caulk 4-by-8-foot sheets of 1/2-inch-thick exterior-grade plywood, if necessary.

- If you are going to over-roof, remove the roofing 6 inches up from the edge. Also remove the ridge shingles.

- The edges of wood and asphalt shingle roofs are often fitted with wooden drip edges that are designed to guide water off the roof and into the gutter. If these show evidence of rot, remove them and replace them with new, aluminum drip edges.

- Make sure all the flashing is sound; have it replaced, if necessary.

- Next, using a staple tacker, tack strips of roofing paper to the sheathing. Start from the edge of the roof and work upwards. Overlap the upper courses over the lower courses by several inches, so the water does not run through the layers.

- If you are using wooden shingles, invest in a shingler's hatchet, which is lightweight so the stroke will not damage the shingles and has a sharp blade on the end for splitting shingles.

- Start installing by placing a double row of shingles at the bottom of the roof. The edges of the shingles should sit flush on the drip edge (if there is one) of the roof. Use two nails for each shingle. Allow a 1/4- to 1/2-inch gap between shingles, and at least 1-1/2 inches between a gap on one course and those on courses directly above and below it (otherwise water will be channeled directly into these gaps).

- Asphalt roofing comes in a variety of colors and shapes. Different colors will manifest the same properties as different colors of paint: a light color will reflect heat in hot-summer areas; light colors will make the house appear taller; dark colors will make it look shorter.

- When installing asphalt shingles, follow the manufacturer's instructions, which may vary with different brands of shingles. Also, some brands of asphalt shingles have self-sticking adhesive backs; make sure you store these away from heat and sunlight.

- When you reach the ridge, or hip, of the roof (where two slopes of the roof intersect to form an outside angle), use special ridge shingles.

EAVES

Eaves, the lower edges of a roof that project past the walls of a house, are designed to channel rainwater away from the roof and away from the walls of the house.

Eaves may be attached to a roof in various ways, depending on the type of construction and the part of the roof on which the eaves sit. Some eaves are incorporated into the house framing; others are assembled independently and hung on the house.

Low-hanging, *open* eaves are a characteristic feature of later Victorian-era homes (Craftsman and bungalow, especially) and of modern construction. Most early and mid-Victorian-era styles, however, have *boxed-in* eaves: the space between the edge of the eave and the side of the house is boarded in (*returned* to the edge of the house), creating a *soffit* space. Water entering this space, if allowed to sit, creates an ideal situation for the formation of rot. This rot can spread from the eave to the house structure, especially if the eave is part of the structural framing of the house. In some

Eaves can be attached to roofs in many ways, including those shown below. The eave on the left is a separate piece that is literally tacked to the side of the house. Center: This eave is actually part of the roof truss and incorporates structural members. Right: *The ends of this eave are the roof rafters. A return piece is added at the top of the studs, leaving a soffit space within the walls.*

instances, the eave soffit opens into the wall space of a house, so water running into an eave will actually be running down the inside of the wall.

EXAMINING THE EAVES Rotted eaves may display a bright-green fungus. Rot may also be growing inside an eave (especially boxed-in eaves) without any exterior manifestation.

Often, eaves that are incorporated into the house framing can be examined and repaired from the inside, if you are planning to remove the plaster from the interior walls. If you are not removing the plaster or cannot examine the eaves from the inside (which is often the case), you will probably have to tear up the roof to examine the eaves. If you suspect the eaves are rotted, do it now, rather than after the eave has rotted through. Also, if you are reroofing, you should remove all the old roofing and sheathing covering the eaves, so you can examine them closely. If you examine the eave and it is sound, treat it with a wood preservative to inhibit future rot growth.

Eave rot frequently occurs in conjunction with deteriorated gutters, so if you have problems with the gutters—especially gutters that have rotted through and are allowing water to sit or seep into the eaves—check the eaves as well. An especially vulnerable situation is where a house has boxed-in eaves and *dutch gutters*: gutters that catch the water before it reaches the edge of the roof and are designed to funnel it into downspouts that come up through the eaves. If the downspout leaks, or if it is missing, the water may be channeled directly into the eave soffit.

Eaves may also rot if ice dams have regularly built up on the roof during heavy freezes and snows. Ice dams add a significant weight burden to the roof, but are dangerous for another reason. Often, due to heat loss from the roof, the roof of a house is warmer than the ambient temperature, and the bottoms of the ice dams will melt. Water is trapped underneath the ice dam and has nowhere to run except into the roof and the eaves of the house, often causing rot.

Ice dams result from a combination of factors, including local climate, composition and configuration of roof gutters and eaves, roof ventilation, and attic insulation. Ice dams can be prevented and broken up in several ways, such as installing heating cables on the roof, creating ventilation, or adding special metal strips to the roof to break up the ice. Consult a professional to determine the best method for your house.

REPLACING ROTTED EAVES Some people maintain that the solution to rotted eaves is to simply cut off the rotted ends. *Don't.* Not only does this destroy the symmetry of the house, if there is no eave to direct the water away from the house, the water will run down the side of the house and possibly into the foundation, creating other serious rot problems.

If you are lucky, the eaves themselves are sound and only the eave boards have rotted. Often, these boards are pieces of wainscoting or tongue and groove flooring that were left over from the house construction. Matching these would probably be expensive; you can substitute plywood, nailed with the grain perpendicular to the rafters. One-half inch exterior grade sanded plywood is good for this, although local code requirements may specify exact size and grade.

How an entire eave is replaced will be determined by the manner in which it is affixed to the house. Eaves that are just hung upon the house may literally be cut away totally, then replaced. In many Victorian-era homes, the eaves are separate members from the rafters, and you will be able to remove them and affix a new eave board without having to disturb the roof rafters.

GUTTERS

Gutters, which are troughs attached to the edges of roofs, are designed to drain water away from the house structure. Gutters that don't work properly, however, can actually channel the water *to* the house and foundation. Also, many roof problems are actually caused by deteriorated or clogged gutters. Gutter problems develop when the gutters do not receive proper routine maintenance. Leaves and debris collect in the gutters, causing the water to back up underneath the roofing material—or to sit in the gutters and rust or rot them out. This is a common problem in Victorian homes, where the gutters are usually several stories above the ground.

Many early gutters were fabricated of redwood. Although redwood is extremely rot resistant, any original redwood gutters have probably been in place for over seventy years, and chances are they need replacing.

If redwood gutters have been well maintained, however, the wood may still be sound. Test it with an icepick to determine if there is any rot (see page 71).

Sound wooden gutters should be coated (when thoroughly dry after the rainy season) with linseed oil, then painted with a water-resistant (marine or epoxy) paint, then covered with two coats of exterior paint.

If your gutters are not redwood, chances are they are fabricated of sheet metal, either galvanized steel or aluminum (a few early gutters were made of copper). Aluminum will not rust, but it is soft and can bend and distort easily. Galvanized steel—probably the most common material—will rust quickly after the protective galvanized coating wears off.

Small areas in galvanized gutters that have rusted can be wire brushed, then primed with a rust-inhibiting primer, then painted. For larger areas or areas that have completely rusted through, you can either replace the rusted section of gutter or patch it. Patching compounds—usually asphalt roof cement—are readily available at hardware stores. Make sure that, in addition to rust-inhibiting primer, you cover galvanized metal gutters with two coats of exterior paint to keep the galvanized coating from wearing off the metal.

If 10 percent or more of a metal gutter is rusted out, you should replace it. If you notice any rot at all in redwood gutters, don't fool with it—replace the gutters, because the rot can spread to the house structure. Replacement pieces for redwood gutters can be found at salvage yards or can be refabricated by a lumber mill. This is an expensive solution, however, and other materials will wear better.

There are several different options for replacement gutters. Inexpensive sheet metal varieties, made up of sections that slide together and are then glued, will last for only three to four years. The best kind of sheet-metal gutters are much heavier and require soldering where the sections join together. These will last for decades with proper maintenance. They are available in several different colors, but they are extremely expensive.

Recently, gutters made of polyvinylchloride (PVC) came out on the market. Although plastic is scorned by renovation purists, PVC gutters make sense for several reasons. Although they cost about three times as much as the inexpensive sheet-metal gutters, they are less expensive than the better sheet-metal varieties. Anyone can install PVC gutters, for the pieces are glued together with PVC cement. Also, PVC requires neither priming nor painting. Unlike their redwood or sheet-metal counterparts, they will not rot or rust away, even when water is left standing in them. PVC is also manufactured in several different colors.

Gutters that are 4 inches wide will suffice for up to 700 square feet of roof space; 5-inch widths are for roofs up to 1,400 square feet; and 6-inch widths are for roof surfaces greater than 1,400 feet.

Gutters should slope towards the downspouts at least 1/2 inch per 20 feet of run. Too much slope (more than an inch, usually), however, will look odd next to the straight line of the roof.

DOWNSPOUTS Downspouts, which carry water from gutters down the sides of the house and into the street or yard, should be inspected to ensure that they are sound and that they are not leaking where they enter the gutters. You should wire brush, prime, and paint rusted surfaces. Don't, however, try to patch drainpipes that have rusted through. Patching will not kill the rust, which will continue to eat through the metal.

Leaves and debris can easily clog a downspout, especially if it makes a sharp bend from the gutter to the side of the house. If this occurs, use a water hose nozzle or a plumber's snake to force the debris through the downspout. To prevent the recurrence of clogged downspouts, install a wire strainer at the top of the downspouts.

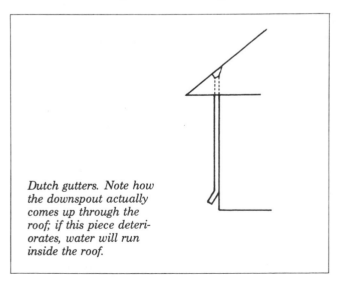

Dutch gutters. Note how the downspout actually comes up through the roof; if this piece deteriorates, water will run inside the roof.

CHAPTER 13

Stairs & Steps

The old-house renovator must take thousands of steps—literally, for the Victorian-era home was built on a vertical axis, and most old houses have several stairways. You may, therefore, encounter problems with those steps: squeaky treads, deterioration, wear, and cracking. Or, you might want to move a stairway or disassemble it for stripping, repair, or modification.

ANATOMY OF A STAIRCASE

Plain, ornate, straight, spiral—there are many different types of staircases, but they all share certain basic features. Each staircase has two *stringers*: pieces of wood or other material running from the top of the staircase to the bottom with the steps fixed between them. *Open stringers*, or *carriages*, are those cut in a sawtooth fashion so the steps can be affixed to them. *Closed stringers* are not cut to hold the stair but may be *rabbetted* (the wood is notched so the stair fits into it). The step may also rest on blocks known as *glue wedges* nailed to a closed stringer. Staircases are often a combination of open and closed stringers.

Each staircase also has *treads*—the horizontal members—and a rise space that is either open or is closed with *risers*: the vertical members. Risers and treads are cut to uniform dimensions and must be proportioned to allow someone ascending or descending the staircase to maintain stride. To achieve this, all steps are built to a precise ratio. (Mathematically, one ratio is $t + 2[r] = 25$, where t is the depth of the tread and r is the height of the rise [including the thickness of the tread]. If the stairway is wide [18 inches wide for 3/4-inch treads or 36 inches for 1-1/2-inch treads], it must have an additional stringer between the primary two.)

REPAIRING STAIRS AND STEPS

TREADS Treads obviously receive more wear, tear, and weight than any other part of a stairway, and they most often need to be replaced or repaired.

Squeaky treads are usually the result of the tread separating from the carriage or riser because of warping, shrinkage, or erosion of the wood where it is nailed to the stairway. To fix this problem, have someone stand on the tread while you reaffix it. Use screw nails (which achieve more purchase on the wood), driving them in at opposing angles so they won't be pulled out by ordinary wear. If this does not work, use screws, first drilling a pilot hole smaller than the screw threads into both tread and riser, then a shank hole the size of the screw shank into the tread only. Countersink the screw head and fill the resulting hole with either wood putty or a wooden dowel.

If the treads are worn, try removing them and turning them over to expose the other, unworn side. If this is not satisfactory, you'll have to replace the tread. To do this, first drill large pilot holes in the tread. Then, using a saber saw or a keyhole saw, cut the tread into two or three pieces and remove it.

Replacing the tread in a closed stringer staircase can be tricky if the stringer is rabbetted to hold the step. Cut the new tread the same length and manner as the old one, less 1/8 inch on either side for play. Using a chisel and a coping saw, cut a 1-inch-square notch in the tread nosing. Insert the notched end of the new tread into the rabbet. The notch will allow enough play so you can maneuver and wedge the tread into the other rabbet.

After the tread is in position, nail it to the riser and carriage with sixpenny or eightpenny galvanized

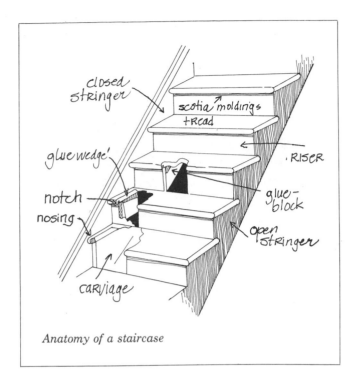

Anatomy of a staircase

finishing nails. Then, replace the notch cutout, using glue and tiny brads.

PROBLEMS UNDERNEATH If the tread seems to be intact but the step sags, this is probably due to deterioration or other problems in the stairway carriages or stringers. The best way to fix these types of problems is from underneath the stairway; if the underneath is inaccessible, you'll have to remove the treads. Once you can view the carriage and stringers, you can assess what is needed to fix the problem. Slight sagging or settling can be remedied by driving wooden shims between the stringer and the tread. If the stringer or carriage has deteriorated or rotted, you will have to treat the wood (see page 71). You can restore strength to a stringer by gluing and bolting another piece of wood to it.

EXTERIOR STAIRWAYS The most common problem in outside stairways or steps is rot due to poor drainage. To avoid this, treat all wood with a pentachloraphyl or copper or zinc napthalate. Shim the treads to slope about 1/8 inch from back to front, so water will not stand on the treads. If you are rebuilding the staircase, design the carriages so the treads are inclined thusly. Make sure the stringers sit on a concrete footing, for this is

another favorite spot for water accumulation. Also, you should design the stair railing so that the balusters are attached to the handrail at the top and to a freestanding shoe rail. This gives the water a place to run off.

BALUSTERS If the stairway balusters are loose, simply tighten them with glue and nails. If they are cracked or badly dented, or if you want to strip the wood or move the stairway, you will have to remove them.

Balusters may be affixed to the stairway in several different ways. If they are set in holes in the tread and railing, you need only push them up deeper into the railing hole until the bottom peg comes out of the tread hole.

Filleted balusters are those that are set in grooves between rails at the top and bottom of the balustrade. To remove these, simply remove the lower fillet. Balusters in the more intricately constructed stairways are dovetailed into notches at the end of the tread, and these notches are then covered by a return nosing. Remove the return nosing and slide the balusters out of their notches. If they don't slide easily, drive them out gently, using a block of wood and a hammer.

Exterior balusters tend to rot at the bottoms. If this occurs, treat the wood; if the problem is severe, cut off and replace the block at the bottom of the baluster. Affix a new block with a waterproof glue and dowels.

Newel post in a house in South Dakota

CHAPTER 14

Dry Rot Never Sleeps

Dry rot—it's insidious, voracious, and almost omnipresent. Before you even know it's there, it can turn even the most massive beam into powdery nothingness.

Dry rot is the name commonly given to a strain of fungus—*Merulius lacrymans*—of the Basidiomycetes family. *Merulius* refers to the bright yellow coloration on the mycelium (reproductive) portion of the fungus. *Lacrymans* means "weeping"—and thousands of miniscule water droplets can be observed where the dry rot fungus is actively growing.

Fungi are plants that do not have chlorophyll and must obtain their nourishment from other organic matter; *Merulius lacrymans* actually eats wood. Dry rot derives its common name from the dry and friable condition of the rotted wood. Beyond that, however, the appellation "dry" is a misnomer, since the fungus requires a wet, humid environment to thrive.

Wood usually contains approximately 12 to 14 percent water, which is present in the cell walls as thin films between cellulose layers. Wood must nearly attain its fiber saturation point of 25 to 30 percent water, however, for dry rot to take hold.

If wet wood is not dried promptly, dry rot is almost a certainty, for the invisible spores are almost always in the atmosphere, and one infestation of dry rot can produce 50 million spores per minute. The mycelium of the fungus sends out long, white, silky threads that can travel across any surface, including brick, metal, and concrete.

Once dry rot is established in a wet area, it can also spread to dry wood, since *Merulius lacrymans* produces water-carrying rhizomorphs that can convey moisture from damper to drier wood. The fungus thrives on warm, stagnant air, improperly seasoned wood, and high humidity.

The areas of a house most susceptible to dry rot are those where wood comes into frequent contact with water—basements, gutters, low spots in roofs, doors and windows, bathrooms, and kitchens—or where wood meets building materials (masonry, brick, concrete) that are capable of absorbing and retaining water for long periods of time. Water may also "wick up" from the earth through a masonry or concrete wall to an interior beam or joist.

In its earliest stages, dry rot is invisible to the naked eye. In mature forms, it causes the wood to crack against the grain in a cuboidal pattern, then to dry and crumble. *Merulius lacrymans* is clearly visible in its advanced stages: the mycelium is a huge white or yellow patch that may reach 5 feet in diameter, and the fungus appears thick and spongy white.

Dry rot may thrive for years in places where it cannot be seen, such as underneath floors and in walls near plumbing. A structural-pest-control report will identify accessible areas of dry rot, but may often miss (and will specifically disclaim responsibility for) hidden spots. The new old-house owner, structural-pest clearance clutched in hand, feels secure until he or she falls through the floor—literally.

There are signs that suggest the possible presence of hidden dry rot, and when you suspect, you should inspect. Definitely examine areas surrounding plumbing, for old pipes are notorious for leaking, and one drip is all that's needed.

One of the first signs of dry rot is a discoloration—usually red or brown streaks—on the floor, wall boards, or joists. The presence of dry rot is also indicated by a fine brown or mustard yellow dust in cobwebs near the infestation site. This is not powdered wood but fructification—the spores of the fungus. Other indications of excess moisture and possibly of dry rot are blistering and peeling paint, cracks in ceramic tile grout, and sagging floors.

If you are uncertain whether a piece of wood has succumbed to dry rot, try the icepick test: lift a small amount of wood with the tip of an icepick. Sound lumber will splinter with the grain; rotted wood will appear spongy and/or will crumble and loosen across the grain.

There is no way to "cure" dry rot once it has been established, since the wood that is infested is probably already ruined, and *Merulius lacrymans* is highly resistant to fungicides.

The first step in treating a dry rot infestation is to eliminate the source of moisture, otherwise the fungus will reappear. The next steps may appear excessive, but it is best to err on the side of thoroughness to preclude recurrence:

1. Cut out and replace all timbers showing cuboidal cracking, brown coloration, or mycelium at least 3 feet on either side of visible decay. Carefully remove this from the house by the shortest route and burn.

2. Using a wire brush, thoroughly scrub a 5-foot radius around the affected area.

3. Heat masonry and plaster surfaces with a propane torch until too hot to touch; this will kill any remaining fungi.

4. Apply a fungicide to the area.

5. Treat with a wood preservative all wood within a 5 foot radius of the infestation.

6. Use zinc oxychloride plaster or paint on nearby plaster or Sheetrocked surfaces.

7. If the rotted area of the wood is located where you cannot remove and replace it, there is a product called Git Rot that removes the moisture from wood and encases rotted fibers in a plastic

An advanced case of dry rot

material to prevent the spread of fungus. Git Rot is manufactured by Boatlife (Old Bethpage, New York) and is available at marine supply stores. It is expensive, however, costing about $8 for a kit containing a pint of resin and a pint of catalyst.

Undoubtedly the best way to deal with dry rot is to prevent its occurrence. Check roofs, gutters, and plumbing fixtures for leaks. Wherever possible, place wood at least 18 inches from any direct source of moisture. Always use well-seasoned wood when building.

There are several different petroleum derivatives that are highly effective, both in poisoning dry rot before it can become established and as water repellants. Creosote, which is used to preserve utility poles, is excellent but is thick and foul-smelling. Copper napthalate is both safe and effective, but it stains the wood green, so it is best used on surfaces that will not be seen or will be painted. Pentachloraphyl was popular for many years as an effective clear wood preservative; but, because of its toxicity, its use has been curtailed. Zinc napthalate, although not as effective, is not toxic and dries clear.

The best way to use these products is to soak the wood in a bucket of the wood preservative. If this is not possible, brush the preservative on liberally until the wood is saturated, let it dry, then repeat the process.

OTHER FUNGI

There are several other moisture-induced fungi that attack wood. Although none of the following is as serious as dry rot, the presence of any of them indicates excessive moisture, signifying that the wood is vulnerable to an attack of *Merulius lacrymans*. In all of the following cases, sand to remove the fungus and treat with a wood preservative.

● *Mildew and mold* appear as powdery, loose masses on the surface of wood or as clusters of small, black spots. Often, these fungi are accompanied with a musty smell. The presence of mold or mildew does not weaken wood.

● *Blue stain* is named for the dark color caused by the attacking fungus. It appears only in sapwood (soft wood between the bark and the heartwood of a tree). While blue stain does not itself destroy wood fibers, it does make a piece of wood extremely susceptible to moisture retention.

● *White rot* receives its name because it causes the affected piece of wood to lose its color and appear whitish. This fungus does destroy the cellulose in the wood, leaving it fibrous and stringy.

● *Soft rot* looks disastrous, creating severe cracks and fissures running along the grain of a piece of wood; but it seldom travels beyond the wood's surface and is usually easily scraped off.

INSECTS

Many different groups of animals contain species that are able to utilize wood as a foodstuff, although very few appear to be able to digest cellulose except in the presence of wood-destroying fungi. On land, the most destructive kinds of wood-eating animals are insects: butterflies and moths, beetles, ants, bees, wasps, and termites.

Insect damage is distinguishable from rot by the presence of well-defined tunnels of constant shape, usually 1/16 inch in diameter. (Sometimes you can actually see the insects or their larvae in or near the wood.) Although both insect damage and rot will reduce wood to a brown powder, the color of insect-damaged wood is usually unchanged, whereas rot will often stain the wood. Also, rot requires wetness to exist, and many insects thrive in dry conditions.

The termite is the insect most commonly associated with large-scale wood damage, and virtually every state in the country (except perhaps Alaska) has a termite problem. A termite is a *symbiotic parasitic* insect; that is, it is actually two creatures: the termite, and a small organism (a *protozoa*) that lives inside the termite's stomach. The termite ingests wood, and the creature in its stomach digests the wood, producing a by-product on which the termite lives.

There are three basic types of termites: subterranean, which live in the ground and come to the surface to eat; dry wood, which live inside walls and woodwork; and damp wood, which live in wood with a high moisture content.

The presence of termites can be detected in several ways. The exterior of the wood will usually show a slight indentation or rippling to the trained eye, and when you cut into it or probe it with an ice pick, there will be hollow tunnels where the insects have eaten the wood. Subterranean termites will construct tubes of dirt and saliva, inside which they travel from their homes in the ground to the wood. Dry-wood termites leave droppings (actually bits of undigested wood) that resemble miniature footballs, each with six ridges running across it. Also, you might see the insects themselves, crawling near woodwork or (in the case of subterranean termites) in the ground.

Termites are classified as crawling insects, but they can fly. Their wings are flimsy and only serve them when they swarm, which will occur on a warm day, usually in the spring, but sometimes during fall. And beware when they do swarm! A colony of termites can infest an entire house in a matter of hours. You should, therefore, have a termite inspection of your house every few years.

Subterranean termites are controlled by digging a trench around the house and filling it with a chemical, then backfilling it; additionally, holes are usually drilled into the foundation and filled with chemicals. Eradication of dry-wood termites is much more difficult (and more expensive), requiring that a tent be placed over the entire house, which is then fumigated. Damp-wood termites are controlled by removing the source of excess moisture.

Termite control (except for damp-wood termites) is best left to a professional company. The chemicals they use are extremely strong and unavailable to the public, and the do-it-yourself remedies that you can find just won't do the job.

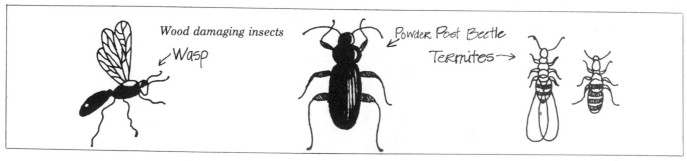

Wood damaging insects
↙ Wasp
↙ Powder Post Beetle
Termites →

PART IV

The Mechanicals

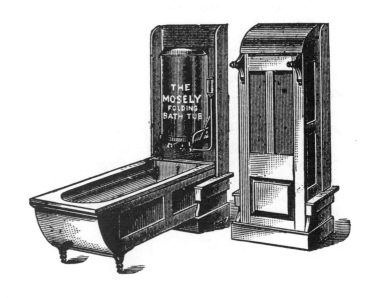

Plumbing

CHAPTER 15

OLD PLUMBING AND PLUMBING FIXTURES

Assessing your plumbing system is one of the first things you should do—ideally before you buy your house. Also, since major plumbing work necessitates tearing out floors, ceilings, and/or walls, it should obviously be one of the first renovation tasks undertaken.

Unfortunately, when you buy an old house, you usually get an old plumbing system, and many of these have to be completely replaced—a major job that can cost from $5,000 to $10,000 for the average (2,000-square-foot) house.

WHAT IS A PLUMBING SYSTEM? A plumbing system is actually two systems: the *supply system* brings water from the well or street (city water supply) into the house. It branches into two pipes, one bringing cold water to fixtures, the other traveling via the water heater to supply hot water. The *waste system* (also known as the DWR: drainage waste removal) takes used water, bodily wastes, etc. from the fixtures to the sewer or septic tank.

When assessing your system, make a layout showing where supply pipes enter the house and service the fixtures, including any *waste clean-outs* (plugs in the waste system that can be unscrewed to clean out waste lines). Also locate the main supply shutoff valve (usually where the water enters the house) and try closing it to determine if it completely shuts the water off, since you will need to turn off the water to do any work on your plumbing and to find leaks. Many times this valve is worn; if so, the water must be shut off at the street or the well.

THE SUPPLY SYSTEM If your plumbing system has major problems, chances are it's the supply system, not the waste lines, that will need to be replaced.

Through the years, the connecting areas of the supply pipes—elbows, T-joints, nipples, and unions—collect various deposits, including rust, calcium, magnesium, and other minerals. There is no way to remove the corrosion from the pipes, and it can eventually completely block the water flow.

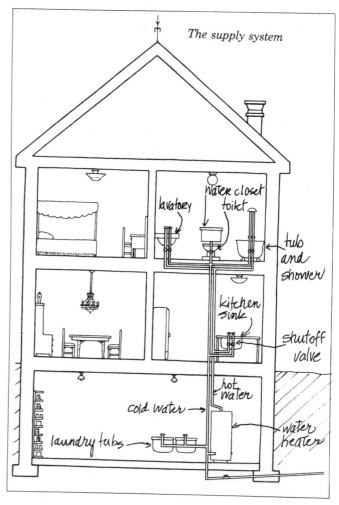

The supply system

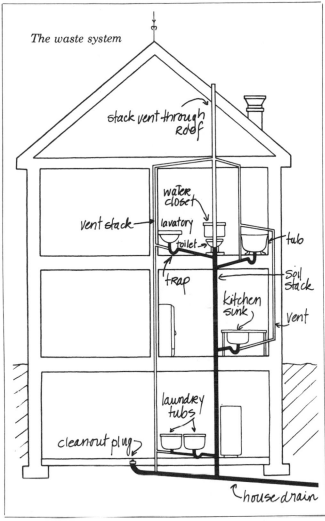

The waste system

stack vent through roof

vent stack → water closet

lavatory

toilet →

← tub

trap

Soil stack

kitchen sink

← vent

laundry tubs

cleanout plug →

house drain

The next type of pipe developed was *galvanized*— a gray metal formed by plating steel with zinc. Galvanized pipe is still used today in many areas, and galvanized plumbing in your house could either be new or it could have been in place for the last eighty years.

Some plumbers insist that all galvanized pipe older than fifty years be replaced. This is not *always* necessary; some old galvanized pipe works just fine, depending primarily on the composition of the water running through it.

Rigid copper pipe is commonly used for supply lines in modern plumbing. Copper does not rust, is less susceptible to corrosion, and, although expensive, is easy to install. Most copper plumbing is great (consider yourself lucky if your house has been replumbed with copper), but it may corrode in some areas, especially when it comes in contact with certain combinations of minerals in the soil. Also, if copper pipe has been joined to galvanized pipe without an electrolytic union (see page 79), electrolysis can occur between the two dissimilar metals, intensifying deterioration.

Flexible copper and brass pipes are also used for supply lines. Their characteristics are similar to rigid copper. Plastic PVC (polyvinylchloride) pipe is used for water supply lines in some areas. It is strong, durable, easy to install, and does not deteriorate. In many areas, however, PVC does not meet code requirements; also, the glue used on PVC is a suspected carcinogen.

EXAMINING GALVANIZED PIPE The only way to really determine if your galvanized plumbing supply lines need replacing is to examine the inside of them for corrosion—although you should be suspicious if you turn the water on full and it only trickles from the faucet.

The easiest place to look is where the pipes come through the wall or floor and join the valves, fittings, etc. for the lavatory, bath, or toilet.

First, consult pages 78-80 of this chapter for tips on working with pipes. Shut off the water to the house at the main shut-off valve. Next, drain as much of the water as possible out of the pipes by turning on all faucets. Place a coffee can beneath either of the supply valves (also known as an *angle stop*) to catch any water that might be left in the line.

There is also no practical way to prevent corrosion and "crud" from accumulating on the inside of the pipes. When newspaper mogul William Randolph Hearst was building his castle in San Simeon, California, he wanted the plumbing to last forever, so he had the pipes plated with tin, which was then almost as expensive as silver. In most older homes, you will probably have to deal with deterioration.

The degree of corrosion will vary according to the water content and the material of which the pipes are made. Replacing the supply pipes may be necessary if they have significantly deteriorated.

The first supply systems were *cast iron* (rough black metal) pipes. These deteriorated and rusted so badly that all but a handful have been replaced. If your house still has this type of pipe (heaven forbid), chances are about 99.9 percent that they will have to be replaced. (This is not the case with cast-iron *waste* systems.)

Using an adjustable or open-end wrench, remove the nut that fastens the flexible tubing to the supply valve. Wrap the supply valve with a rag to protect it; then, using a pipe wrench, remove it.

Look inside the pipes. If they are relatively clean (less than 1/8-inch buildup of gunk on the inside circumference) there are probably no problems with the supply system. If the pipes are filled with crud—enough to reduce the pipe's diameter by half its size—this does not *necessarily* mean the pipes will have to be replaced, but you should examine them further. If you have a basement crawl space, you can probably do this without tearing anything out; otherwise you may have to remove some floorboards or a section of the wall to expose the pipes.

Again, first turn off the water and drain the pipes. Saw through one of the supply pipes with a hacksaw, then remove one of the cut pieces with a wrench to get a look at the inside of the pipes.

Examine especially any joints: if the diameter has been reduced by buildup to half the original size, the pipes probably should be replaced.

When replacing the cut sections of pipe, use two new threaded pipes and join them with a union. That way you can tighten both ends down; also, you have a convenient place to inspect your pipes in the future.

Reverse the first steps outlined above to replace the supply valve. Replace the rubber washer in the supply tubing when doing this.

THE WASTE DRAIN SYSTEM Fortunately, old waste drains rarely present problems of the magnitude of supply systems. The 4-inch-diameter waste pipes are not subjected to the high pressure that supply pipes are, plus detergents and roughages going through the system inhibit buildup inside the pipes. If you do have to replace the waste systems this is usually quite costly (especially if you have to use cast iron).

Because of the reliability of cast-iron waste drains, it is not necessary to tear out walls to inspect them, but if any of the pipes are visible, check for cracks and leaks. Several cracks and leaks suggest the entire system is deteriorating and will probably need replacing within a few years.

Many plumbers even prefer cast iron over the black ABS (acrylomitrile butadiene styrene) plastic pipe used for modern installations. They believe the 3-inch diameter allowed by most codes for ABS is insufficient: power augers can tear right through plastic pipe, making clearing of clogged drains virtually impossible by that method. Plastic will not take the stress that cast iron will, and settling of the ground underneath a house might crack it, or break the joints.

Because it is much less expensive than cast iron and is very easy to install, ABS has been widely accepted for modern waste drains. It is not allowed by code in many East Coast locales, however, and it is usually prohibited in any structure higher than two stories.

VENTS AND P-TRAPS Early plumbers had to contend with deadly sewer gas: offensive fumes that came up from waste drains and that caused many fatal explosions. Finally, someone determined that sewer gas could be safely vented through long, open pipes that ran along either the insides or outsides of the walls and up through the roof. Combined with these are P-traps—sharp S-shaped bends built into toilet bodies and incorporated into waste pipes directly beneath sinks and tubs. The bottoms of these bends always "trap" a little water; this prevents the gases from escaping back into the room through the fixture.

P-traps and vents were routinely incorporated into plumbing systems installed from the turn of the century on. Systems installed earlier, however, may not be adequately vented, and very old toilets, especially, may not have P-traps incorporated into their bowls. If your system is pre turn of the century, check it out—so you don't have a sewer gas explosion.

TYPES OF DETERIORATION Forces that cause deterioration in pipes also wear down faucets and fixtures, necessitating repairs and/or replacement.
- *Friction* primarily wears faucet threads.
- *Water pressure* will eventually wear virtually any metal.
- *Hot water* accelerates decomposition, especially of rubber (washers on the hot water faucet, for example, wear much faster than do those on the cold water tap).
- *Oxygen in the water* accelerates metal deterioration.
- *Sand and grit* erode metal and rubber.

● *Atmospheric corrosion* Pollutants in the air act on pot metal (an inexpensive metal alloy), slip joint nuts, jam nuts, and metals with high zinc content.

● *Chemicals* Both those added to purify the water and those used for cleaning can deteriorate metals and rubber.

● *Electrolysis* Also known as galvanic action, this is a process whereby stray electric currents between dissimilar metals cause corrosion.

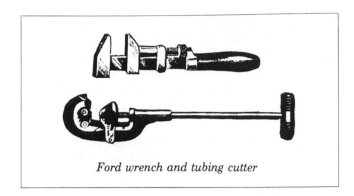

Ford wrench and tubing cutter

GENERAL PLUMBING REPAIR

DO IT YOURSELF OR HIRE A PRO? There are many good books on do-it-yourself plumbing that can teach even the beginner to install and repair fixtures and hardware. Plumbing is actually quite simple—until it doesn't work. Then it's a frustrating mess.

Unfortunately for the would-be home plumber, old plumbing frequently does not work. Old materials deteriorate over the years, causing leaks; poorly installed plumbing additions also cause problems.

Another frustrating factor for the do-it-yourselfer is the unavailability of old plumbing parts.

In areas where cast-iron drainpipes and caulked wiped joints are mandated by code, repairing the waste drain system should be left to a pro.

If you opt to pay someone to do your plumbing work, however, you may receive a nasty shock. Just because you hire a pro doesn't mean that person knows anything about old plumbing systems or fixtures. He or she may spend many expensive hours looking for that obsolete part or trying to repair a deteriorated fixture.

Whether you choose to hire a plumber or do the work yourself, find a person who has worked on old plumbing systems. Even if you want to do the work yourself, a plumber who knows old plumbing can assist you in finding (or making) that obsolete washer—or stopping your ninety-year-old faucet from gushing.

TOOLS FOR PLUMBING REPAIR

● *Pipe wrenches* For working with all types of pipe, removing or replacing valves, faucets, or other rounded fixtures, you will need two pipe wrenches. I prefer one 8-inch wrench and one 10-inch wrench: sometimes you'll need the smaller one to fit in tight places; the larger one gives you more torque and leverage.

Never use just one pipe wrench at a time; this causes undue stress on the pipes. Use one wrench to hold one pipe in place, the other to turn the other pipe and fitting.

If you don't have a strap wrench (see below), you can use a pipe wrench on a faucet, valve, or fitting. Wrap the fitting first with a rag to prevent the teeth of the pipe wrench from chewing up the metal. Never use pipe wrenches on nuts or on a chrome finish; the teeth will destroy these. Always turn the pipe wrench in the direction of the teeth to avoid damaging them.

● *Adjustable (crescent) or open-end wrench* For loosening nuts holding fixtures. Although adjustable wrenches are more versatile, open-end wrenches fit better on nuts and won't destroy the edges of the nuts.

● *Strap wrench* Has a handle with a smooth belt attached. Grips valves and fittings to remove them without damage.

● *Ford or monkey wrench* A large adjustable wrench without teeth—ideal for large slip-joint washers on tubs and sinks.

● *Slip-joint pliers* These are an alternative tool for slip-joint nuts. Wrap the pipe first before you use slip-joint pliers on it to prevent damage to the chrome plating. Not as good as a monkey wrench—many have a tendency to bend nuts out of round.

● *Screwdrivers* An assortment of Phillips-head and slothead screwdrivers.

● *Tubing cutter*

● *Small hammer*

● *Cold chisel* A chisel made of hard, tempered steel, necessary for cutting cast-iron pipe. You may be able to break some frozen connections by tapping the fitting with a cold chisel and a hammer.

- *Chain wrench* Most of the tightest connections will succumb to pipe wrenches or large adjustable wrenches, but some fittings or fixtures may be rusted or frozen on so tightly that nothing seems to work. A chain wrench provides a tight grip on a fitting or fixture, enhancing your leverage. These wrenches are available at rental yards for only a few dollars.
- *Small, fine-bristled wire "toothbrushes"* These, which can be found in large hardware and welding supply stores, are perfect for cleaning rust, deposits, and old pipe-joint compound from the threads of old pipes and fixtures.
- *Large wire brushes* Useful for cleaning rust and crud from cast-iron waste pipes and bathtubs.
- *Reciprocating saw* This is good for cutting cast-iron pipe.
- *Mini side grinder* This is an indispensable tool for cleaning rust and corrosion from the outside of footed bathtubs. The Bosch company manufactures a model that is fitted with both sanding disks and a wire cup brush; Skil also makes a small model.
- *Wire brush attachment for electric drills* For cleaning rust and other deposits off toilet hubs, underneath bathtub drains, etc., you can use a wire brush attached to your drill. Do not use the drill for large areas and avoid running it for long periods of time; the small motors were not meant for heavy-duty jobs.
- *Pipe joint compound or Teflon plumber's tape* To seal threaded connections.
- *Caulking compound* To seal faucets to fixtures, fixtures to floors, etc. Most brands either don't adhere, become brittle and crack, or remain sticky and collect dirt and dust. One type, however, Poly-seamseal by the Darworth Corporation (P.O. Box K. Tower Lane, Avon, CT 06001), hardens without becoming brittle and is available in several colors.
- *Liquid Wrench* Manufactured by Radiator Specialty Company (Charlotte, NC 28237) and available at any hardware store. Try several applications and wait fifteen minutes after each one. Great for loosening old rusted or corroded connections.
- *Lacquer thinner* This is useful for cleaning old plumbing parts. Don't use it on plastic pipe.
- *Hacksaw* with medium-toothed blade. For cutting all types of pipe.

- *Rat-tail file* for cleaning burrs from ends of cut pipes.
- *Plumber's putty* This is used to adhere a faucet, drain, overflow, or other fixture to a sink or tub. Putty always works best when it is warmed and softened. Work a lump in your hand like modeling clay, then spread it generously on the base of the fixture. As you tighten down the fixture, the putty will squeeze out the sides. Cut away any excess.
- *Rags* Lots! These are useful for protecting the finishes on pipes and fixtures from wrench teeth—and they're obviously necessary for water spills and drips.
- *Single-edged razor blades* Use these to clean deposits, crud, excess putty, etc. from china and porcelain fixtures.
- *Coffee cans, nut cans* Place these under pipes and valves to catch drips.

SOME PLUMBING TECHNIQUES

WORKING WITH GALVANIZED PIPE Galvanized pipe is available in 1/2- to 4-inch diameters, although most supply lines are either 1/2 or 3/4 inch. Galvanized pipe is commonly purchased threaded at both ends and comes in lengths from 1 inch to 20 feet; lengths shorter than 1 foot are commonly referred to as *nipples*.

When joining pieces of galvanized pipe, coat the threads of both pipes and fittings with pipe-joint compound or wrap a couple of times (in the opposite direction of the threads) with Teflon tape; then use pipe wrenches to tightly join the connections.

WORKING WITH RIGID COPPER PIPE Rigid copper pipe comes in lengths up to 20 feet, and in diameters ranging from 1/2 inch to 3 inches. Pipes most commonly used for water supply systems are 1/2 and 3/4 inches in diameter.

Copper pipe is cut with a tubing cutter; fittings are joined to it by sweat soldering: heating the pieces with a propane torch until solder placed on the copper melts and forms a seal between the pipe and fitting.

You will need the following tools for sweat soldering copper pipe:
tubing cutter
propane torch with regular nozzle

fire extinguisher (just in case)
solid wire solder (50 percent tin and 50 percent lead)
flux (any type made for use with solid wire solder)
small brush to apply flux
medium-grade steel wool

When sweat soldering copper pipe:

● Make sure all cuts in pipes are straight and the ends are free from burrs. Clean the last inch of the pipe with steel wool for a good surface onto which the solder can bond.

● Clean and polish the ends of the fitting with steel wool, inside and out.

● Using a small brush, apply flux to the end of the pipe and to the inside of the fitting.

● Insert the pipe into the fitting until it butts against the edge in a smooth fit.

● Wrap nearby sweat-soldered joints with wet rags so that the solder joints won't become hot and melt.

● Heat the pipe and fitting with the propane torch. When they become sufficiently hot, touch the solder to the joint and it will melt and flow into the joint.

● Continue this until you have built a ridge of solder all around the joint.

● To unsolder a joint, wrap the surrounding joints with wet rags. Heat the pipe and fitting with the torch until the solder in the joint melts. Gently tap the pipe from the fitting with a rubber or wooden mallet or small hammer.

Note: When adding copper pipes to a galvanized system, you must join them with an *electrolytic union*. This is a fitting that resembles a normal union but on one side is galvanized metal (threaded) and on the other side is copper (to be sweat soldered). The two pieces are joined by a rubber gasket. This fitting significantly lessens the galvanic action between the two dissimilar metals; it is required by code in many places.

WORKING WITH PLASTIC PIPE Plastic pipe is available in 1/2-inch to 4-inch diameters, although 1/2 or 3/4 is preferred for PVC supply lines, and most ABS waste lines run 1-1/4 inch to 3 inches diameter. The pipe comes in lengths up to 30 feet; PVC also comes in varying thicknesses, depending upon the amount of pressure the pipes will have to bear (building codes may specify a certain thickness).

Plastic pipe is easily cut with a hacksaw. Most fittings are joined to the pipe via a special cement, which bonds the molecules of the plastic (you must use PVC cement for PVC pipe, ABS cement for ABS pipe). Where fittings join threaded fixtures or galvanized pipe, special couplings (plain on one side, threaded on the other) are available.

To join pipe and fittings: Make sure the pipe is cut straight and smooth and filed to remove any burrs. If you are using PVC pipe, use a primer first on the surfaces to be joined. Using the proper cement, coat the inside of the fitting and the outside of the pipe with cement about 1 inch up the pipe. Immediately slide the fitting onto the pipe, turning it slightly to ensure that the cement covers both surfaces. Set the piece aside and don't touch it. PVC will set up permanently in a matter of minutes; do not run water through ABS pipe for one to two hours after you glue it. When joining a threaded fitting, use either pipe-joint compound or Teflon tape.

Cast-iron no-hub neoprene connection

WORKING WITH CAST-IRON PIPE Although *caulked joints* in hubbed cast-iron pipe and *wiped lead joints* are best left to old pros, virtually any do-it-yourselfer can join cast-iron pipe with *no hub:* a neoprene sleeve that joins two pieces of pipe and is held in place with gaskets and clamps. This can be found at any plumbing supply store.

The easiest way to cut cast-iron pipe (not in place) is to take it to a plumbing store. You can also cut it with a reciprocating saw with a heavy-duty blade. To cut cast-iron pipe, mark with yellow or white grease pencil around the entire pipe where you want to cut it. Brace underneath the pipe with blocks of wood. Using a hacksaw, score about 1/16 inch deep all around the perimeter of the pipe. Use a cold chisel and a small hammer and tap around the pipe at the score until the pipe breaks.

EXTRA GENERAL PLUMBING TIPS

● When you visit the plumbing supply store to buy parts, always take the old parts (including deteriorated washers) with you. This is essential with old plumbing, for you might need a part the salesperson has never heard of.

● When measuring pipe for installation, make sure you allow enough extra pipe (an amount equal to the diameter of the pipe) so that the pipe will fit clear up into the fitting.

● When cutting plastic, copper, or cast-iron pipe with a hacksaw, make sure your cuts are straight, otherwise the pipe will not fit flush into the fitting. A miter box is good for this purpose. After cutting the pipe, remove burrs from the ends with a rat-tail file.

● Always clean and save old nuts and other plumbing parts. Many are obsolete!

LEAKS

If you come home one day, as I did, to find several inches of water on your kitchen floor, chances are you have a plumbing leak. Many leaks are slow, however, and go undetected for years. Dampness or water marks on floors, ceilings, or walls are indications of leaks, as is wetness around pipes or fixtures.

If you live in an area where the water is metered, check for leaks in the supply system by turning off all faucets and watching the water meter for about ten minutes. If the pointer needle on the meter moves at all, there is a leak somewhere in the system. Remember that water damage—including dry rot—goes hand in hand with leaky plumbing. If you find a leak, or even evidence of an old leak (such as dried water stains), always check the surrounding wood for soundness.

PIPE LEAKS

● *Cast-iron waste pipes* Because of the reliability of cast-iron waste drains, leaks seldom occur, but watch for any telltale dampness or water marks.

Joints in cast-iron pipes are *caulked* (tamped with a substance called *oakum*) and filled with molten lead. These are both complicated procedures that not one do-it-yourselfer in a thousand can do well. Since they necessitate special skills, if your cast-iron pipe joints leak, call the plumber.

Cracks within the pipes are often caused by the house settling. These are relatively easy for the do-it-yourselfer to repair. If the crack runs vertically and is less than 1/16 inch wide, you can fill it. Two-part epoxy works for this task; even better, however, is a product, formulated for this purpose, that fills the crack, then expands as it dries to form a tight seal. This product is marketed under various names, including Crack Seal.

If the crack runs laterally down the length of the pipe, or if it is wider than 1/16 inch, it probably cannot be successfully filled, since lateral cracking will continue, and large patches tend to be weak. The best way to repair these is to cut out the section of the pipe around the crack and replace it with *no hub*: see preceding page under "Working with Cast-Iron Pipe."

● *Galvanized supply pipes* Leaks may occur at joints. Use two-part epoxy and fill the area where the elbows, T-joint, etc. meet the pipe.

● *Sweat-soldered rigid copper pipe* Leaks will occur at joints if the solder bond is poor. Heat the joint with a propane torch until the solder melts (wrap nearby joints with wet rags to prevent them from melting). Tap the pipe with a hammer to remove the fitting from the pipe. File both thoroughly to remove any excess solder, then buff with steel wool. If the fitting is bent, use a new one. Resolder. (Note: Water must be completely drained from the lines so the copper pipe can heat enough to melt the solder.)

● *Copper pipe (flared fittings)* Leaks, which occur at joints, are most often caused by an improper fit between the flare fitting and the pipe. Remove the fitting, recut and reflare the pipe. You may have to add a new section of pipe.

● *Copper pipe (compression fittings)* Leaks may occur at joints if the compression rings are not tightened down enough, or if the pipe does not fit flush into the fitting. Try tightening the fitting with an adjustable wrench. If the joint still leaks, remove the fitting and recut the pipe.

● *Plastic pipe* Both ABS (waste) and PVC (supply) pipes may leak at joints if the glue bond is not perfect. Cracks may also occur along the lengths of pipes that have been subjected to undue stress.

The cure for either of these maladies is to cut out the leaking area with a hacksaw and replace it with new pipe and/or fittings.

BATHTUB AND SINK DRAIN LEAKS These commonly occur because the chrome-plated pipes directly under the sink or tub are crimped or deteriorated, or because the slip-joint nut washers have worn out. If the pipes are worn through or are crimped, you will have to replace them. Worn washers, also, must be replaced, but these may not be easy to find. Although some old bathtubs and sinks utilize standard (1-1/4-inch) waste drains, many footed bathtubs, especially, run into 1-3/8-inch drains. You will have to buy a *thin* 1-1/4-inch washer and stretch it to fit. These will be hard to seal; make sure you don't over tighten the slip joint nut.

In an old bathtub, where the waste drain enters the floor, the tube, which is 1-3/8 inches, fits into a 1-1/2-inch pipe. This connection requires a 1-1/2-inch slip-joint nut and a special 1-3/8-by-1-1/2-inch reducing slip-joint washer. Few plumbing stores carry these or even know what they are.

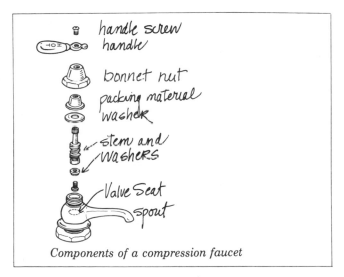

Components of a compression faucet

LEAKING FAUCETS

● *If the faucet leaks at the spout* This may be merely a worn washer or it may be the result of a deteriorated valve seat.

1. If the faucet has individual hot and cold spouts, you will obviously be able to determine which one is leaking. If it does not, you will have to determine which side is leaking (most often it is the hot water valve, but with old plumbing you never know). Turn off the supply valve to either the hot or cold water. If the drip stops, you know you've found the right side; if it does not, the opposite faucet is leaking.

2. Turn both supply valves off. Turn on the faucet until all the water has drained from the lines.

3. Remove the screw from the top of the faucet handle. If this screw is worn, it should be replaced at this time.

4. Remove the handle.

5. Using either an adjustable wrench or slip-joint pliers, remove the *bonnet nut* (protect the finish by first wrapping the nut with a rag).

6. The *stem* may come out with the bonnet nut. If not, place the handle on the end of the stem and turn to loosen the stem.

7. Remove the screw from the bottom of the stem (replace it if it is worn).

8. Remove the washer and replace it. A washer exhibiting normal wear will be hard and shiny. If the bottom of the washer is pitted and torn, this signifies that the *valve seat* has deteriorated. If you're lucky, it can be ground—take it to a plumber. Regrinding a valve set is an exacting task that requires a special reseating tool; but even if you find this implement, it is easy to ruin your entire faucet if you don't know what you're doing.

9. Reverse steps 1 through 8 to reassemble the faucet. Turn the water on at the supply valve and check for leaks. If the faucet still leaks at the spout, the valve seat may need regrinding.

● *If the faucet leaks near the handle or bonnet nut stem leaks* This is usually caused by a deteriorated bonnet washer or bonnet packing.

1–5. Follow steps outlined for spout leaks.

6. If the stem comes out with the bonnet nut, place faucet handle over the stem and turn counterclockwise to remove it.

7. Remove the old packing from the bonnet nut.

8. Replace with the same kind of packing, spinning it in a counterclockwise direction. Make sure it fits snugly into the bonnet.

9. Remove and replace bonnet washer.

10. Reverse steps 1–6 to reassemble faucet; check for leaks.

● *If the faucet handle is loose* The *broaching* on the stem where the handle is fastened may be worn out, and you will have to replace the entire stem. Many times it will be difficult (or even impossible) to find replacement stems.

LEAKING SUPPLY LINES Supply lines will leak at either the supply valve or where it enters the fixture, and this is often the result of a deteriorated washer. To replace the washer:

1. Turn off the supply valve.

2. Open the corresponding faucet or flush the toilet, whichever is appropriate, to drain the lines.

3. If the water continues to run, the supply valve has probably deteriorated and does not seal off the water. If this occurs, shut off the water at the main shutoff valve, then drain the line, remove the supply valve with a pipe wrench, and either replace it or have it repaired. (Since many of the older supply valves were brass, having them repaired and stripped may be worthwhile).

4. Using an adjustable wrench, remove the nut holding the supply tube to the supply valve.

5. Remove the washer from the end of the supply tube and replace it with a new one (if the supply tube has a brass *farrell,* a small ring about 3/8 inch wide, replace that—do *not* combine a farrell with washer).

6. Reinsert the supply tube into the valve. Make sure it is straight, flush, and inserted as far as it will go.

7. Replace the nut holding the supply tube to the supply valve.

8. Turn on the water at the supply valve. If the water drips from the valve, you may have a crimped supply tube and will have to replace it—or you may not have adequately tightened the nut over a brass farrell.

Note: A relatively new kind of plastic supply line, available at hardware and plumbing stores, can be installed without any tools and is virtually leak-free.

REPAIRING OLD PLUMBING FIXTURES

Your house might still have some of the original marble, china, or porcelain fixtures. Repairing these, however, may or may not be worthwhile.

OLD MARBLE Marble was widely used in bathrooms before 1900 and was popular during the first two decades of the twentieth century in the South (in New Orleans, especially). Old marble is beautiful, but it is very porous and may be broken or cracked.

If you do not like the old look of dulled marble, some companies (try those who manufacture gravestones) can repolish it. Small cracks in marble can be filled with patching compound mixed with latex additive (available at large floor-covering stores). If the color of this filler does not match the marble, tint it with a small amount of pigment. If you have large cracks to repair, don't expect to restore the tensile strength of the marble with a patch.

CHINA FIXTURES may show cracks, crazing (intricate spiderwebs of hairline cracks), or dullness and wear. There is really no way to repair these lovelies; take their imperfections as character lines. Some people try to cover the surface with a coat of clear epoxy paint, but this soon peels.

PORCELAINIZED CAST-IRON bathtubs and sinks are made by heating the iron fixture until it is red-hot, sprinkling a glass-based mixture over it (this melts) then allowing the piece to cool. Although stains come off porcelain fixtures fairly well with pumice (try a very dilute hydrocholoric acid solution for stubborn spots), there is really no way to permanently restore chipped porcelain other than to reheat and reporcelain the fixture. A newly developed method recoats the fixture with a special, commercial epoxy-acrylic finish. The resulting surface is smooth, but it is shiny and not original-looking—and its longevity has not yet been verified.

If you have an old footed bathtub that is in bad shape, you might want to replace it, since these are common and relatively inexpensive (you can find one, without faucet, for under $150). You may be able to find one at a garage sale or in a country pasture. Old sinks are rarer, however, and since they don't receive nearly the friction that bathtubs do, you might try to patch even sizable chips.

● *To repair chipped porcelain:*

1. First sand the chipped area, feathering the edges where the original porcelain remains. Use wet and dry sandpaper with water, starting with 200 grit (anything coarser will scratch the porcelain) and working up to 600 grit. Sand until you have a glass-smooth surface.

2. Next, clean the surface thoroughly with lacquer thinner and a clean, lint-free rag.

3. Many companies manufacture good-quality porcelain repair products, and any of these will do.

The stark white color of these paints usually does not match the more muted, bluish cast of old porcelain. To replicate the old color, add a tiny amount of black enamel to the patching paint. Do this in a discarded bottle top and measure the amount added so you can duplicate the exact proportions.

4. Test the color match in an inconspicuous place on the porcelain; let it dry thoroughly because the color may change.

5. After you have a good match, apply a very thin coat of the paint to the cleaned, chipped area, covering both the chip and the feathered edges.

6. Shine an ultraviolet or infrared lamp on the spot from a distance of about 10 inches for thirty minutes. After the spot has cooled, clean it again with a tack rag and repeat the process. Ten or twelve applications of the paint may be necessary before the patch is built up to the level of the original porcelain, but you will then have a baked-on finish that is as durable as possible for a patch.

OLD FAUCETS You may wonder about the value of saving old bath, kitchen, and lavatory faucets. Most faucets made more than about thirty years ago are top-quality brass, with heavy stems and deep threads; these are actually better constructed than their modern counterparts.

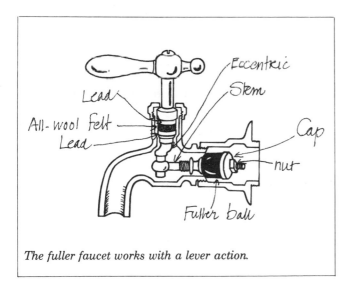

The fuller faucet works with a lever action.

Faucets made prior to World War I were primarily of two types: *compression* and *fuller*. If the faucet was made before 1900, chances are it has a slender spout with ornamental decoration.

Because compression faucets are still being manufactured for today's tubs and sinks, most parts are readily available, and most compression faucets can be repaired. For some faucets, such as the old Crane or Mueller brands, you may have to grind down a new washer to adapt it to the old faucet.

Unfortunately, fuller-type faucets are a different story. This type, which works via a lever and ball action that shuts off the water through the spout, was made by virtually every major plumbing manufacturer. Because they are no longer made, however, parts are difficult to find; if you have fuller faucets with problems, the best thing to do is to take them to a plumber who knows old plumbing. Perhaps s/he can find spare parts from another old faucet.

OLD HIGH-TANK TOILETS As mentioned above, buying a reproduction high-tank toilet may be preferable to the real McCoy. If you do buy an antique, have the dealer guarantee that the parts work—or, ideally, that they have been replaced.

The trouble with most old high-tank toilets is that they use outmoded components that are nearly impossible to repair or replace (whereas parts for modern toilets are available even in supermarkets and virtually anyone can install them).

Most plumbers will not repair an old toilet ballcock. The labor to repair seat washers and packing as originally used costs more than it does to replace them. In addition, the old materials, even after repair, will continue to deteriorate, and the toilet may continue to leak.

Old *syphon flush valves* are also virtually impossible to repair due to the unavailability of proper washers. Today, most good-quality toilets use the Douglas flush valve, developed by John Douglas at the turn of the century. You can't just replace an old syphon flush valve with a Douglas valve without major work. This involves boring the hole for the downtube from approximately 1-1/2 inches (the size of old syphon flush valves) to 2-3/4 inches (for the Douglas), then fitting that hole with a special reducing fitting to adapt the Douglas flush valve to the original downtube.

Liners in old high-tank toilets, which were originally made of lead, copper, or galvanized metal, also present problems, since the metal corrodes and wears over the years. More than 90 percent of them need to be replaced.

To examine the liner of a high-tank toilet, clean it first with dilute muriatic acid to remove as many of the deposits as possible. Then, examine it carefully in the light (especially around the holes for the ballcock and flush valve) for thin spots and holes. You can have a new liner made by a plastics company from either fiberglass or Plexiglass—these will last virtually forever.

Also, check the distance from the center of the waste drain to the wall. Most modern toilet installations are "roughed in" (as this is known) 12 inches from the wall; high-tank toilets were often roughed in at 10 inches; and old low-down toilets were routinely set at 14 inches. Always measure the distance!

And don't forget to check the toilet bowl to make sure it is fitted with an integral P-trap.

Rebuilding an antique high-tank toilet costs about $200. After it's completed, your toilet will be as good as a new one, though.

CORROSION ON OLD FOOTED TUBS Since cast iron rusts easily, most old footed bathtubs will show some evidence of corrosion, and will have deteriorated badly. Painting over this leaves unsightly pits and lumps, and the rusting will continue beneath the paint.

The best way to remove this corrosion is to grind it off, using a mini side grinder fitted with a wire-cut brush. Follow this with a sanding disk to obtain a glass-smooth surface. Treat with a rust-inhibiting primer, then paint.

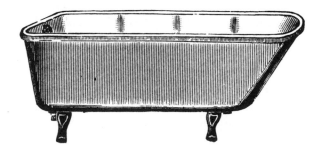

CHINA FAUCET HANDLES Most faucets made before 1930 were equipped with china lever or cross-arm handles. Unfortunately, today, many of these have broken or chipped. Replacements are hard to come by—antique-plumbing dealers covet them—and are extremely expensive when you can find them.

Mac the Antique Plumber in Sacramento, California, is perhaps the only source of reproduction china handles, and he manufactures them to fit any faucet. For more information, write him at 885 Fifty-seventh Street, Sacramento, CA 95819.

A FEW LAST HINTS If you install a shower ring (a circular or D-shaped apparatus holding a shower curtain in a footed tub), try sewing or gluing tiny magnets into the hem of the curtain. This will cause the curtain to stick to the tub instead of your body.

When you clean old bathroom fixtures on a daily basis, use only Bon-Ami, the least abrasive of all cleansers. You don't need to erode the finish of your fixtures any more than they already have been.

SEPTIC SYSTEMS AND SEWER LINES

SEPTIC SYSTEMS If your septic tank is of adequate size (1,000–1,500 gallons) it can service an average family of four people with a dishwasher and a washing machine.

If your house is on a septic service, have it checked before you buy. A septic system report will usually cost less than $50, and then you'll know the state of your system. If the report recommends that you have the system pumped, do it—if it backs up into the house, you will have a real mess.

To find the septic tank: most of the time it's located under a steel plate. If not, trace the main drain where it exits the house and look for the lushest part of the yard. Septic tanks may be located right up next to a house—or even directly underneath a porch.

You can usually determine if the septic tank is in good shape just by looking at it. If the sides are falling in, it's gone. While you have the lid off, flush the toilet and run the water in several areas of the house. If the water flows well into the septic tank, the lines are clear; if it just trickles, they're obstructed (usually by tree roots) or they're cracked.

The septic system works by bacteria that break down, digest, and liquify wastes. Do not put anything into your drains that will kill bacteria, such as lye (Drano) or other harsh chemicals. Special enzyme additives are available and should be added periodically for preventive maintenance.

Avoid overloading a small septic system. If yours is less than 1,000 gallons, don't run a dishwasher and washing machine and take a shower at the same time.

Most septic tank manufacturers advise against installing a disposal on a septic system, since food wastes—especially fats—are difficult for the bacteria to decompose. Also, for this reason, avoid pouring grease down the sink.

SEWER LINES In most old houses, the lines running from the house to the sewer or septic system are made of clay. Hard-fired clay is durable and can last for centuries. Like old bricks, however, clay that is fired at temperatures below 1,700 degrees F. is susceptible to cracking and to decomposition from water and freeze-thaw cycles. It is best to have your lines checked by a pro—preferably before you buy your house. Also, be suspicious if any areas in the ground seem perpetually damp.

If your house has been converted from a septic to a sewer system, check to make sure that the sewer lines were not run through the old septic tank. If so, the old tank, once emptied, will eventually collapse and can crush the sewer lines. This happened to an acquaintance of mine. For months, the waste ran into the collapsed septic tank, then eventually into his backyard.

Electricity

During the current era of electric can openers, toothbrushes, trash compactors, and shoeshine contraptions, the miracle of illuminating an entire room with the mere flick of a switch is taken for granted. Yet, less than two hundred years ago, the only sources of light were ill-smelling fish and animal fats, candles, and the open fireplace. Natural gas was not developed until 1812, and not until 1860 were gas and kerosene widely used for illumination. The Victorians, though, recognized the need for good lighting, and homes of the wealthy often had their own gas generating plants.

Although Benjamin Franklin developed working electrical circuits by 1749, and small battery-powered motors were in operation during the 1830s, electricity did not become a common house-hold phenomenon until the 1880s and 1890s.

The marvel of electricity was introduced to the populace at the Philadelphia Centennial Exposition of 1876. In 1878, Philadelphia received the first commercial electrical installation, and, during the 1880s, most major United States cities installed electric streetcar systems. Electricity became a nationwide fad and was celebrated by carnivals of lights in the streets.

In 1889, the first utility company—the Edison General Electric Company—was formed. Early electrical generators only worked during the evening hours, however, and they often failed, so, until the early twentieth century (later in remote areas), light fixtures combined electric sockets with either gas or kerosene jets. After electrical service became reliable, some of these fixtures were retained for atmosphere—now, they're collector's items.

In 1893, the Palace of Electricity at the Chicago World's Colombian Exposition featured an all-electric kitchen, complete with electric range, fry pan, coffee percolator, dishwasher, and toaster.

These gadgets, however, were prohibitively expensive for all but the very wealthy. The utility companies did not promote the use of electric appliances, either, since they were being forced to make huge capital expenditures for additional generators just to meet residential lighting demands.

In 1893, however, the Niagara Falls Power Project swung into operation. During the ensuing decades, hydroelectric and other methods of mass generating of electricity made electricity readily available, and by 1920 most houses had an array of electric gadgets.

Despite the growing popularity of electricity, much of the public harbored a distrust of it, and they had good reason to be wary. Much early electrical wiring was run without any sort of insulation, causing devastating fires; and there were many horrifying tales of death by electrocution. Ironically, the same Palace of Electricity that dazzled World's Fair visitors in 1893 caught fire; poor quality wiring—no insulation, no grounding, crossed and overloaded circuits—was blamed.

By the end of the nineteenth century, the need for electrical safety standards was well recognized, spawning both the National Electrical Code and also the Underwriter's Laboratory. The latter is an independent testing group concerned with ensuring the safety of electrical components and appliances; their UL trademark is still valued as a mark of quality.

HOW ELECTRICITY WORKS

Electricity occurs when electrically charged particles, known as electrons, flow between two points of a wire, completing a circuit from a *hot* wire, through the appliance, light, etc., and then through a *neutral,* or *cold,* wire.

Three terms are commonly used to describe measurements of electricity:

● *Voltage,* or *volts,* are the force of the electrons going through the wires. Lights and most appliances in the United States run on 120-volt circuits. Heavy appliances such as stoves, clothes dryers, heaters, etc. require 240-volt circuits.

● *Amperes,* also known as *amps,* are the measure of the rate of flow of electrons through electrical wires: the current a particular electrical device draws.

● *Wattage,* or *watts,* measure the total amount of electricity a light, appliance, etc. consumes per hour.

To explain the relationship of these terms, electricians often compare electricity flowing through a wire to a river flowing downstream. Volts are similar to the volume of water in the river; amps are like the speed at which the river flows; and watts represent the total amount of water that flows past a given point during an hour. These measurements are related as follows: *Watts = Volts (Amps)* per hour.

Electricity travels through commercial power lines at over 10,000 volts into transformers, which reduce the power to lines of 120 volts, which then enter a house.

Electrical entrance head. Note how "drip loop" wires hang below the level of the curved head to prevent water from running down the pipe and into the electrical box.

Two or three wires (a neutral line and one or two 120-volt hot wires) enter the house at the *entrance head,* travel down through a large metal pipe and through the utility company's power meter, and then into the *service fuse* or *circuit breaker panel box.* There, the electricity feeds various circuits that power receptacles, lights, and appliances in the house. Each circuit is controlled by a safety device: either a fuse or a circuit breaker. The entire service panel is controlled by a *main* fuse or breaker.

FUSES AND CIRCUIT BREAKERS A fuse has a metallic strip that, when exposed to excessive heat, melts and breaks (*blows*) the circuit. A blown fuse must be replaced with a new one.

There are two types of fuses: *Edison* (or *screw in*) and *cartridge.* The Edison fuse has a clear glass top through which the metal strip shows, and a threaded base similar to that of a light bulb. You can determine, by examining a blown Edison fuse, what caused it to blow. If the circuit overloads, the metal strip melts. If a short circuit causes the fuse to blow, the strip bursts, scattering flicks of metal on the inside of the glass. (A *short circuit* occurs when two hot wires touch each other or when a hot wire touches bare metal. If a hot wire touches a piece of metal that is grounded, such as a junction box or conduit, this is called a *ground fault.*)

A cartridge fuse does not indicate why it blew— the metal strip on top of the fuse melts whether there is a short circuit or an overload. The advantage to cartridge fuses is that they are manufactured in graduated sizes corresponding to ampere ratings. The fuse holder in the panel box will only hold one size, making it impossible to use an incorrect size fuse. Edison fuses are the same size and are therefore interchangeable, unless you purchase a special *stat* fuse, which consists of a permanent holder that screws into the Edison fuse base, into which only a certain size fuse fits.

Circuit breakers, which were developed about thirty years ago, also have small, thin metal strips. These bend with an electrical overload, causing the breaker to *trip* and break the circuit. A tripped breaker may be reactivated by switching it to the OFF position, then back to ON.

WIRE GAUGES Electrical wire is manufactured in different thicknesses or *gauges* capable of carrying different-sized electrical loads. The thicker the wire (and the smaller the gauge number), the more amperes the wire can carry without overheating.

Wire has a certain resistance to current flow, which, over a long distance, results in some leakage of current from the circuit. At the end of a long *run,* an electrical wire can only deliver about 90 percent of the power that entered the wire at the beginning of a circuit. This puts considerable strain on electrical appliance motors; therefore, smaller-gauge wire should be used for long runs and also for extension cords.

SAFETY GROUNDING Electricity always travels through the path of least resistance: through the material that is the best electrical *conductor*. Metals are good conductors—so is water, and so is human flesh! Wood is a poor conductor. Plastic and rubber are among the poorest conductors, so they are commonly used to insulate electrical wiring.

Mistakes in installation or deteriorated or damaged insulation (from age, friction, overheating due to circuit overloads) can cause electricity to leak from a hot wire into an appliance, electrical box, receptacle, etc. If a person touches a place that has come in contact with leaking current, s/he can receive a shock; if enough current travels into a combustible material, a fire can result.

As a safeguard against leaking current, all modern electrical installations are grounded. Grounding literally means to provide a path of least resistance by channeling any leaking electrical current into the earth, where it will be harmless.

A bare copper wire is used for grounding. It runs from special ground terminals on receptacles and junction boxes, and a bare *grounding* wire runs with the hot and neutral wires in the circuit to the electrical service box. A bare *ground* wire is also run from the inside of the service box to a pipe or stake running deep into the earth or to a length of steel that is buried within the foundation of the house.

Most modern appliances are also safety grounded, with three-wire circuits and three-pronged plugs that fit into special receptacles. Old circuits and old appliances, however, were run without grounding wires. The receptacles for these will accommodate only two-pronged plugs, and you will therefore need special adaptors (available for less than a dollar each at hardware or variety stores) to plug three-pronged plugs into your old circuits.

(The exception to this is the newest "double-insulated" appliances, in which the motor and circuitry are totally encased in plastic; manufacturers claim this prevents contact with any current-carrying part of the appliance, even if there is current leakage. These double-insulated appliances have two-pronged plugs.)

Unfortunately, there is no way to add a grounding wire to an old two-wire circuit. Code requires that if you tamper with an old electrical circuit, you must replace it.

ASSESSING YOUR ELECTRICAL SYSTEM

The electrical system is one thing you should definitely check before you purchase an old house. Minor electrical repairs are relatively easy, and even adding circuits usually poses no problem; but any work required at the *service entrance* (the entrance head where the wires enter the house and the service box) will be costly. A new electrical service box, for example, will cost $150 to $300, and circuit breakers are $5 to $10 apiece.

Until the 1920s, electricity was more of a novelty than a necessity, and early electrical systems powered very little: lights, a few receptacles, and maybe some small, early-model appliances. Thus, unless your Victorian-era house's electrical system has been updated, it will be insufficient for modern appliances that require large amounts of electricity, such as electric ranges, clothes dryers, and televisions, and you probably should replace it.

When assessing your electrical system, first check the entrance head. If only two large wires (one 120-volt line and a neutral) enter the house from the street, your electrical system has only 120-volt capacity and can only power lights and small appliances—not an electric clothes dryer, range, air conditioner, etc. A three-wire hookup at the service entrance indicates two 120-volt circuits and the capacity to power 240-volt appliances.

Next, check the rating of the service box. This is

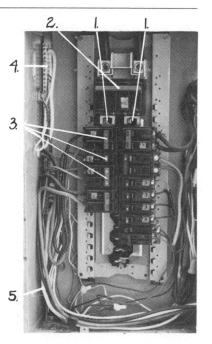

A 200-amp electrical service box: (1) Service wires; (2) Main breaker; (3) Circuit breakers on a hot busbar; (4) Neutral busbar; (5) Grounding wire.

a number, stamped somewhere on the box, that indicates the maximum amperage capacity of the box. Many old service boxes are only rated for 20–30 amps, which is not even sufficient for powering small appliances. A new house requires at least 100 amperes—ideally 200 for an all-electric installation.

With any luck, the electrical service to the house has been stepped up adequately to meet current demands—perhaps the entire house has been rewired. Indicators of this are a large-capacity service box and circuits run in conduit or sheathed cable (see pages 90-91).

The real gray area, however, is the patch job: the house that has undergone various remodelings. Perhaps the electrical service has been stepped up and new circuits have been added, but the old ones remain. You will notice, perhaps, a circuit breaker box in addition to an old fuse box—or several different types of wiring coming into the service box. If the additions were done according to electrical codes, you won't have to redo them all.

Unfortunately, this is not always the case. I've encountered insufficient gauge wire to carry the amperage on a circuit, poor splices made to add new circuits to old ones, grossly overloaded circuits—even 240-volt circuits run with two hot wires and no neutral!

If you plan to live with a patched electrical system, familiarize yourself with the different types of wiring (see below) so you can spot overloaded or deteriorated circuits and potential dangers. You also might want to consult an electrician who can help you determine what in your electrical system is safe and what needs to be replaced.

Continue your assessment by checking the electrical service box and ensuring that all ground wires are connected, and that the box is grounded to the earth via a pipe or stake.

Examine your attic, basement, or crawl space, and any other location where you have access to electrical wires. A big danger in old wiring is deterioration or damage to the insulation, which produces fire-causing shorts. Virtually any type of old insulation will fray or crack over the years and is subject to the preyings of birds, insects, and rodents. All a rat, for example, has to do is complete a circuit by touching a piece of grounded metal as he bites through a wire, and *zap!*—fried rat and your house is in flames.

WHEN TO HIRE AN ELECTRICIAN

Basically, the same guidelines apply to hiring an electrical contractor as to hiring a general contractor (see Chapter 6).

Of all the tasks in working on an old home, wiring is among the easiest for the novice do-it-yourselfer to grasp. Wiring is basically simple, and many how-to books on the market explain away the mysteries of electricity. Perhaps the best of these is H. P. Richter's *Wiring Simplified* (Park Publishing Company, 1999 Shepard Road, St. Paul, MN 55116), which is available at hardware and electrical supply stores and costs less than $2. A new edition of this book, which even electricians use as their "bible," is published each year, giving new code requirements and describing new products on the market. The book explains the fundamentals of electricity, describes all the materials and tools used, and provides enough information so you can wire an entire house.

If you choose to do your own wiring, you will not have to invest a fortune in tools, since a basic renovation workshop contains the tools required for most wiring jobs. Even the few you may need to buy (wire strippers, conduit bender, etc.) cost less than $20 apiece.

Many people, however, avoid electrical work—primarily because they do not understand it. Some fear the electricity and the danger of working with something that, although you can't see it, can kill you.

Running and repairing electrical circuits should pose no danger—if you are careful and remember to always turn off the electricity before you begin! You might want to hire an electrician if you have to increase the electrical service to the house and/or replace the service panel box, however, since this necessitates working with 240-voltage wires—and possibly even with energized wires. Also, whereas wiring a room (or even a house) where the studs are exposed is little problem, "fishing" electrical wire through existing walls is time-consuming and potentially frustrating—and may therefore be better left to a professional.

Check your local code requirements. Although most areas utilize the National Electric Code (available at most large bookstores), some municipalities impose additional more stringent requirements. Some areas require the do-it-yourselfer to consult with a licensed electrician.

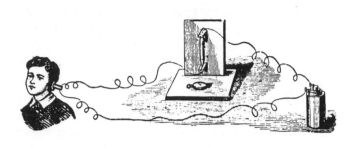

OLD WIRING

KNOB AND TUBE WIRING In modern wiring, all the wires—hot, neutral, and safety ground—are run together encased in either heavy plastic insulation (known as *non-metallic sheathed cable* or by its trade name, *Romex*) or in metal pipe known as *conduit*. In the first type of wiring developed, however—*knob and tube*—two wires run independently of each other, and each is covered with hard insulation. Where the knob and tube wires run through joists, they are encased in ceramic tubes to prevent the wire from chafing on the wood; where the wires run over the joists, they are looped around ceramic knobs, which resemble a stack of poker chips.

The ceramic knobs were often nailed to the joists with *date nails,* common nails stamped with two-digit numbers indicating the year in which they were manufactured—and therefore the year when the electrical circuits were added to your house.

In some homes, the knob and tube wire was run without insulation. Unfortunately, most of these houses burnt down. Also, sometimes an additional sheet of loose insulation, or *loom,* was placed over the hot wire.

If you have knob and tube wiring in your house, don't summarily tear it out (unless, of course, the wires are not covered by insulation, in which case it is a miracle that the house is still standing). Most knob and tube wiring is safe—safer, even, than some more modern installations. The first electrical craftsmanship was excellent, and high-quality copper wire was used, along with durable insulating products. You should, however, inspect any wire to which you have access for cracked insulation, since it has probably been in place for over seventy years. Also, remove any dust or debris that has collected near the wires.

Junctions (where circuits bisect each other or where wires are spliced) in knob and tube wiring were made by twisting the wires together and covering them with friction tape. This tape becomes brittle and may have peeled off over the years. Examine the junctions carefully.

Another problem with knob and tube wiring occurs in basements, where the wire, strung between exposed floor joists, was often used as clothesline. If the wires were pulled or stretched inordinately, something could have become loose down the circuit, since knob and tube receptacles and lights were run in a series, like early Christmas tree bulbs, and if one plug or light develops a problem, there go the rest of the ones on that circuit.

Actually, the biggest danger of knob and tube wiring is not the construction itself, which is remarkably durable, but a potential overload from extra receptacles and lights that may have been added to the circuit over the years.

Most wire used in knob and tube circuits is 14-gauge, which is capable of handling an electrical load of 15 amperes. Some previous owner of your house may have tapped off an old knob and tube circuit for some additional receptacles or lights. If you start plugging irons and toasters into an overloaded circuit, fuses will blow for sure.

CONDUIT INSTALLATIONS Some of your circuits may be run in pipe known as *conduit,* which comes in three different forms: *rigid* (heavy, threaded, elbow fittings used at corners), *thinwall* (the most common, this is joined by compression fittings and may be bent with a special conduit bender), and *flexible* (for tight corners, this is usually corrugated and may be encased in plastic for exterior installations).

Since the wires have to be run through the conduit pipe, if this is done without care, the insulation can be stripped from the wires, causing shorts.

SHEATHED CABLE Approximately thirty to forty years ago, the first sheathed cables—insulated wires manufactured in protective material—appeared. Metallic *armored* cable is a flexible metal cable containing two insulated wires. Although it has no third, bare wire, the cable itself acts as a safety ground, since it is metal and is connected to junction and receptacle boxes via metal connectors.

Another variety of cable combines insulated wires wrapped in paper and covered with a fabric (usually cotton) braid. This braid frays easily and is a favorite material for bird and rodent nests, thus posing a substantial fire threat. There is also no method of adding a safety ground to this two-wire cable, short of running a bare ground wire the entire length of the circuit. Again, you may as well redo the entire circuit.

ALUMINUM WIRING Another potential danger source is aluminum wire, which was used during World War II (when copper was scarce) and has been used during the past fifteen years in some modern installations. Recent allegations charge that aluminum wire overheats and melts its insulation, causing fires. Although aluminum wire is considered safe for some service connections, if your home contains even recently installed aluminum circuitry, you should consider replacing it.

WIRING PROBLEMS

TRACING OLD WIRING If you are attempting to live with an old electrical system, you should first map out the circuits in your house to determine if all the circuits are alive, which receptacles or lights or appliances are on which circuit, and if additions have overloaded circuits. The easiest way to do this is with two people: one to stand by the electrical service panel and the other to check the circuits.

Work one room at a time. Have one person stand in that room and use a circuit tester to determine first whether the circuits are alive. (If the receptacle or light is dead, check also the wires feeding it, since the receptacle or fixture itself may be damaged or improperly wired.)

Turn on all the lights in one room; plug a light or a circuit tester into each receptacle. Have the person at the service box flip off circuit breakers or remove fuses, one by one. When the lights or testers go dead, you know which circuit they are on. Mark these at the panel box. Do not be surprised if the lights and outlets in a room are on different circuits.

LOCATING SHORT CIRCUITS If your electrical system is continually blowing fuses or tripping circuit breakers, and you don't have an overloaded circuit, then you have a short circuit. To locate the short, if you have a plug-in fuse box:

1. Unplug everything from outlets and turn off all lights on the circuit.
2. Remove the fuse from the fuse box.
3. Insert a 100-watt light bulb in the fuse socket.
4. If the bulb lights, the circuit has a short, and the wiring must be traced.
5. If the bulb does not light up, the short is in a light, appliance, etc. that was plugged into or is on the circuit. Turn these on one at a time. If one does not work but the light bulb lights up, you've located the short.

If you have circuit breakers or cartridge fuses:

1. Turn off all lights and unplug everything from the circuit.
2. Replace the fuse or turn the breaker to ON.
3. If the fuse blows or the breaker trips, the short is within the circuit.
4. If the fuse or breaker does not react, the short is in a light or appliance that was plugged into or is on the circuit. Turn these on one at a time. When the circuit breaker trips or the fuse blows, you've located the short.

OTHER TIPS
FOR WORKING WITH OLD WIRING

● Check to ensure that the gauge of the wire is sufficient to carry the number of amperes indicated on the circuit breaker or fuse. An unknowing or lazy former owner may have just changed the fuse or breaker, without changing the wire, to increase the amps of a circuit.

● As you work on your electrical system, make a map showing what circuits power what, where the wires go, and what may have been added to original circuits.

● When tracing knob and tube circuits, since both wires may be black in color, mark the one that is hot.

● Look for telltale signs of outlets, lights, or appliances being tapped on to an old circuit: junctions formed from different types of wiring, receptacles that are wired with sheathed cable and are on the same circuit as old knob and tube.

● Many electrical fires occur at a receptacle, junction, switch, or appliance. Therefore, check your old switches and outlets carefully to make sure that they are not cracked or loose, that they are free from lint or debris, and that the wires are not loosened. Check also to ensure that the hot wire is attached to the brass terminal screw on the receptacle, the neutral to the silver screw, and the safety ground (if any) to the green screw and to a screw in the receptacle box.

● Retape junctions joining knob and tube wires. You really should add junction boxes; however, electrical code prohibits working on old wiring— "if you touch it, you replace it" is the maxim. Talk with your local building inspector; s/he may permit the additions of junction boxes if you convince him/her they're solely for safety purposes.

● Check to make sure all the connections in the service panel box are tight (turn off the power at the main first). Are the fuses (if this is what you have) screwed in tightly? Are the set screws that affix wires to circuit breakers or to the *neutral busbar* secure?

● With the power on, carefully (don't touch any metal) wiggle each circuit breaker (if you have them). Sparking behind the breaker indicates that it is not attached properly to the hot busbar and is arcing. This can damage both busbar and breaker.

● The electrical service wires entering the house are slack so they hang below the entrance head to prevent rain water from flowing into the wires. Check out these *drip loops,* as they are known, to ensure that they fall below the level of the entrance head. If not, call the utility company.

● When an appliance compressor or large motor starts, it initially draws an extra load of current. If you notice your lights dimming momentarily when a major appliance starts, this indicates an overload. If the lights and the appliance are on the same circuit, chances are the circuit is the culprit. If not, and if your entire electrical system seems to be in order, have the utility company check the cable and transformer that service your house. Many old transformers and cables were installed to serve a few small amperage services. The addition of larger services and new homes could render the system inadequate. Light dimming may also be caused by an *open neutral*: a neutral wire between the transformer and the service panel box that is broken or has a poor connection.

● Check to see that all white (neutral) and safety ground wires are connected tightly to the neutral busbar, and that a ground wire runs to earth.

● Since every house wiring system is unique, these suggestions cannot begin to cover the countless situations you might encounter with your wiring system. Your local building inspector can help you locate problems in your wiring and give you advice and consultation; work closely with him or her.

RUNNING NEW ELECTRICAL CIRCUITS IN EXISTING WALLS

To gain access to the joists, you must pry up a few floorboards. Look along the floor for planks that have already been cut for prior wiring and either screwed or renailed in place. When removing

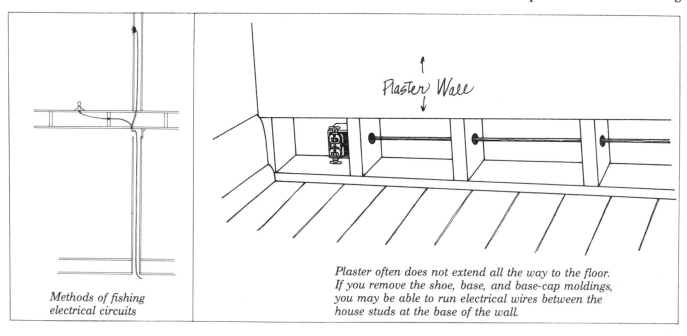

Methods of fishing electrical circuits

Plaster often does not extend all the way to the floor. If you remove the shoe, base, and base-cap moldings, you may be able to run electrical wires between the house studs at the base of the wall.

floorboards, ideally you should use a nail puller, which does not damage the wood.

Fishing circuits is easiest with two people: one who gently pulls the fish line at one end of the circuit; another who guides and feeds the wire at the other end.

If you are replacing old cable with new cable of approximately equal diameters, you can use the old wire as a fish line by splicing the end of the new cable to the old at the end of the circuit.

Another way to add circuitry to a masonry wall is metal raceway surface wiring, a two-part square metal pipe. The back part of this pipe screws into the wall with masonry fasteners; individual black, white, and safety ground wires are run through it; and the front of the pipe then snaps into the back, covering the wires. Metal raceway is manufactured in 5- and 10-foot lengths and, like conduit, must be cut to fit. The raceway will be visible; however, this may be the only way to run wiring in a solid wall. You can try to hide it, however, by covering it with a decorative molding.

For instructions on cutting holes in plaster or drywall to accommodate new outlet boxes, see Chapter 19. Do not locate the receptacle between laths—instead, move it until it sits part of the way into the laths and can be anchored on them.

SAFETY TIPS FOR WORKING WITH ELECTRICITY

- Make sure the current is turned off at the main breaker before you begin working with electricity. Use a circuit tester to verify that the power is actually off before you start touching wires.
- Always unplug an appliance before working on it. Make sure it is turned off before you plug it back in.
- Water is perhaps the best conductor of electricity. Make sure *all* areas where you work are dry; avoid working on the service panel or entrance head outside in damp weather.
- Decrease your own electrical conductivity and protect yourself against shock by wearing rubber-soled shoes and rubber-lined gloves and using tools with rubber handles when working with electricity.
- If you are sawing through or drilling into a wall,

turn off all electricity to circuits within the wall. If you need electricity to power a tool, run an extension cord from another circuit.
- If you blow a fuse or circuit breaker, don't just replace it (or turn the breaker back to ON) without determining the cause. If the blow was caused by plugging too many appliances into a circuit, avoid doing this again. If not, you should suspect a short and trace the circuit until you locate it.
- Check the condition of cords on tools and appliances. Poor connections can overheat and cause fires.
- Assume that *all* electrical wires are hot. Although the white wire is supposed to be neutral, a previous owner might have erroneously used a white color for hot wire—or might have improperly wired a circuit.

TOOLS

- *Circuit/voltage/continuity tester* This is necessary even if you plan to hire someone to do your electrical work. One type is a light bulb attached to two insulated wires; at the end of each wire is a wire prong known as a *wiggins*. When one prong is placed on a neutral or ground wire and the other on a hot wire, a circuit is completed, and the bulb lights. Purchase a good model (about $20) that will also tell you the number of volts traveling through a circuit.
- *Wire strippers* These remove insulation from wires to allow connections to be made between wires; they are necessary for any wiring, including minor repairs. Buy the type with graduated holes designed for different-gauge wires (about $7), which will strip insulation from any gauge wire without damaging the wire. Automatic wire strippers, which strip and remove insulation in one movement, are available for about $60 per pair.
- *Needle-nosed pliers* These are essential for bending wires to fit around terminal screws and are useful for pulling, bending, or straightening wires in cramped spaces.
- *Bull-nosed pliers* These, which are heavier than needle-nosed pliers, are useful for twisting wires for splices and junctions.
- *Wire cutters/diagonal pliers* Most needle-nosed and bull-nosed pliers and wire strippers have

sharp edges for cutting wires; however, a pair of wire cutters is necessary for nonmetallic sheathed cable and for any wire heavier than 10 gauge.

● *Screwdrivers*

● *Wire nuts* In early wiring, junctions and splices were made by soldering or taping wires together. Modern methods utilize wire nuts: dome-shaped pieces of plastic with metal threads inside them, which safely join two or more wires without soldering. Different-sized wire nuts are available for different gauges of wire. Keep an ample assortment on hand, and use the correct size.

For running electrical circuits in existing walls, you will need a:

● *Fish line* This is a long (most are 100 feet) coil of thin, flexible, metallic banding for running wires through conduit or for running sheathed cable through existing walls. You can substitute a wire for a fish line, but it is not nearly as flexible and tends to get caught at bends.

● *Long auger bit for drill* For running wires between floors (see illustration).

● *Keyhole, saber, or reciprocating saw* For cutting holes for new receptacle boxes.

● *Wood-boring bit* For running cable through joists.

● *Chisel and hammer*

For jobs requiring the use of rigid or thin-wall conduit:

● *Conduit benders* These are available in various sizes for different-diameter conduits.

● *Pipe cutter, hacksaw, or reciprocating saw* For cutting conduit.

● *Rat-tail file* Sawing conduit leaves metal burrs at the ends of the pipe. These must be filed smooth or they can, as wires are pulled through the conduit, damage the insulation.

CHAPTER 17

Heating & Energy

BUILT-IN ENERGY SAVERS

With the energy crunch upon us, the old-house owner may feel a draft throughout both house and pocketbook. Tall ceilings that trap warm air, thin wooden sash windows that provide little protection from the cold, and inefficient heating systems are all part of an old home.

But wait. Don't, in your conservationist zeal, destroy properties of your house that were originally designed for energy efficiency. Don't tear out those double-hung sash windows, which may be drafty during the winter but are a boon in summer. Open both top and bottom sections halfway. The hot air will rise up and out of the top opening and a fresh breeze will be sucked in through the bottom.

Refrain, also, from pouring insulation in your inside walls. This interferes with the natural circulation inside the house and can trap moisture within the walls, resulting in rot and peeling paint.

The Victorians were especially concerned with fresh-air circulation, which they believed to be vital to health, and most older houses have better air circulation than do contemporary homes. The first screen doors were developed during the late nineteenth century. Fireplaces, especially those in bedrooms, were installed as much to bring fresh air into a house during the warm months as to heat the rooms.

Attic vents are another good energy-saving method for summer months. Look first in your house for the Victorian counterpart of the attic vent: a movable board on hinges along the eaves or roof ridge, which can be opened in the summer months to dispel trapped hot air that has risen from lower floors.

The Victorian fireplace, in contrast to many modern units (where most of the heat is lost up the chimney), was often engineered to trap the hot air and circulate it to other rooms, usually via vents in the chimney chases on upper floors. Many of the old coal fireplaces also had doors or grates to prevent drafts from entering the room.

Lath and plaster are fair insulators, and brick and stone houses are difficult to beat for holding warmth during the winter and coolness during the summer. Many brick houses have air spaces (the best insulators) built into their outer walls to help trap heat and stimulate air circulation.

ENERGY-SAVING METHODS

Since they couldn't just flick the thermostat and obtain instant comfort, the Victorians devised methods for lessening the chill of winter—and some of these are just as effective today. Comforters, quilts, and hot bricks placed at the foot of the bed brought warmth at night. Shutters, window shades, heavy draperies, storm windows, and wall tapestries were also used. These have a surprisingly effective heat-saving result. During the late nineteenth century, "portiers" (curtains or draperies hung in arches and doorways) were fashionable to help keep the heat in some rooms and out of others. Winter door draperies were usually made of two layers of velvet and were replaced by lightweight silks during the hot months.

To reduce drafts entering double-hung sash windows, the Victorians used "draft excluders"—1-1/2-inch sausage-shaped rolls of cloth, stuffed with cotton or sand—along the width of the windows between the upper and lower sashes.

Most of the tips that environmental and energy groups provide about home energy efficiency are as applicable to Victorian-era houses as they are to modern dwellings.

One of the most important of these is caulking. If you were to add up all the little cracks, gaps, loose joints, and crumbling mortar or caulking in the average old house, they would amount to a 5-foot-square opening. Imagine how much heat is lost through that! Stroll through your house on a cold day and note where any frigid air is entering. A candle flame will help detect drafts. Caulk around windows and doors (outside as well as inside), electrical outlets, and spaces between the shoe moldings and the floor.

Those old-fashioned wooden ceiling fans, first popular after World War I and currently enjoying a revival, are useful in both summer and winter. During the cold months, the fan, which uses only as much electricity as a large light bulb, redistributes warm air that collects at the top of the room and might otherwise escape through the ceiling. In summer it circulates the air.

If your house does not already have an attic vent, an attic fan or turbine vent can, during the summer months, disperse hot air that is trapped underneath the roof. Wrap hot water pipes, the water heater, and any heating ducts with insulation. Add weather-stripping to the bottoms of all windows and along doorways.

FIREPLACES

Fireplaces were the main source of heat in American homes until 1833, when Jordon Mott of New York City received the first patent for a base-burning (oil) heating stove. Use of this type of stove was limited at first, however, and the fireplace continued to be the predominant source of heat for several decades.

Victorian tastes were a large influence on the design of heating stoves. Large, elaborate cast-iron stoves with nickel-plated trim that burned either coal or wood stood in splendor in Victorian-era parlors. These stoves have regained popularity during recent years, but they are inefficient for heating.

Although many of the fireplaces built in Victorian-era houses were designed to maximize heating efficiency, those in the less expensive homes (especially Victorian row houses) were, like their modern tract-house counterparts, built cheaply and quickly, without any thought to saving energy. To improve these, you can cover the openings with grates or glass doors to stop downdrafts of cold air from the chimney. Or, you can add a *flue heat exchanger*: C-shaped pipes that fit into the firebox and attract cold air into the bottom openings, warm it, then "exchange" it into the room.

SMOKING FIREPLACES If your chimney won't draw, make sure the damper (if there is one) is open. If this is not the problem, the flue might just be cold. Build a small kindling fire at the back of the fireplace and open a window opposite the fireplace to increase the cross draft.

If the chimney still smokes, chances are the firebox is proportionately too large for the flue. The depth of the firebox should be two-thirds the height of the opening, and the flue diameter should be at least one-tenth the size of the open area of the fireplace.

Several factors might have combined, over the years, to either reduce the size of the flue or to increase the size of the firebox. Bits of mortar or bricks could have chipped from the surface of the firebox; old brick surfaces might have spalled from years of exposure to the heat. Also, there could be obstructions or soot buildup constricting the flue of the chimney.

To reduce the size of the firebox, place several rows of firebricks on the bottom of the fireplace. If these stop the smoking, you may want to have them set permanently.

If this does not do the trick, the problem could be that something—a television antenna, a tree that has grown too large, or a nearby roof—is disturbing the air flow around the chimney. A device known as the Vacu-Stack (manufactured by Improved Consumer Products, Inc., Towne Street, P.O. Box 1264, Attleboro Falls, MA 02763) can be installed at the top of the chimney to improve the draft of the chimney.

CHIMNEY CARE Take care of that old chimney! Soot builds up in a short period of time, especially when a fireplace is used regularly for heating. Deteriorated chimneys and chimneys clogged with dirt, soot, and debris can also cause serious chimney and roof fires—which in 1980 alone caused $60 million damage in the United States.

Modern chimney cleaning methods utilize huge vacuum devices that suck soot and debris from the chimney. This is efficient and can be done with a minimum of mess, but the modern method may not be the best for an old chimney.

Chimney sweeps, who use materials and methods developed centuries ago in Europe, not only clean chimneys but will examine them for soundness of construction—including the condition of bricks and mortar—which is crucial in old fireplaces. A practiced chimney sweep can determine whether a chimney has holes, or what's inside it (from soot to pieces of kindling, newspapers, or bottles), just by the sounds the brushes make as they go down the chimney.

Most chimney sweeps perform their trade on the rooftop, using wire brushes on the ends of poles (plastic brushes are used for coal-burning fireplaces, since sparks from metal can cause coal dust to explode). Some chimney sweeps, like their ancient counterparts in England, even dress in top hat and tails!

If you would like to try your hand at cleaning your own chimney, the book *Be Your Own Chimney Sweep* by Christopher Curtis and Donald Post (Charlotte, Vermont: Garden Way Publishers, 1979) is a well-illustrated guide. Although you probably can adequately clean your chimney, since you lack the experience of a pro, you will not be likely to detect flaws in it.

Holes or cracks in the chimney are perhaps the greatest cause of chimney fires. Old fireplaces are especially vulnerable to this problem, since the lime mortar used before the advent of portland cement is prone to crumbling.

Another dangerous condition encountered in many old fireplaces is *incipient paralysis*. Nearly all chimneys older than twenty years are composed of a single layer of brick. Over the years, heat from the chimney can heat the surrounding wood, blackening it and literally turning it to charcoal. Ordinary wood ignites at 451 degrees F.; charcoal ignites at 250 degrees F. Since, when a fireplace is lit, the chimney temperature ranges from 250 to 500 degrees F., fires caused by incipient paralysis are common.

One cure for both incipient paralysis and holes or cracks in a chimney is to insert a flue liner in the chimney. A stainless steel liner, available at fireplace stores, costs $500 to $700 and should last thirty to forty years. Make sure you replace any blackened timbers.

Another problem with brick fireplaces and chimneys is spalling, or deterioration, of the old bricks (see Chapter 11). Seriously spalled bricks in a firebox should carefully be removed, using a cold chisel, and replaced with firebrick. The entire firebox area and/or bricks not seriously damaged can be covered with a coat of *refractory mortar* (available at masonry supply stores). This mortar, specifically formulated to withstand high temperatures (it will probably last longer than your entire chimney), will protect the soft bricks from further heat damage.

Many Victorian fireplaces, especially those with small fireboxes, were originally designed for burning coal. With the current energy crisis and the high cost of wood, coal may seem like a viable alternative for wintertime heat. Coal prices vary throughout the country. One ton of coal usually costs twice as much as a cord of wood; however, a ton of coal will produce as much heat as four cords of wood. In addition, whereas a few logs will burn out on a cold night, you can put four or five lumps of coal in a fireplace, and they will last all night.

You can't burn coal in just any fireplace, however, even if it was originally made to burn coal. Coal burns at a much higher temperature than does wood. It can quickly melt all but cast-iron fireplace grates, and it may damage the fireplace itself. If your chimney and firebox are in A-1 condition, you can probably burn a mixture of 75 percent coal and 25 percent wood; however, consult a chimney sweep or coal dealer before you try this.

Many old fireplaces originally were constructed without dampers. Rather than rebuilding the entire chimney, try installing a *butterfly valve,* which fits at the top of the stack and can usually be ordered through Wards or Sears catalogs.

Fireplace screens that install at the tops of chimneys are another good idea. Use 1/2-inch wire mesh, cutting and bending it to form a box, which is then inverted and stuck into the chimney flue. Any larger-sized mesh won't trap sparks or burning debris; anything smaller quickly gets clogged with soot and debris.

Old oil heater

OLD HEATING SYSTEMS

With the exception of fireplaces and perhaps old oil-burning and steam heating systems, the heating systems in most Victorian-era homes were added as afterthoughts. Old heating and cooling systems are seldom energy efficient, since only during the last five years has any concentrated attempt been made in this century to conserve energy. In fact, heating systems developed more than fifty years ago may be better even than those of the 1960s and 1970s—when we believed we had perpetually cheap and unlimited sources of energy.

STEAM HEATING Water is heated in a boiler until it becomes steam, which rises under its own pressure to radiators with metal pipes, where the heat is dissipated into the rooms. The water then cools and returns via gravity to the boiler. Water has to be added to the system every few days.

This type of system is safe to use, as long as the boiler and radiators are in sound condition (have them checked). Steam heating is expensive, however; one homeowner in the Midwest, for example, paid over $300 per month to heat his house in the winter with steam.

Old steam radiators, if not level, often trap cooled water, preventing it from heating and causing a hammering noise. If this occurs, raise the vented end of the radiator and place small shims underneath it, so that the cold water can flow back to the boiler.

RADIANT HEAT Hot water heat, which is created by hot water flowing through pipes in ceilings or floors (radiant heat) or through fins in baseboard perimeter units. Like steam heat, it is usually expensive to operate.

If you have a hot water system that is not heating, it may be because air is trapped within the system. All hot water radiators have valves on them to bleed off the air. Open this valve and let the air escape until you can see water flowing from the valve.

GAS WALL UNITS These were often installed about forty years ago to modernize older homes. Some of them are actually dangerous: the gas regulators often do not work, and many of them leak gas. Earlier models were often connected to the gas supply with copper tubing. This is now illegal (but was probably not against code when they were installed), since a chemical reaction occurs between the gas and the copper that can cause leaks or explosions.

Although new gas wall units are more efficient and safe, you might not be able to replace an old wall furnace with a new one. Older gas heaters were usually engineered to fit between narrow stud spaces in the wall. New wall heaters are built to fit walls with 18-inch or greater stud spaces; installing a new wall heater might mean tearing up your whole wall.

GRAVITY-FED FURNACES The precursor of the modern central heating and air system is the gravity-fed furnace, which was developed in the 1930s. These are large, square metal boxes, with tapered domes, containing furnaces. Many originally had a layer of sand on top, perhaps as a first attempt at insulation.

These furnaces are located in the basement. Cool air settles into returns and is then heated by the furnace. When hot, the air expands and rises through a large floor register to heat the room.

Although not an efficient system, most of the heat that escapes rises to the floor above and is there "lost" to the area that needs heating.

Since heat cannot travel far by convection, the furnace has only a minimum amount of ductwork and can effectively heat only a few rooms. The balance of the house, including upper floors, remains cold.

Many people have chosen to retain these gravity-fed furnaces, supplementing them with space heating, fireplaces or freestanding stoves, or a central unit for the upstairs.

Most old gravity-fed furnaces are well built, with good automatic shutoff mechanisms and adequate fire safeguards. These old units are perfectly safe (watch that you don't stand on a register too long and burn your rubber-soled shoes, though), as long as the firebox has not been tampered with.

Sometimes, however, previous owners have attempted to add extra ducting and have cut into the firebox, creating a potential fire hazard. If your firebox has been cut into, don't use it; consult a heating and air conditioning contractor about repair or replacement.

Many gravity-fed furnaces are still in use. The registers for the earliest of these were beautiful oak latticework. The old thermostats and control valves are collectors' items also.

EARLY FORCED AIR SYSTEMS The first forced-air systems, developed just after World War II, added to the gravity-fed system a blower, which forced air through longer ducts to other parts of the house. Since there were no set standards for heating systems in those days, many companies experimented with forced-air systems, changing sizes and locations of the blower, ducting, etc., so that many customers virtually had a custom-made system.

Old forced-air systems operate in essentially the same manner as modern central heating systems. The components, in some instances, may have been even better made than those of modern units. Ductwork, for example, was all custom-made sheet metal.

MODERNIZING YOUR SYSTEM

Experts concur that, for most homes, a central heating and air conditioning system is the best bet, although the most economical and efficient designs combine central heating and air with good passive solar measures and with some auxiliary solid fuel system, such as a wood or coal stove.

The particular type of system that is best for you will depend on the price and availability of fuel and energy in your particular area, so before you choose a system, check with local experts. Natural gas furnaces are popular throughout the country, but gas may be unavailable or prohibitively expensive in certain locales. Oil (which costs more than natural gas but provides more heat) is popular in cold climates, as are hydronic systems, which use heated water. The electric heat pump, recommended for temperate climates, is inefficient in colder areas and at high altitudes. Some systems, such as the "Five-in-One" by the Williamson Company (3500 Madison Road, Cincinnati, Ohio 45209), will run on different fuels, even wood, with a turn of the valve.

The recent energy crisis and resultant push towards conservation has created a revolution in heating and air conditioning technology. Virtually every system on the market is much more efficient than its predecessors, and experts recommend that if your system is more than seven years old, you should replace it—the increase in efficiency will pay for the new system within a few years.

Among recent innovations is a computerized system developed by the Sta-Tech company in California (4530 Putah Creek Road, Winters, CA). The system, which operates on an Apple computer chip, utilizes a heating unit only one-half the size normally required. It controls the heat in different areas of the house, either on a timed basis or by sensing when a person enters or leaves a room. Only one-half of the computer's capacity is used for this, allowing it to serve such auxiliary functions as a burglar alarm (which will sound and will also dial five telephone numbers to report an intruder), a light timer, and a sprinkler system that is activated by the moisture content of the ground.

IDEAS FOR DUCTING

● Some houses have laundry chutes from upper floors to lower; use these for chases for ductwork.
● Some older homes have unused chimneys, such as for a trash burner in the kitchen that is no longer in use. Ductwork can easily be run in these chimneys. Do not run ducting in a chase next to a hot chimney!

- Old lath and plaster walls may contain enough space to run small ducts within the house.
- You can build a boxed-in chase in a corner of a room, incorporating it into a closet or a set of bookshelves.
- If you plan an ultramodern or avant-garde decor for your house, you might even consider exposing the ductwork.
- Many heating and air conditioning companies will suggest lowering hallway ceilings and placing the ducting below the original ceiling. This may be a viable solution if the hallway is inconspicuous, but don't ruin the symmetry of the house.
- If you are planning to remove a gravity-fed heating system and replace it with a central system or systems, the old floor register is a natural location for the return air register for the new system. Old floor registers were centrally located where air flows well. Often they are an integral part of an old house and might therefore be less conspicuous than a wall return.

INSTALL IT YOURSELF—WHY NOT? Installing your own central heating and air conditioning is not impossible. First you will need to determine what size system you will need. Until recently, this was "a matter of sticking your finger up in the air to detect a draft," according to one heating contractor; now, it involves precise room-by-room calculations of the amount of heat gain and loss in your house.

A heating and air conditioning dealer will help you plan the system. Installing it is no problem. Modern systems require no sheet metal work, since duct pipes come in modular sections that just snap together. Also, whereas old units had to be charged with freon, new ones come fully contained and precharged.

You will, however, have to hire a pro to warm up the system and turn it on. This is extremely important; if it is not done correctly the entire system could burn up.

ALTERNATIVES TO CENTRAL HEAT AND AIR Central heating and air may not be the answer for your old house. Some of the new gas wall units are extremely efficient, as are perimeter baseboard heaters. Several companies have recently introduced closed-water perimeter heating systems, where each baseboard unit is individually controlled and designed to heat quickly and maintain a preset temperature. This is more efficient than a central heating and air system, and baseboard units provide an answer to the ducting dilemma.

An option for the bathroom is an infrared heat lamp that installs in the ceiling, although this may not be compatible with an antique decor.

PROBLEMS WITH GAS FIXTURES

GAS LEAKS If you smell gas in or near your house—or if you have old gas fixtures—you should check your fixtures for leaks. Your local utility company will visit and tell you whether you have a leak; many will light your pilot lights and tell you if an old fixture is safe. The companies have sensitive testing gauges that will register minute gas leaks too small to show on a gas meter. The utility company will only tell you that you have a leak—they won't locate it or fix it for you unless it is in their pipes outside the house.

To locate a gas leak, coat the pipes and the areas where the gas enters the fixtures with soapy water and watch for bubbling.

OLD COOKING STOVES Old gas and electric cooking ranges are a delight to cook on. Most cook more evenly than their modern counterparts and are better insulated and therefore save you money. Many of the old gas stoves were combined with wood burners or trash burners. Make sure you do not vent the stove and trash or wood burner into the same chase, since this can cause explosions or fires (and is also illegal).

Also, codes in certain areas now require that if a gas stove is added or moved, it must be vented with a special *metalbestos* pipe: an expensive ($40 or more per linear foot) pipe that has a built-in air chamber to keep heat from the stove from starting fires.

Getting In & Digging Down

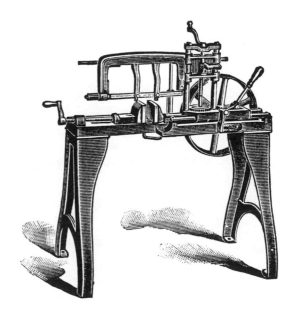

PART V

CHAPTER 18

Tear Those Walls Down Gently

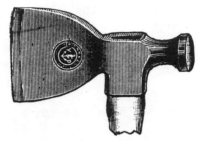

At times the old-house renovator must become a house wrecker to undo the thoughtless or incompatible additions made by previous owners. It's a great feeling—like a surgeon removing a tumor—and a good way to release aggressions.

Just because you are using a wrecker's tools, however, does not mean the house has to look like the victim of a wrecker's ball. Protect the wood and plaster by working slowly. Look carefully at what you're going to tear out, to determine where and how the nails sit and how the joints are made, since many moldings and casings are mortised into each other, and if you jerk one out, you could easily damage it or the one to which it is attached. Be careful cutting into walls; some people have found intact stained-glass windows or decorative woodwork that had been added to the original structure. If possible, turn off the electricity serving that wall—since you don't want to zap yourself by cutting through a live electrical wire. (There may be wires even if there are no switches or receptacles.) Cover your furniture (remove it if possible), and use sheet plastic and duct tape to seal off doors to other areas of the house.

You'll definitely need a couple of pry bars: a very small one (the kind with a screwdriver handle) and a medium-sized one with a flat (rather than a hooked) end. Also useful are a claw hammer, a couple of wide, thin-bladed putty knives, a saber saw or reciprocating saw or keyhole saw, a large slothead screwdriver, a nail puller, a pair of vise grips, a large nail punch, small bolt cutters, and a variety of small blocks and boards.

REMOVAL TECHNIQUES

REMOVING NAILS Illustrated are several ways of removing nails from walls and woodwork. Each is designed to minimize the amount of damage to the wall, since plaster, especially, will dent and crack easily. The locking-grip pliers will pull nails with the least amount of damage, but they do not provide the leverage of blocks and pieces of wood or protect the area surrounding the nail from being dented.

If a nail is too firmly embedded in a wall (especially a masonry or concrete surface) to

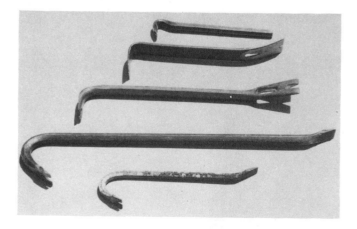

Prybars, from top: A cat's paw, with a curved end, is especially good for removing nails. A flat, non-tempered prybar is thinnest and therefore the best for use with moldings; however, it will bend under heavy pressure. A flat prybar, made of tempered steel, is good for slipping behind things with minimal damage. Small and large crowbars (sometimes called wrecking bars) are also made of tempered metal; the configuration gives good leverage.

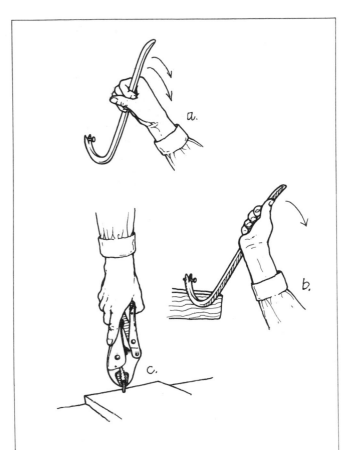

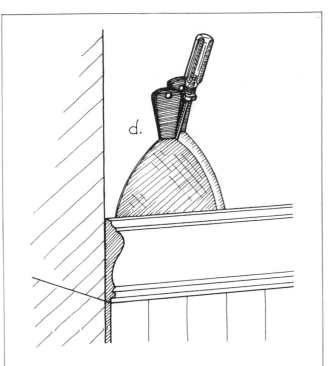

Using pry bars: (A) For maximum leverage, pull with a downwards motion. This will remove an object quickly; however, you might damage both it and the wall. (B) When removing nails, always protect the wall by slipping a piece of wood between the end of the prybar and the wall. (C) Small nails can be pulled with locking grip pliers.

(D) To remove moldings without damage: Start at one end (not in the middle and not at an end that is covered by a coped molding); hammer two wide-bladed putty knives between the molding and the wall. Slip a screwdriver between the putty knives and gently pry the molding away from the wall a fraction of an inch. (Don't try to pull it too far: old moldings may be very brittle and can break easily.) Work your way to the end of the molding using this procedure. If you have a pair of bolt cutters or a reciprocating saw, slip it between the loosened molding and the wall and cut the nails. If not, repeat the prying process until the molding is free from the wall.

remove, an alternative is to cut it off with a pair of bolt cutters, then use a nail punch and drive the remaining nail shaft into the wall. For embedded nails in drywall, plaster, or wood, use a small nail puller or a thin, flat screwdriver and dig in back of the nail until the head sticks just far enough above the surface to utilize one of these other methods. If at all possible, avoid digging for a nail head, since this will gouge the surface considerably.

REMOVING MOLDINGS Some people remove moldings to match them or to have the paint commercially stripped from the molding. Don't do this indiscriminately, however. Delicate moldings splinter easily, and when you nail them back into place, you will have twice the number of nail holes to fill—and these nearly always show.

To remove moldings, if you must, start at one end: if you're removing a casing, start at the top, since many are embedded at the bottom in either the window or doorsill. Hammer two wide-bladed putty knives behind the molding. Work an old slothead screwdriver between the putty knives and pry gently until you can feel the molding pull away from the wall a fraction of an inch. Work your way along the molding, then repeat the process. Don't pry one section of the molding or it might break. When the entire molding has been pried an inch away from the wall, use a pair of bolt cutters to snip the nails.

Pull what's left of the nail from the wall with a pair of locking grip pliers; pound the rest of the nail through the molding from the back to remove it. If your house was built with square nails, you should

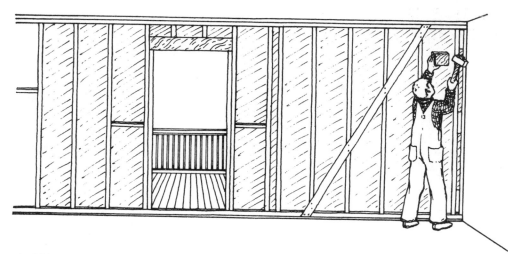

To remove sheet goods (siding, drywall, lath, and plaster) when you have access to the back: Work from the back, using a scrap of 2-by-4-inch lumber and a sledgehammer. Start at one corner. Place the two-by-four on the wall and hit it with the hammer to loosen the nails a fraction of an inch. Work your way a few feet down from the corner, then a few feet across.

Repeat this procedure, starting at another corner, then another. When the entire section is loosened a fraction of an inch, go back to the first corner and either cut the nails with a reciprocating saw or a pair of bolt cutters or pound the wall again to further loosen the nails.

probably cut them off from the back of the molding and leave the heads in the wood, for the heads of square nails embed themselves. They leave large holes when removed and can even splinter the wood.

REMOVING PLYWOOD AND DRYWALL If possible, work from the back. Starting from one end, use a large block and a sledgehammer and knock the wood out from the back. Use a keyhole saw or saber saw to cut around delicate moldings first.

REMOVING LATH AND PLASTER First, score the wall with a chisel, then cut away sections between studs with a saber saw, a reciprocating saw, or a keyhole saw. A sledgehammer will badly crack the plaster.

REMOVING CABINETS Before you start with a crowbar, brace the cabinet with lengths of two-by-four so it will not suddenly tear away from the wall when it is loosened.

REMOVING LINOLEUM Working from the edges inward, heat a small area with a propane torch, lifting the hot tile from underneath with a rigid putty knife and tearing pieces off with a large pair of pliers. You will probably be able to scrape off most of the cement that adheres the tile to the floor; any residue can be removed with paint remover. Avoid overheating the tile, since many types were made from asbestos, and fumes are toxic and perhaps carcinogenic. Make sure the room is well ventilated; wear heavy gloves and a respirator.

CHAPTER 19

Plaster

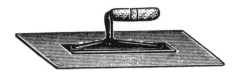

Plastering, one of the earliest-known building techniques, was developed prior to Egyptian times and took the place of the mud or slime used to protect buildings from fire and the elements. The materials and procedures used in ancient plastering were nearly identical to those employed today. The primary element is plaster of paris, a crystalized form of calcium sulfate commonly known as gypsum plaster. It is made by heating gypsum rock (calcium sulfate dihydrate) to 120 to 130 degrees Celsius. At this temperature, nearly three fourths of the water in the gypsum dissipates, leaving a white powder. Lime was occasionally used as the cementing agent in areas where gypsum was not readily available. Modern stucco utilizes portland cement. Pure plaster is extremely brittle and is usually strengthened with various additives.

A plaster wall is composed of two or three coats. The first, or *scratch* coat, will generally be a 3/8-inch-thick mixture of gypsum plaster, sand, and either perlite, vermiculite, or (in the oldest houses) animal hair. This is also known as *hardwall plaster*. The surface of this first coat is *scratched* with a tool called a *scarifier* (from the word *scarify*: to scratch or puncture).

The *float*, or *brown*, coat (so named because additives turned the plaster a muddy brown—modern varieties are usually off-white) is the second layer in a three-coat application, or it may take the place of the scratch coat in a two-layer job. This coat is also strengthened with sand and perlite, vermiculite, or animal hair.

The *finish* coat, applied last, combines a special type of plaster of paris known as *gauging plaster* with a mixture of lime, which imparts plasticity and is smooth and chalk white.

Plaster in Victorian homes was applied over *wood lath*—small, thin (usually 1/4 inch thick), 1-inch-wide strips of wood—usually fir. Modern lath consists of sheets or strips of thin metal. The plaster squeezes through the spaces between the wooden strips (or the holes in metal lath), forming *keys* that anchor the plaster to the lath.

REPAIRING PLASTER

CAN THIS WALL BE SAVED? Although sizable holes in plaster can be patched successfully, large areas covered with a network of spiderweb cracks are another story. Balanced against the obvious preference of saving as much of the original plaster as possible is the horrendous possibility that you will patch together and paint a whole wall, only to have it crumble later. Press on the wall with the heel of your hand. If the plaster underneath feels spongy, it's gotta go. If it feels solid, you can probably patch it.

Sometimes the plaster will be sound, but the keys holding it to the lath will have deteriorated. The plaster will then bulge away from the wall or ceiling. This is a common occurrence in plaster ceilings; it is very noticeable; and, yes, you could be showered at any moment with falling plaster.

Bulging or loose plaster *should* be replaced, but if you are determined for some reason to try to save it (if it contains some decorative stenciling, for example), you may be able to anchor it to the lath with flat-headed wood screws. Use fairly long screws with thin shanks and drill a pilot hole first (to avoid shattering the plaster). Countersink the screw heads and fill the holes.

TOOLS AND MATERIALS Plaster patching compound, available at most hardware stores, is sufficient for repairing small holes in walls and ceilings. Although you can adequately patch holes less than 2 inches in diameter with a single application of patching compound, for larger holes a two-coat application is preferable.

For two-coat applications, *neat plaster* (a special type for mixing with aggregates), sand, perlite or vermiculite, gauging plaster, lime putty, and other supplies and tools may be obtained from a stucco or plaster supply house. Most times, the dry ingredients will be premixed for you.

You will need a plasterer's trowel for mixing and applying the plaster, a *hawk* for holding the plaster while you work (a 1-foot-square board of 1/4-inch plywood mounted on a 1-by-1/2-inch-diameter dowel will suffice), plus several different sizes of putty knives. I prefer those with flexible blades, but this is purely personal taste. Ideally, the blades of the putty knives will be wider than the diameter of the hole; if not, you'll need a piece of sheet metal or a smooth board for larger patches.

MIXING PLASTER Mix only a small batch of plaster or patching compound until you gain some experience and can determine how much you can use before it sets up (hardens).

● Always add the plaster to the water, never vice versa, or it will set up too quickly.

● Sift the plaster through your fingers and stir it lightly with the tip of the trowel. Stir as little as possible, since motion will accelerate the setting process. Plaster absorbs about its equal volume in water. Try using one part of each, then adjust to achieve the consistency of soft mud.

● When mixing a brown coat, mix the additives with the plaster (if they aren't premixed) before you add the water. For the brown coat, you will need the following proportions (if not premixed):

OVER LATH 25 pounds of neat plaster; 5/8 cubic foot of sand; 5/8 cubic foot of vermiculite or perlite.

OVER MASONRY 25 pounds of neat plaster; 3/4 cubic foot of sand; 3/4 cubic foot of perlite or vermiculite.[6]

● When mixing a large batch of plaster, form a round ring on a table or board with the dry ingredients and pour the water into the middle of it, then mix.

PLASTERING TECHNIQUE Filling holes in plaster is not difficult; the knack comes easily with practice. At first, to get the feel of working with plaster, try

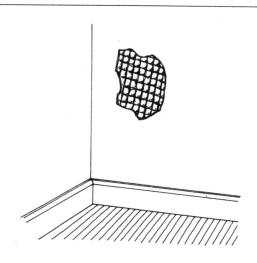

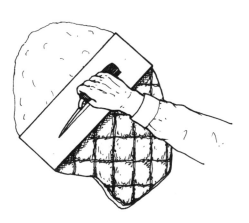

Patching cracks in plaster. Left: Apply the scratch coat to the inside of the hole, filling it to about 3/8 inch below the surface. Scratch it with the edge of a putty knife in a crisscross pattern so the finish coat will adhere to it. Let it dry. Right: Cover the hole with the finish coat, ideally using a putty knife with a blade wider than the hole, so you can cover the hole with a single, smooth swipe. Leave as little excess plaster on the area as possible, since it will have to be sanded off.

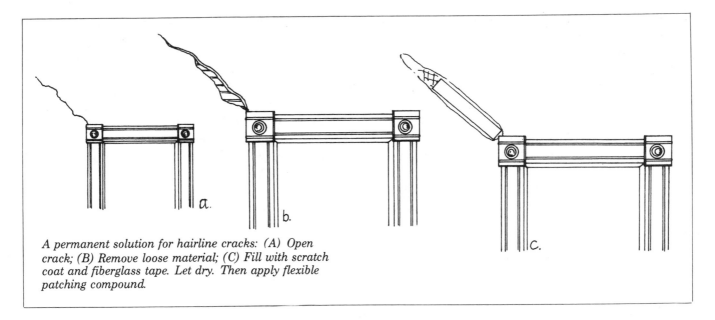

A permanent solution for hairline cracks: (A) Open crack; (B) Remove loose material; (C) Fill with scratch coat and fiberglass tape. Let dry. Then apply flexible patching compound.

applying just the scratch coat to several patches; luckily, the finish coat can cover a multitude of sins.

● Always clean out any loose crumbs of plaster before you patch, and wipe the area lightly with a tack rag.

● For the scratch coat, use a small-bladed putty knife to apply the plaster. You are trying here to apply the plaster smoothly and uniformly, covering the entire hole to a depth of about 3/8 inch.

● You can, instead of buying a scarifier to "scratch" the bottom coat, use the edge of your putty knife to etch diagonal crisscrossing lines in the plaster. Let this coat dry thoroughly.

● For the finish coat, mix the plaster smoothly to a consistency somewhat thicker than toothpaste. Trowel some of the finish plaster onto the wall; use slightly more than you think you'll need to cover the hole. Then, using a putty knife with a blade wider than the diameter of the hole (or a piece of sheet metal or a smooth board), make a pass over the entire area, spreading the plaster over the hole and beyond its edges on the wall. (Until you get the hang of this, you may have to make several passes before you get a smooth, even surface.) Try to leave as little excess plaster as possible, since sanding it down will be time-consuming.

● After the plaster has dried thoroughly, sand lightly with a sanding block, a pole sander (a flat board attached to a pole with a swivel for sanding walls—available at most paint stores), or a finishing sander, using fine-grit sandpaper.

HAIRLINE CRACKS These seem to be the old-house owner's constant companions. Basically, there are two types: some are caused by impact, such as hammering a nail into plaster or hitting the wall with an object. These cracks are easy to patch and should not recur. Use a thin mixture of plaster patching compound and water; I apply the mixture with my finger.

Diagonal or vertical hairline cracks in plaster—especially those radiating from the tops of door or window casings—are caused by movement of the house. Since house movement does not stop, the cracks usually reopen after being patched. Some sources suggest opening the cracks with a chisel or drilling small holes at the end of the crack to relieve the stress before patching.

Joint tape and vinyl patches are easy and popular shortcuts for covering hairline cracks, but these will invariably show beneath a coat of paint. Joint tape will usually split if the house movement is significant. Vinyl patches may lift away from the wall in time, leaving a real mess.

The only method that really works to cure hairline cracks permanently combines stress relief with two flexible products: a flexible patching compound (available at large paint stores—be sure to purchase the smooth variety) and an open-weave fiberglass tape.

1. Using a small chisel, carefully open the crack to its full depth in a V-shape. (You'll notice that the crack is much wider underneath; this is one reason it recurs.) This will help the patching compound

adhere to the edges of the crack and will relieve the stress on the area.

2. Next, use coarse sandpaper and sand a 1/4-inch-deep indentation all around the crack and 1/2 inch out on either side. Also, sand the surrounding area with fine paper to prepare it for painting or papering, since you will not be able to sand the flexible patching compound.

3. Brush or blow the plaster dust from the crack, then clean it thoroughly with a tack rag. Fill the crack (but not the surrounding area that you have sanded) with the patching compound.

4. Cut a strip of the fiberglass tape to fit into the indentation. "Butter" it with the patching compound and lay it over the crack.

5. Let the patch set up for at least twelve hours—it will not harden. Using a wide-bladed putty knife, trowel flexible patching compound smoothly over the entire area, feathering it into the wall. After it has set up, the area is ready to paint. The patched area should be virtually unnoticeable, and it will flex—not crack—with future stress.

Another method is to use newspaper as backing for the patch (I dislike this but it is popular). Wet the paper and crumple it into a firm ball, then stuff it into the hole. Make sure none of it protrudes past the level of the surrounding plaster, then patch the hole.

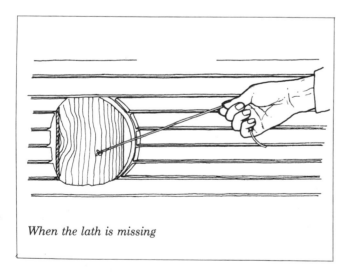

When the lath is missing

WHEN THE LATH IS MISSING If you have an area to patch where the lath is missing, you can tack a replacement piece to the surrounding lath (lath can be obtained from most lumberyards). Or, you can take a piece of wire mesh or 1/4-inch plywood, 1 to 2 inches wider than the hole and narrow enough to fit into the hole. Drill into the center of the wood and run a piece of string through the wood, knotting it in back so that it will not pull through. Slip the wood through the hole, holding onto the string, and patch with a brown coat. Continue to hold the string until the plaster has set up, and let the patch dry thoroughly before you apply the final coat.

COVED CEILINGS Many ceilings in Victorian-era homes are "coved": curved in a concave arch. If you have to repair or replace the plaster, you will also probably have to replicate this cove. Even if you replace the plaster on the walls and ceilings with wallboard (see section following), you will still have to plaster the cove.

A professional Sheetrock hanger can soak a piece of 1/4-inch drywall until it becomes pliable, then bend it to conform to the ceiling cove. I tried this once with disastrous results: the drywall decomposed when it became wet, then broke when I tried to bend it.

A professional plasterer will also have no problems with a coved ceiling, but the novice will probably have a hard time plastering a cove with complete precision—and every fraction-of-an-inch deviation will create a conspicuous flaw.

Sean Fitzpatrick, however, has developed a method that even the first-time do-it-yourselfer can use to achieve a perfect-looking ceiling cove:

1. Apply a small amount of scratch coat to the cove, keying it into the lath. Use enough to make a patch about 4 inches wide. When you work this small an area, judging the curve of the cove accurately will be no problem. Take care to keep the patch below the surface of the final plaster coat.

2. Repeat this approximately every 15 inches all along the length of the cove; you will be able to leave more space between patches as you become more proficient judging the curve.

3. After these first patches have dried, fill them in with more scratch coat. When the cove has dried thoroughly, cover it with the finish plaster coat.

DRYWALL VS. PLASTER

If you must replace a large expanse of plaster wall or ceiling, you will have to decide whether to replaster the area or replace the plaster with *drywall*: boards formed of plaster of paris and paper, also known as *plasterboard, wallboard,* or by the trade name *Sheetrock*.

Replastering is obviously more authentic, and purists won't have anything else. The hard, smooth surface of plaster is elegant, and, to many, is more aesthetically pleasing than drywall. "Plaster just belongs in an old house," one friend of mine insists. I believe plaster walls are one of the most appealing elements of an old house, and I try to retain as much of the original plaster as possible. Patching plaster is not a difficult task, either, and the web of old, patched cracks are character lines that add to a house's personality.

As much as I like old plaster, I suggest that you *not* try to replaster an entire wall—or even an area larger than 3 square feet—yourself. Working with large amounts of plaster is not easy. Sometimes the plaster will be too runny; sometimes it will harden too quickly. Some areas will sag; others will crack. Achieving a smooth, level surface is difficult.

And, whereas a professional can apply two coats of plaster to an entire room in a single day, it took me several days to apply just the scratch coat to one wall that was 20 feet long and 12 feet high. Also, unless you mix the plaster to exactly the right consistency, it might not set up for days or weeks. This is a task that is better left to the pros.

There are people who don't like old plaster. Many people would rather install drywall on an entire wall than repair even small holes in lath and plaster, so they either remove all the plaster (even when it is sound) or add drywall over the existing plaster.

There are two problems with installing drywall over plaster. First, the added thickness will usually bring the walls flush or nearly flush to the window and door casings, yielding an unsightly appearance. Second, if the drywall is added over crumbling plaster, chances are that the plaster will continue to crumble underneath; if it falls away from the lath it could cause the wall to bulge or buckle. Drywall can be installed directly over the lath, or the lath can be removed and the wallboard affixed to the studs.

Plaster and drywall hammers. The drywall hammer (bottom) *has a hatchet blade for splitting wallboard and a waffle face for driving nails. The rare lath hammer* (top) *has a hatchet end for splitting wood lath; the face is square and the same width as lath.*

Drywall has obvious practical advantages. It is quick and easy to install—especially by a novice. If you are hiring people to work on your house, neighborhood carpenters can Sheetrock a room for you, whereas replastering a room requires a trained professional plasterer—at four to ten times the cost. Drywall will not crack as readily with house movement or impact as plaster. Materials and tools for installing it are available at almost any hardware store.

If the wall is even, all you have to do to install the drywall is to nail 4-by-8-foot sheets to the house studs, cover the seams with joint tape, and feather in the joint tape and nail heads with several applications of joint compound, sanding the areas smooth between applications. Directions for installing drywall are printed on most sheets of wallboard, on bags and tubs of joint compound, and in virtually every handyman book.

What these instructions do not tell you is how to install drywall when the wall is not even, which is often the case in old houses. Rough-cut lumber manufactured during the Victorian era is not always cut to consistent dimensions. Studs were set flush on the outside of houses for application of siding. Inside, however, there were often differences of plane, which were exacerbated because the lathing was often varying thicknesses. Plaster was applied to the lath in different thicknesses with a huge leveling trowel, so that the result was a smooth, even surface upon which the trim was installed.

Therefore, if you are planning to add drywall, you will have to check the plane of each and every stud and casing. To achieve a surface of an even plane, you may have to shim so the drywall can sit flush to all studs, or you might even have to use several different sizes of sheets of drywall.

VENEER PLASTERING—A COMPROMISE One way of retaining the appearance of plaster with the ease and simplicity of Sheetrock is *veneer plastering.* This method, used prior to the advent of drywall, incorporates a thin skim coat of finish plaster over *gypsum base,* a specially treated wallboard. This wallboard, then known as *gypsum lath,* was originally developed as a replacement for wood lath and was covered with a coat of finish plaster.

Veneer plastering yields beautiful results. Because you start with flat, level wallboard, even the novice is assured of obtaining a flat surface, and applying the finish coat is not difficult. Many professional plasterers even opt for veneer plastering of interior walls. The single application of plaster does not take much longer than does drywall taping and finishing.

Gypsum base comes in 4- by-8-foot sheets, with a special face paper that chemically bonds to the plaster. The United States Gypsum Company manufactures a special Imperial brand of plaster specially designed to use with this wallboard.

If you are stuck with already-installed ordinary drywall, there is a special liquid bonding agent (also available at your friendly plaster store) with which you can treat the walls so a coat of plaster will adhere. Before you apply this solution, prepare the walls as if for painting (see Chapter 25), since plastering over chipping paint will yield nothing but a mess.

Note: Many of these specialized drywall products are not available at local hardware stores, and you will have to gain access to a wholesale house to obtain them. A small number of houses built at the end of the Victorian era were constructed of early wallboard (known as *lathboard*), which was either 1/4 or 3/8 inch thick.

An ornamental plaster ceiling medallion

DECORATIVE PLASTER

There are several types of ornamental plasterwork. *Frescoes* are paintings applied over fresh, wet plaster. The colors dry with the plaster, becoming part of it, and they are extremely durable.

Decorative friezes (so-named because they were cast on the frieze area of a wall) were either cast from elaborately carved scenes (such as those on the exterior frieze barges of Queen Anne–style homes) or were delicate, repeating patterns, similar to stenciling, that often complemented a Victorian wallpaper.

Many wealthier homes boasted *ceiling medallions,* which were cast and then affixed to the ceilings; light fixtures were characteristically hung from their centers. Ceiling medallions, along with other types of decorative plaster, were often left unfinished; or they were painted the same color as the surround-

ing walls and ceilings, shellacked, or given an antique finish.

Ceiling medallions, mantels, capitals (the tops of pilasters or columns), frieze sculptures, and other three-dimensional or relief plaster ornaments are cast from rubber, fiberglass, or plaster of paris molds. Virtually any object can be molded, and this is not a difficult process for the do-it-yourselfer. Hobby shops and ceramic studios can assist you.

Many houses with ornamental plasterwork also feature *run plaster moldings* or *cornices*, so named because the plaster is placed in a glob on the wall or ceiling, then "run" with a template across the length of the area. First, a mold is *horsed*: sheet metal templates are cut to the intended profile. These are affixed to a block of wood, which is nailed to a wooden jig, known as a *skipper*. Next, a wooden strip is tacked level along the entire length of the wall. The brown plaster coat is troweled onto the wall, and the mold is placed against the tack strip and run the length of the wall, forming the plaster. This generally requires two persons: one to run the mold, the other to remove excess plaster and place additional plaster in front of the template. Miters at corners are always done by hand, using blocks of wood and old saw blades to shape the miter.

CONSTRUCTING RUN PLASTER MOLDINGS If you are going to create a plaster cornice or you have a large section of molding to replace, hire a professional. This is an extremely exacting process; if you attempt it yourself, you're liable to have goopy plaster falling in your eye while you ruin your ceiling.

If you only have a small area of plaster molding to replace, a do-it-yourself job might be viable. There are two ways you can approach the task.

First, if you are missing only a small piece of a run molding, you can replace it with a combination of wooden moldings.

1. You will need a piece of the molding. If you do not have one, make a template.

2. Take a 1/8-inch lead *came* (available at stained-glass supply stores) and bend it over the contours of the molding. (You can also trace the configuration of the molding with a special contour gauge, available at most hardware stores.)

3. Once you have the outline of the molding, carefully trace it on a piece of cardboard.

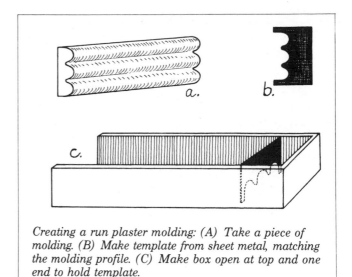

Creating a run plaster molding: (A) Take a piece of molding. (B) Make template from sheet metal, matching the molding profile. (C) Make box open at top and one end to hold template.

4. Cut out the design and check it against the actual molding to ensure that you have drawn the lines accurately.

5. Take the molding or pattern to a lumberyard or molding manufacturer and buy a molding or combination of moldings that match. Mount these, using brads on a piece of 1/4-inch plywood, cut to the length of the molding piece you are missing. Countersink the brads and fill the holes with wood putty. Sand, then prime with alkyd primer.

6. Affix the board to the ceiling joists with wood screws. If the ceiling bends or bows, use small wooden shims to obtain a flush fit. Fill any gaps with plaster and feather the joints.

If you can't match the molding or would rather try to run your own plaster, you can try the *stick* method—also known as *benching* the mold—wherein the molding is run on a bench or table in a wooden trough.

1. First, build a three-sided wooden box. Make the bottom dimension of the box equal to the height of the molding, plus the thickness of two 1-by-8-inch boards.

2. Using a jeweler's saw or metal-bladed saber saw, cut a sheet metal template to match the profile of the intended cornice (use your cardboard pattern). Cut another one 1/4 inch larger. The larger template is used for the first (brown coat) run. It will run a slightly smaller molding, leaving room for the finish coat.

3. Spray the inside of the trough with a mold release before starting. Mix the plaster until it is smooth and the consistency of soft mud: too soft,

Plasterers "running" an ornamental molding at the California State Capitol restoration project. The plasterer in the foreground, holding a hawk, literally throws the plaster on the ceiling; his companion runs a template along the ceiling, forming the molding.

and it will not hold the shape of the mold; too stiff and the template won't mold it.

4. Position the template at the closed end of the box. Trowel a large amount of the brown coat into the box, then run the template down the length of the trough. The excess plaster will be forced out the open end of the box, and you should be left with a good length of run molding.

5. Let the molding dry for approximately six hours, then repeat the process, using the smaller template and the finish coat of lime putty and plaster. Don't be disappointed if you have to make several runs before you achieve a good length of molding. Also, run more than you'll need, since you might break some getting it out of the mold or cutting it—and any excess you save can be used for future repairs.

6. After the molding has dried thoroughly, cut it to shape (including miters) with a fine-toothed saw. Butter the molding with some plaster, stick it in place, and hold it for a few minutes.

HANGING OBJECTS ON PLASTER WALLS

As you can probably discern from the cracks you have had to patch, pounding nails into plaster walls should be avoided.

● The Victorians loved to hang pictures on their walls. Most often, they suspended them from the frieze moldings on long wires attached to the molding with elaborate hooks. These are still being manufactured (check your local picture-framing store), and pictures may be suspended from them with ordinary fish line.

● Lightweight objects can be hung from modern stick-on picture hangers.

● If you must hammer a nail or screw a fixture into a plaster wall, put a piece of cloth-backed tape on the wall first, drive the nail through the tape as you would ordinarily drive it for the picture, then remove the tape (it will pull easily over the nail). This minimizes cracking.

● To make a large cut in plaster or drywall, mark the cut with a pencil or pen. Then drill pilot holes every 3 to 4 inches along the mark and saw between the holes.

● When you cut into a wall to affix something such as a light fixture or receptacle box, try to place it so that the edges fit *into* the lath top and bottom, which provides better anchorage than can be achieved trying to attach it between laths. Drill a pilot hole into the wall first to locate the position of the lath.

CHAPTER 20

Wood Stripping & Finishing

Natural wood is an appealing contrast to today's proliferation of plastic, but before you convert your house into an exposition of bare wood, consider seriously whether you actually want to strip the surface.

Until the late nineteenth century, most wood ornamentation was painted rather than stained. (The exception to this is fine wood, such as cherry or walnut, which has always been prized—and expensive.) Good pigmented stains were unavailable, and berry juices had to suffice for some Victorians.

Not only were painted woods scrubbable and therefore easier to keep clean, they fit the Victorian penchant for covering everything "naked." Another Victorian mania was the practice of making something look like what it is not, and wood was often grained or marbleized: painted to resemble other wood or marble.

Also, underneath all that paint may be an ugly hodgepodge of different woods. Craftsmen chose a particular wood for its intrinsic properties: redwood for exteriors and for doors and windows because of its resistance to rot and insects, fir for its hardness and durability, pine for availability and economy. Victorian rooms may have pine moldings, oak wainscoting, fir doors, and redwood window casings.

How much effort will stripping the wood require? If many layers of paint, varnish, or whatever (glue, wallpaper, etc.) cover the surface, you are going to face a time-consuming job that may yield disappointing results. Sometimes it is impossible to remove all the paint or whatever from the surface, and stripping can raise the grain or discolor many old and porous wood surfaces. Redwood, for example, usually darkens when it is stripped. Definitely try a test patch before you begin; it may be enough to deter you forever. Painted or grained surfaces are more appealing than damaged wood. You could remove your moldings, doors, etc. and have them commercially stripped—some wasteful novices spend more money on paint remover than commercial stripping would cost them. Also, if you're dealing with a wainscot or other flat surface, you could remove it and reverse it. This could damage plaster, but you'll probably have a virgin wood surface when you're finished.

Sometimes stripping is advisable even when the wood is going to be painted, in order to enhance decorative detail that has become obscured by many coats of paint, or to do away with chipping and alligatoring.

STRIPPING METHODS

Chemical stripping is probably the most preferred method, although it is messy and requires the use of caustic and noxious chemicals. Heat—electric paint softeners, torches, or heat guns—is a good method to use if you are going to repaint a surface, for it avoids the possibility of residual chemical stripper ruining the paint job. Cleanup is easy, since the softened paint dries after it is removed and can be swept up with a broom. Heat methods scorch the wood easily, however; and removing all the paint without damaging the wood is often impossible. Heat stripping tends to cost less than chemical paint removal, since it requires only an initial capital investment for the paint gun, torch, or whatever—plus costs for electricity or propane.

Another way to remove paint is by abrading it from the surface. Sanding is a time-consuming and horrid project, however; and the only way I would recommend it is for those working with a belt-sander on a flat surface having only a coat or two of paint. Even then, the heat from the sander causes the paint to become sticky and gummy, and the sanding belts quickly become clogged with paint.

Another tool on the market is a drill-powered paint stripper (available for less than $10 at most hardware stores), which is composed of small steel rods that whirl in a circle, abrading the paint. This is another method I would not recommend: the metal fingers easily damage wood or metal, and this tool can put undue stress on your power drill.

Varnish, shellac, urethane and other clear finishes should be removed from wood with chemical stripper; these usually come off quite easily.

CHEMICAL STRIPPING

Chemical stripping is not difficult or expensive (everyone should try it at least once), and if this is your choice, approach it confidently. Arm yourself with newspapers, paper towels, rags, all grades of steel wool, old toothbrushes, old putty knives, paint scrapers (the kind with replaceable blades, since they dull quickly), plastic garbage bags, rubber gloves, a drop cloth to protect the floors, goggles to protect your eyes, and a copious supply of chemical remover.

TYPES OF STRIPPERS There are many different types of chemical stripping agents available. Lye, a caustic alklyd that is used by commercial "dipping" or "tanking" outfits, is tremendously destructive to the wood and should therefore be avoided. It destroys the vital oils in the wood, raises the grain, and very often leaves a residue on the wood that prevents the wood from later accepting paint or varnish.

Other strippers are solvent-based and have little or no deleterious effect upon most woods. Solvent-based strippers also contain activators, fillers, wax, and (in the case of paste removers) thickeners. The solvent dissolves the paint or varnish; the wax floats to the top of the wood and retards the solvent evaporation; thickeners keep the remover from running. If you're a novice or are working on primarily vertical surfaces, you may find the paste type easier to use, since it permits heavy application without runoff. On the other hand, the liquid type is less costly, far less messy to clean up, and, with practice, works just as well as the paste. You can thicken liquid stripper yourself by adding a cornstarch and water paste to it.

The most commonly used stripping solvents are acetone, alcohol, aromatic spirits, and methylene chloride. (Prior to January 1978, most removers on the market were benzene based, but benzene was determined to be carcinogenic and was outlawed.) Acetone is the least caustic of these and won't burn the skin, but it evaporates much quicker than other agents. Methylene chloride, the "Cadillac" of strippers, costs more, but it is more efficient (especially on latex paints) and is the only remover that actually attacks the pigment in the paint.

Chemical stripper is expensive, and prices can fluctuate from $4 to $18 per gallon, so shop around. Your best bet is to find a manufacturer who supplies commercial stripping businesses and buy directly in at least 5-gallon quantities. Also, many times a stripping agent purchased directly from the factory will contain a higher percentage of solvent than those sold at retail hardware and paint stores. If you have a sizable area to strip, you could save scores of dollars. There is no accurate way to estimate how much chemical stripper a job will require, since this will vary widely, depending on the type of remover you use, the types and conditions and number of layers of paint you have to remove, the ambient temperature, and your proficiency. The best thing to do is to strip a test patch, calculate how much chemical you used, and estimate your needs from there.

Also, pay attention to the labeling of the cans. Some removers are water soluble, and therefore the residue is much easier to clean up. Others require neutralizing with mineral spirits, which is much messier and adds greatly to the cost of the job. *Please* avoid strippers that are flammable. These not only pose a fire risk from careless smokers, shorts in electrical circuits, etc., but that half-filled can you store on your shelf needs only a rise in temperature to become a lethal bomb.

PREPARATION Protecting surrounding walls, floors, ceilings, etc. before you use chemical removers is important not only to avoid damaging finishes you don't intend to remove, but to minimize time-consuming cleanup when you're finished.

To mask a portion of a wall or ceiling to protect it from the chemicals, use 2-inch-wide Scotch-brand masking tape (many solvents will eat through other brands). For the best protection, run tape around the perimeter of the area you wish to mask, then tape newspaper (a single layer will suffice) over the area. When masking a wall, start from the bottom and work upwards. That way, the laps of the newspaper will be facing downwards, and the stripper will run off them, rather than between the layers of paper.

Before applying stripper, determine how the air flows in the house. Walk around the house with a lit cigarette or candle, watching which direction the air wafts. Start your stripping where the air is stagnant or where it collects—this is where fumes from the stripper will accumulate. If you start elsewhere, by the time you reach these areas, vapors will have already built up there.

SAFETY Most chemicals used to strip paint from wood are both caustic and noxious, so protect yourself. Wear clothing over your entire body (rubber gloves are a must) so the chemical won't splash onto your skin. Also, use a respirator, if possible (they're available at paint stores) to prevent inhalation of the vapors. Keep a bucket of clean warm water close by at all times when working with chemical stripper, just in case some of the solvent gets on your skin or in your eyes. If this does happen, there is a few seconds' delay before the solvent starts to work; keeping water handy might prevent a serious chemical burn.

Also, cover any electrical switches and outlets with duct tape, as the solvent can eat through the insulation covering the wires, and fire could result from the combination of electrical current and heat released by the solvent.

APPLICATION Stripping technique is a personal thing, and even professionals don't agree on tools or on methods for application. You, too, will develop your own knack and preferences with practice.

Perhaps the most accepted method is to brush the stripper onto the wood. Pour the solvent into a 2- or 3-pound coffee can. Using an old paint brush, apply the chemical liberally to the surface of the wood. Brush in one direction only; a back and forth motion will remove some of the stripper you've just applied.

Another method is to spray the stripper onto the wood with a heavy-duty garden sprayer (courtesy of Jack the Stripper, alias Brian Reardon, who perfected this method and who has stripped paint from old houses and furniture throughout the United States and in his native England). Use liquid methlyene chloride (paste or semipaste stripper won't fit through the nozzle in the sprayer) and use a plastic sprayer, since solvent will pit a metal cannister.

Start with a small area at first, although after you've worked a while you should be able to strip a large (10-square-foot) area at one time. You don't want to have to wait for the solvent, but you also don't want the solvent to dry.

After you have applied the stripper, wait—until the solvent has worked through all the layers of paint (you'll see them, one by one, bubble and actually lift from the surface of the wood). If you don't wait long enough before scraping the residue, you are thwarting the stripper in two ways. First, you are not giving the solvent time to adequately dissolve the paint. Second, if you disturb the stripper, the protective wax in it cannot float to the top, and the solvent will evaporate much faster. Either way, you will have to use much more remover and a lot of unnecessary elbow grease to do the job.

Note: One exception to leaving stripper on until all paint has lifted is latex paint over oil-based paint. The latex will lift off of the surface in large strips only a few minutes after application. You should remove this layer of latex, then reapply a coat of stripper on the paint underneath.

When the paint has bubbled and lifted from the wood, take a putty knife or scraper and scrape a little off (work with the grain and don't gouge the wood). All the paint should come off easily, although

some rare, thickly painted surfaces may take two coats of remover. The solvent may take half an hour to bubble and lift from the wood; or it may take all night.

When the mess is ready to remove, lift as much of it as possible from the surface, using an old putty knife, into a heavy plastic garbage bag. Experiment in corners and on moldings with toothbrushes, steel wool, putty knives, and scrapers. Wipe off the residue with paper towels, and throw them into the garbage bag as well.

If you leave the stripper on too long, or if the ambient temperature is too warm, the stripper, along with the paint, will dry on the wood, and you will not be able to remove it.

Note: All types of solvent—mineral spirits, paint remover, lacquer thinner, etc.—evaporate quickly when exposed to the air. Therefore, always keep solvents tightly capped; replace the cap immediately when using a solvent.

Heat enhances the efficiency of the solvent to a point; if possible, work on a warm day, and try warming the wood first with a propane torch or an electric heater. Don't bother to heat the stripper, since it produces an endothermic reaction, absorbing warmth from the surface that it meets.

Holding a wallpaper steamer next to a surface coated with remover is a great aid, and I have been able to strip three layers of paint from a 1-square-foot area per minute with this method. The steam not only provides heat for the remover, but creates a moisture barrier that retards the solvent evaporation. But avoid too much of a good thing: if you leave the steamer on too long it can warp the wood and raise the grain.

To neutralize the stripper, brush the wood vigorously with a nylon or natural-bristle brush and either mineral spirits or a mixture of TSP and *hot* water—1/2 cup TSP per gallon of water. Start from the bottom and work upwards, otherwise the neutralizer will turn any excess stripper left on the wood to a tarry substance that is extremely difficult to remove (you'll have to strip it all over again). Also, after the wood has been stripped, before finishing, brush the wood again with a mixture of 1/4 cup of TSP per gallon of hot water. This will clean the wood, so you will have to do much less sanding.

WHEN NOTHING SEEMS TO WORK If you encounter a dry, dull paint that nothing seems to remove, it is probably *refractory* or *milk paint,* one of the earliest paints made, which is composed of casein glue properties and milk or buttermilk. The best way to remove it is with a mixture of equal parts of ammonia, TSP, and hot water, using it like any other chemical remover. Sometimes, unfortunately, even this method fails.

Also, chemical paint removers are ineffective on some opaque stains. Try sodium hypochlorite (pool chlorine) applied full strength. Don't forget your respirator and goggles—this stuff is fierce.

STRIPPING PAINT FROM METALS Stripping methods used for woods can also be utilized to strip paint from metals. Remember, however, that heat will tarnish brass and other finishes, and that sanding or other abrading can scratch a surface and even ruin plating.

I prefer to strip paint from small pieces of hardware with chemical remover, putting a piece into a tin can and barely covering it with solvent. Put a lid on the can and let it sit for a few hours, then brush the hardware with a small wire-bristled brush.

CREATING YOUR OWN STRIPPING TANK Jack the Stripper, famous for his spraying method of applying chemical paint remover, has also invented a good method for removing paint from loose moldings or other pieces of wood:

Build from two-by-four studs a frame large enough to accommodate the pieces of wood to be stripped. Nail or staple to the inside of this frame a large sheet of heavy-duty plastic (the same weight used for water bed mattresses—you can usually find this at water bed repair stores or plastic supply houses), folding it at the bottom so that it forms a basin that will hold both wood and solvent. Put the pieces to be stripped into the "mini-tank" and barely cover them with methlyene chloride stripper. When the paint has lifted from the wood, scrape or brush the pieces and wash them well with hot water and TSP. This is a much better method than commercial tank stripping operations, which utilize lye to remove paint and which can seriously damage wood.

HEAT STRIPPING

Heat stripping is becoming a popular paint removal method among old-house owners, since it is much less messy than chemicals and, with practice and care, can yield good results.

A propane torch is the fastest way to melt paint, but the flame is usually too hot for wood. By the time it melts the paint, it has also scorched the wood. Also, some building codes prohibit burning off paint, since this can release harmful vapors from old lead-based paint. For this reason, always use a respirator when heat stripping.

An electric paint softener is composed of an electric heating element partially encased in a metal shield affixed to a wooden handle. This works well on flat surfaces but cannot be used without damaging the wood on most raised surfaces, such as moldings.

The electric heat gun (available from the *Old-House Journal Catalog* for about $60) is probably the best heat method for stripping paint from wood. The heat gun resembles a blow dryer for hair and provides flameless heat that can be directed to small areas or convex surfaces.

The J. C. Whitney Company (1917–19 Archer Avenue, P.O. Box 8410, Chicago, IL 60680) markets a device that attaches to a propane cylinder and converts propane fuel to infrared, flameless heat. Although this is not as easy to use as an electric heat gun (it is much larger and heats a bigger area, therefore it cannot be directed as well), it is considerably less expensive ($20) and is convenient where there is no electricity.

USING HEAT ON WOOD Experiment before you start to determine how far away from the wood you should hold the gun, torch, or electric paint softener. You want to avoid scorching the wood and still be able to melt all layers of paint with a single application of heat.

For flat surfaces, use a putty knife with a scraping (heavy, chisel-edged) blade. As soon as the paint starts to bubble, slide the paint scraper underneath it and lift the paint from the surface. If you do not do this quickly, the paint will cool, harden, and adhere again to the surface.

For moldings, corners, and other tight places, use a small (toothbrush-sized) wire brush, with fine brass bristles, and vigorously brush the melted paint from the surface of the wood.

If you are working on a vertical surface, work from the bottom up, since heat rises and can easily scorch bare wood above the areas where you are working. Use chemical remover to remove paint residue left on the wood.

WOOD FINISHING

This small section does not intend to supplant the large volume of literature about wood finishing or the teachings of the hardware store sages, but instead offers a few tips for working with old wood, a topic that many of these sources neglect.

Woods are classified either as *hardwoods*: those from broad-leafed, deciduous trees, or *softwoods*: those from evergreen conifers. The appellations *hard* and *soft* have nothing to do with the woods' intrinsic properties. (The United States Department of Agriculture publishes two booklets that provide detailed, illustrated descriptions of the colors and properties of different woods: *Wood—Colors and Kinds*, Handbook No. 101 for $.75; and *Selection and Use of Wood Products for Home and Farm Building*, Handbook No. 311, $.80. Both are available from the Superintendent of Documents, U.S. Government Printing Office, Washington, D.C. 20402.)

When working with old wood, finishing has an added purpose beyond just enhancing the wood's natural beauty; protecting it against cracking, warping, and dirt and moisture absorption.

Proper preparation and treatment of the wood is vital to achieving a good result. Defects should be removed, since stains, especially, will magnify any flaws. Dirt, grease, and other foreign matter should be removed, since they inhibit the action of any finish.

The right way to finish wood depends entirely on the type of wood and its condition. Old wood, especially, tends to be dry and cracked or split; in extreme cases, the grain rises. Finishing and working with old wood is a trial-and-error process, for wood will react differently to different treatments—depending upon its condition, the previous finishes that it has received, and chemicals that were used on it for cleanup or paint stripping.

TREATING DAMAGED WOOD

Overexposure to the elements, chemical bleaching or stripping (especially tank stripping), and old age take their tolls on wood. Like neglected hair or skin, damaged wood loses its natural oils, becomes dull, and splits and cracks. In extreme cases, wood fibers are actually destroyed, the grain rises, and the surface of the wood feels spongy and fuzzy. Although the first impulse may be to discard wood that is this badly damaged, you may *have* to resurrect it, since sometimes that old molding, door or windowsill, or whatever would be very expensive to replicate.

If the wood is the victim of a tank stripping operation, you will first need to neutralize the lye or other alkyd paint remover. Coat the wood with a mild solution of white vinegar and water; repeat this process several times.

If your wood shows evidence of damage, give it a hot oil treatment. First, cover the wood with loose burlap—either wrapping the fabric around the wood (for loose planks) or staple-tacking it to the wood. Saturate the fabric with boiled linseed oil, tung oil, or Danish oil heated to about 120 degrees in a double boiler. Reapply the oil over a two- or three-day period until the wood won't absorb any more; let it dry thoroughly. The Indians, who developed this recipe, would cover the wood and burlap with a coat of mud and let the wood dry in the sun. (Caution: some stains will not penetrate oiled surfaces, so either check before you buy the stain, or stain the wood *before* you treat it.)

FILLING WOOD

Small dents in wood can be removed by placing a damp cloth over the area and pressing it with a hot clothes iron. Larger dents, cracks, nail holes, and flaws should be filled.

Early-day wood finishers made wood fillers from glue mixed with sawdust from the actual piece of wood. The color matched, but the texture was poor.

There are many wood fillers on the market. Some are applied before staining, some after. Some fillers boast that they will accept stains. Even those that do accept stains, however, are not usually as porous as old wood, and you'll find that once you've stained the wood, the patch will appear lighter.

There are two solutions to this problem; perhaps the easiest is to test the stain on an inconspicuous part of the wood to determine the color your wood will become. Using oil-based pigments (available at paint stores), tint the wood putty to match the color that the wood *will be.* Another, less-satisfactory method is to approximately match the color before you stain, then, after the wood is finished, to use a tinted putty stick (available at paint stores). (Note: Do not use paste wood fillers before you use an oil-based stain.)

A small, flexible-bladed putty knife is best for filling wood. Since the solvent in fillers dries quickly, keep the top on the can while you are working. (Some companies manufacture solvents for softening old putty.) Use fillers sparingly to avoid having to sand.

The best way to fill nail holes is to stuff a small bit of wood filler in the hole with your finger. This is an especially good method to use after the wood has been finished (if, for example, you have just nailed in place a prefinished molding), since you won't leave any putty residue on the wood. Fill cracks in wood with wood putty thinned almost to liquid with wood putty solvent.

REMOVING BLEMISHES

CIGARETTE BURNS Remove by rubbing vigorously with Crest toothpaste.

BLEACHING STAINS If the wood is too dark or if the surface has dark marks, these may be lightened or removed by bleaching. Use bleach sparingly, however, since it tends to damage the wood.

For small jobs that don't require color changes, use household bleach mixed to a paste with cornstarch or trisodium phosphate (TSP) mixed with a touch of water. For large areas or stubborn spots, use a commercial wood bleach, available at most paint and some antiques stores. Bleaching times will vary according to the stain and the wood. Test every few minutes.

SANDING

There is nothing tricky about sanding wood—it's just a lot of work.

Buy several different grades of sandpaper. Silicon carbide paper, the most expensive kind, lasts longer and does not clog as fast if there is grit, dirt, paint, or stripper residue on the wood. Experiment with different grades of paper and choose the finest grit that will remove any scratches or foreign material from the wood. Paper that is too coarse will scratch the wood; too fine won't remove the flaws. Sand the whole piece of wood thoroughly, working with the grain; repeat the process with finer and finer grits of sandpaper until you're at 400 grade and the surface is satiny smooth. Always use a sanding block on flat surfaces.

Electric sanders are marvelous inventions (especially the Rockwell Bloc Sander), but practice on a scrap of wood before you attack a cherished antique. Apply even pressure, keep the pad or belt flat on the surface, and keep it moving. The slightest hesitation could leave gouges and dents. Never turn the sander on or off while it is in contact with the wood.

Generally, a belt or vibrator sander is limited to flat surfaces, but a thick pad attachment, available for the Bloc Sander, enables you to power-sand even moldings and curves.

To remove raised grain and that "fuzz" from damaged wood (treat it first, please), use a very fine sandpaper and work by hand. This is an extremely time-consuming job, but don't take short cuts: using a rougher-grit paper will only intensify the problem and raise the grain to a greater degree.

If you are working with a disassembled object, sand it before you reassemble it, to avoid having to sand in tight corners.

STAINING

Virtually any color can be achieved by staining, but don't trust the color chips in the paint store, especially if you're working with old wood. Wood's porosity and resultant ability to absorb stain will vary not only by its type, but by its age and condition as well.

Test the stain first, either on the back of the piece you want to stain or on a scrap of the same kind of wood. To increase color intensity of a stain, let the stain sit on the wood longer or repeat applications; to lighten it, thin with mineral spirits. Colors can be mixed, as long as the types of stain are the same. When choosing stain, match the *color* of the wood—not the kind of wood.

Stains are classified as water-, alcohol-, oil-, or lacquer thinner-based. Water-based stains are inexpensive. They penetrate deeply and evenly, give the clearest tones of all the different types of stains, and they won't fade. Cleanup is easy, too. If the wood is old, dry, and porous, however, a water-based stain might contribute to the grain rising.

Alcohol-based stains are also water soluble, and they don't raise grain, but they are more expensive. They are also the hardest type of stain to apply, since they dry quickly and tend to bleed.

Oil-based stains penetrate well, but they may seep too deeply into soft spots in the wood, causing dark splotches. Oil-based stains may fade with time, also. They are easy to apply and dry slowly, so they can be reworked. The Watco Company combines oil-based stains (medium and dark walnut) with a fine-quality Danish oil for a beautiful, one-step finish, although Watco tends to bring out red hues in wood.

Pigmented oil stain is actually a thin paint. It doesn't fade or bleed and is easy to apply. Unlike other types of stains, however, it gives an opaque finish and covers the grain of the wood.

The type of stain you use is mostly a matter of preference. Choose a type you like to use and practice with it. As you become familiar with it, you will be able to better judge how it will work on different woods.

Before staining, wipe the wood lightly with a tack rag (a cloth dampened with lacquer thinner). Stain may be applied with either a brush or a cloth—experiment on scraps of wood to determine which you prefer. Work in logical sections. Don't, for example, stain halfway up a molding, then stop for a rest. You'll end up with a line where you stopped and then restarted.

Note: Many times, especially with old wood (particularly wood with torn grain), stain will not absorb evenly, resulting in a blotching of the color. To avoid this, before you stain, apply a thin coat of 60 percent denatured (wood) alcohol and 40 percent white shellac. After this has dried, use an oil-based stain (one without a varnishing or finishing agent).

FINISHES

Finishes are classified as either penetrating or surface. Penetrating finishes are usually oils that are rubbed into the wood. They may be combined with stains for a one-step application. These include:
- *Danish oils* Watco brand is the most well known. It comes in plain, medium- and dark-walnut colors and tends to impart a reddish cast to the wood.
- *Linseed oil* Use the boiled type. It tends to remain sticky.

- *Tung oil* is a great finish that gives a good protection against moisture, but requires a lot of elbow grease.

Surface finishes include *shellac, lacquer, urethane,* and *varnish.* Lacquer is used infrequently. It dries quickly but does not last long and provides poor resistance to water and grease. Shellac was a common finish during the nineteenth century and is often favored for its authenticity. Shellac is fast drying but soon yellows and flakes. Urethane is perhaps the most popular finish used today. It has less tendency to yellow than shellac or wax and is easy to apply. Urethane will not bond to old shellac, however. Use it sparingly, to avoid giving a plastic appearance to the wood.

Varnish is used over old finishes (especially shellac) or for exterior application (spar or marine varnish, preferably). It is extremely slow drying and may be difficult to apply.

Hint: Surface finishes spread most evenly when warm, which reduces their viscosity and makes them thinner. If you are working in a cold climate, warm the finish in a double boiler before you apply it.

WAXES

Some people prefer wax to oils or surface finishes. Wax imparts a beautiful, satin sheen to wood; however, it requires a lot of rubbing, and must be renewed in a shorter length of time than other finishes. It also tends to waterspot easily. Avoid spray waxes, which build up and yellow quickly, as well as beeswax, which shows fingerprints.

CHAPTER 21

Wood Moldings & Wainscoting

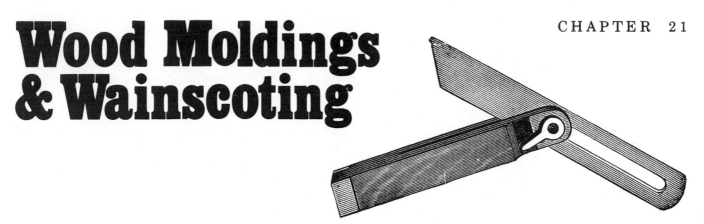

A molding is a decorative strip of wood milled with a continuous straight or curved surface. In addition to serving decorative purposes, moldings may also be protective (chair railings, for example, keep furniture from marring walls), structural (door and window jambs), or cosmetic (shoe moldings and wainscot caps hide raw edges and gaps between moldings and floors or walls).

The first use of moldings is attributed to the early Greeks, who devised decorative patterns to create interest and variety in otherwise plain areas, and to produce aesthetically pleasing highlights and shadows. The Romans continued this fashion, perfecting the symmetry of moldings by the use of mechanical tools and compasses.

Classical traditions prevailed throughout the Colonial and Victorian eras. This was largely due to the influence of Andrea Palladio (1518–1580), who measured the Roman ruins and published the proportions and sizes of classical moldings in the widely read *The Four Books of Architecture*. Many American Colonial architects, however, received little formal education in architectural drawing or practices. This, combined with the American spirit of independence and pride in innovation, fostered many new molding styles.

The early molding tools were planes carved from wooden blocks, with metal blades set in them. A woodworker would often carry as many as thirty different planes. Larger moldings were fabricated on huge planes too large to be taken from the shop. These required several people to operate: two or more apprentices to pull the boards through the plane, and the master craftsman, who set and guided the blades.

In the 1850s the Industrial Revolution saw the development of the mechanized molder and other woodworking machines. This, along with the Victorian penchant for detail and ornamentation, led to the widespread (some claim excessive) use of moldings in nineteenth-century houses.

Moldings in the Victorian-era home were often made of varying types of wood chosen for their practical properties, rather than for color or grain;

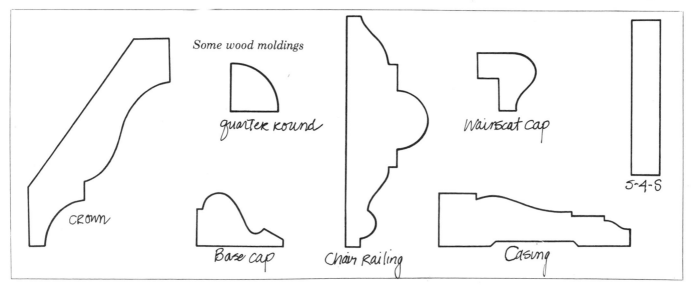

Some wood moldings

crown

quarter round

Base cap

Chair Railing

Wainscot cap

Casing

S-4-S

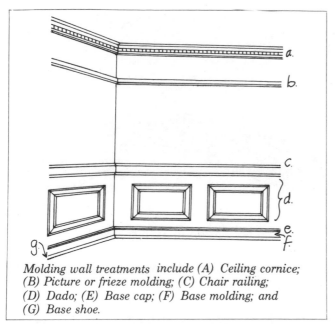

Molding wall treatments include (A) Ceiling cornice; (B) Picture or frieze molding; (C) Chair railing; (D) Dado; (E) Base cap; (F) Base molding; and (G) Base shoe.

in most cases, moldings were painted or grained. Redwood was a favorite for exterior moldings (especially in the West, where it was abundant), since it is most resistant to the elements and to wood-boring insects. The hardness of fir made it a good candidate for structural moldings; pine was used liberally throughout many homes, since it was relatively inexpensive and easy to work with.

REPRODUCTION MOLDINGS

Modern moldings come in varying grades, although you, as a retail purchaser, will rarely have a selection. Buy your moldings at a quality lumber store or molding manufacturer, so you can be reasonably sure of obtaining top quality.

Molding may also be either solid or *finger jointed*. In the latter process, undesirable characteristics or defects are trimmed away, leaving select strips of clear wood that are glued together with interlocking finger-shaped joints. Since these joints show, finger-jointed moldings are suitable only for painted or other opaque finishes.

Most reproduction moldings are fabricated from ponderosa pine. Other woods commonly used include sugar pine, Douglas fir, white fir, hemlock, and redwood.

Many intricate Victorian moldings were planed from single pieces of wood, but you may not be able to find similar moldings today. Some companies are manufacturing reproductions of old molding patterns (check *The Old-House Journal Catalog*) and some lumberyards will produce anything you want—but you'll pay righteously for this. Often, however, you can combine several different simple moldings and obtain a decorative molding as intricate as any fabricated during the nineteenth century. Top an S4S molding for example, with a flat astragal, surround it on each side with a small piece of quarter-round, and voilà! you have a chair railing as fancy as they come. A large crown molding topping base and shoe moldings, with small pieces of lath tacked on for dentils, makes a beautiful, ornate ceiling cornice.

WORKING WITH MOLDING

Working with wood moldings is not difficult, but every little mistake you make—even if your saw cuts are a minute fraction of an inch off—will show glaringly. There are several ways to minimize errors. First, thoroughly prepare the surface to which you're going to nail the molding, ensuring that it is as flat as possible.

Next, use the right tools. Use a miter box with a backsaw to cut moldings; you can't expect true accuracy with a large saw. Another tool that is a must is a brad pusher, which will drive small nails (brads) into the molding without splitting it or leaving hammer marks. (For especially delicate moldings, pre-drill the hole and/or blunt the tip of the nail by rapping it with a hammer. A blunt nail will tear the fibers of the wood, whereas a sharp nail will split them, cracking the molding.) Other tools you will need are carpenter's wood glue, a couple of spring clamps, and a coping saw.

MEASURING MOLDING After determining the types of molding you want, estimate how much of each type you will need. Most moldings are available in lengths from 3 to 16 feet. Make a list of the lengths you need to determine if shorter lengths will suffice, since they tend to be less expensive. Round measurements up to the nearest foot to allow for cutting and trimming, since the ends of moldings are often ragged and should be cut off. To estimate for mitered or coped edges, add twice the width of the molding to the desired length.

MITERING This is probably the most common method of joining moldings, and it's probably the toughest to master. Although it's not the best way to join inside corners, all outside corners must be mitered.

If possible, miter the corners before you cut the length of the molding. This allows you to adjust the miter cuts, if necessary, so they fit better if (heaven forbid) you goof or if the wall is uneven.

First, set the miter box at 45 degrees. Trim each of the molding ends at opposite angles so that, when fit in place, they form a tight right angle.

But what if they don't? Hopefully, you've left some extra length on your molding. Old houses notoriously sag and bend and bow—but don't despair. There are several ways of handling this problem.

Take a picture frame clamp and clamp the mitered corners at a tight fit, if you can. If you note a place where the molding bows away from the wall, insert thin wooden shims. If the molding refuses to come together at a 45-degree angle but it gaps only a little bit, you can fill the gap with wood putty. If the gap is large, remove one side of the molding from the picture clamp, turn it upside down on top of the other side, and trace the exact angle of the one side onto the other. Then, cut carefully with a coping saw.

COPING A coped joint has the end of one piece cut flush to the wall and the other piece shaped to match its face. This is a relatively easy procedure and is a great way to join moldings at inside corners, especially since many walls aren't perfectly square, and miters (as you have probably discovered) tend to gap.

First, back-miter the piece to be coped; set the molding in the miter box exactly as it is to be installed on the wall—upright against the back plane—and trim it at a 45-degree angle. Following this profile with a coping saw, cut at a 90-degree angle with the face of the molding. This results in a duplication of the pattern, which should fit perfectly against the face of the adjoining molding. Practice this three or four times, and you should have the hang of coping.

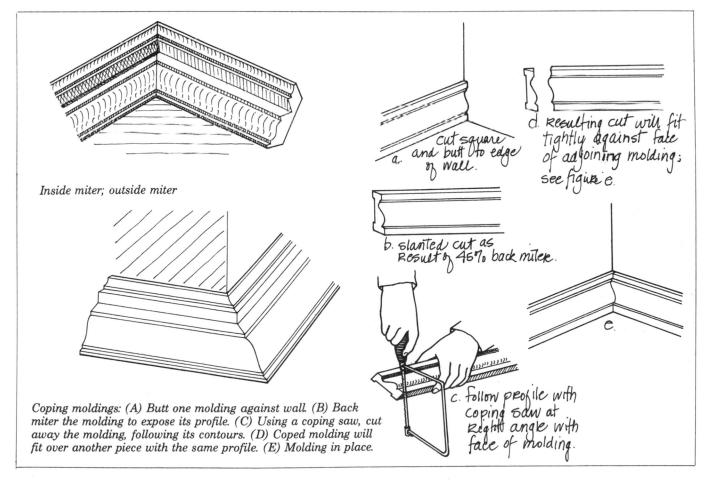

Inside miter; outside miter

Coping moldings: (A) Butt one molding against wall. (B) Back miter the molding to expose its profile. (C) Using a coping saw, cut away the molding, following its contours. (D) Coped molding will fit over another piece with the same profile. (E) Molding in place.

a. cut square and butt to edge of wall.

b. slanted cut as result of 45% back miter.

c. follow profile with coping saw at right angle with face of molding.

d. Resulting cut will fit tightly against face of adjoining molding; see figure e.

e.

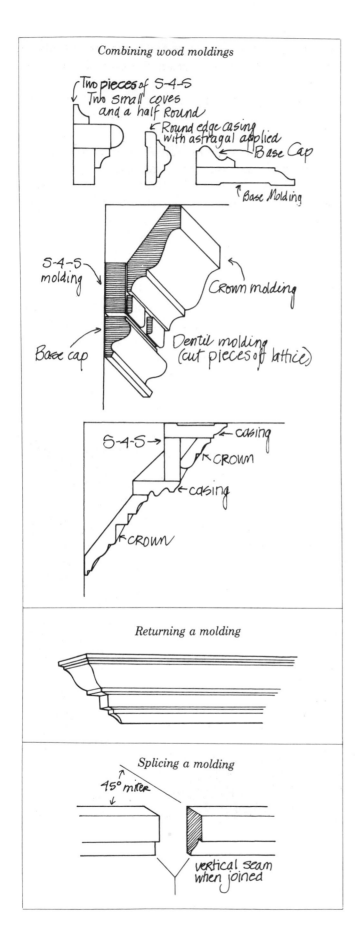

Combining wood moldings

Two pieces of S-4-S
Two small coves
and a half Round

Round edge casing
with astragal applied

Base Cap

Base Molding

S-4-S molding

Crown molding

Base cap

Dentil molding
(cut pieces of lattice)

S-4-S

casing

CROWN

casing

CROWN

Returning a molding

Splicing a molding

45° miter

vertical seam
when joined

PLINTH BLOCKS These are square or oblong blocks, used commonly at corners and at bottoms of doors and windows. They are especially useful where two unlike types of molding meet, such as where a base molding joins a door casing. The moldings butt against these blocks, which are usually molded or carved themselves, avoiding the necessity of miter joints.

Many plinth blocks were decorated with bull's-eyes: concentric circles carved into square pieces of wood. These were originally manufactured on a wood lathe, but do-it-yourselfers can achieve a fairly good replication using an electric drill fitted with hole saws (attachments that cut circles in wood). If you don't already own several different sizes of hole saws, you might profit by buying a flycutter type, which is adjustable. Practice cutting various concentric circles in a piece of wood. When you achieve the desired results, use a wood rasp and sandpaper to round the edges of the circles.

RETURNS Ends of moldings, such as strips used under windowsills, can't be left with raw edges, but are usually finished in one of two ways, both called *returning* the molding. For large or especially intricate moldings, first cut an outside miter on the piece. Cut another outside miter on a small piece and fit the two together. The molding will look as if it has turned the corner.

For flatter or less intricate moldings, place a sample of the molding perpendicular to the piece (decorative side out) and trace the profile onto the molding. Cut the return with a coping saw.

SPLICING There are two ways to splice a molding. Practice them both and determine which you prefer. The first method creates a *scarf joint* with a *vertical face seam* in the finished installation. To accomplish this, orient the moldings on the edge of the miter box, just as they will be applied to the wall. Miter the joining ends at 45-degree angles from front to back. One member will overlap the other. The second method creates an *angular face seam* and is made by orienting the moldings on their backs in the miter box.

Adding moldings to a room is like icing a cake—it's generally one of the last touches. Working with moldings, especially in an older house, can be frustrating. Try to work carefully and slowly, for precision comes with practice and diligence.

WAINSCOTING

A wainscot is a wooden lining on an interior wall. Although modern paneling is technically a wainscot, it is set flush to the wall, whereas most of the wainscoting found in old homes projects out from the wall at least 1/2 inch and is decorated with trim and/or molding. The wainscot may cover the entire wall or may extend up from the floor only a few feet.

When used in old kitchens, pantries, and bathrooms, wainscoting was primarily protective, shielding the walls from grease, dirt, and water. Most of these protective wainscots were tongue and groove boards that extended 3 to 5 feet up the wall from the floor and were capped by a chair or plate railing or another type of decorative molding. They were commonly painted or grained and varnished so they could be scrubbed.

Different types of purely decorative wainscoting, sometimes painted and sometimes left natural, were used in opulent homes of the era; elaborate wood dadoes were common treatments for libraries and parlors. Natural wood became fashionable and common, even in modest residences, during the last quarter of the nineteenth century. The Queen Anne baronial hallways, for example, were adorned with beautiful wood dadoes, often fabricated of black walnut. Craftsman and later homes used simpler treatments, usually of oak or redwood.

CREATING A WAINSCOT

Adding authentic-looking wainscoting is a simple process, and this may be the perfect decorative touch, combined with wallpaper and decorative moldings, to break the monotony of a large wall.

Although several companies manufacture reproduction wood dadoing and wainscoting (check the *Old-House Journal Catalog* for these), you can create your own wainscoting from flooring, paneling, and moldings for much less money.

To replicate a partial-wall wainscot, try tongue and groove fir flooring. Some lumber stores carry flooring with a V-groove at one edge, which adds interesting detail. Quarter-inch tongue and groove cedar paneling also makes a good decorative molding.

You can replicate an elaborate dado with readily available materials. Sheets of veneer or quarter-inch plywood provide the background. Affix them to the wall with paneling adhesive and nails. Then nail S4S molding over the seams and along the tops and bottoms to form moldings at the bottom, and plate or chair railing (if only a partial-wall wainscot) or ceiling cove (if it covers the entire wall) on top.

Caution: Too much wood or wood that is too elaborate can easily dwarf a small room, so before you begin, plan carefully. Draw a scale rendering of each wall and plot your wainscoting. This will help you gauge proportions and also estimate how much material you will need (remember to add extra for mitering). If you have difficulty visualizing your project, try drawing it on the wall.

The simple wainscoting in this renovated bathroom is tongue and groove redwood planks.

Elaborate wainscoting

CHAPTER 22

Windows

REPAIRING DOUBLE-HUNG SASH WINDOWS

Unfortunately, after a century or so of use, old double-hung sash windows frequently do not work. Problems include broken sash cords, broken or missing pulleys, windows sticking in their channels, and rotting wood. The bottom sash usually receives more use than the top and is therefore most likely to require work.

REMOVING WINDOWS FROM THEIR CASINGS The bottom (inner) half of a double-hung sash window is held in place by a small, decorative molding; the upper (outer) half rests between the outside window casing and a flat length of wood (approximately 1/4 to 3/8 inch thick, 3/4 to 1 inch wide) that is wedged into a channel between the two halves of the window. This *window bead, screen bead, or stop,* as it is called, is press-fit into the channel. You can usually remove the bead by grasping it with a pair of pliers (protect the wood with a cloth when you do this) and gently pulling it out of the channel.

Although the window bead was never originally glued or nailed in place, this is often done later by well-meaning but uninformed renovators. If the bead is nailed or glued, you will have to destroy and replace the window bead.

(Don't remove the casing if it is an elaborate one.) To remove the window bead, drive an awl or chisel into the bead and pry it from its channel. But remember, before you destroy it: window bead is not a stock item in lumber stores, so to replace it you will have to have a new one custom milled—an expensive proposition.

If the window bead fits too loosely in its channel, resist the temptation to glue or nail it, since you will only be creating future problems. Instead, remove it and soak it for a few days in water. This will cause the wood to swell, and it should then fit snugly into the channel.

SASH WEIGHTS The four sash weights—one hung from each side of each half of the window—are suspended from the edges of the window by sash cords or chains. The sash weights produce counterweight against the window, keeping it in its channel and facilitating easy opening and closing of the window.

Most double-hung windows contain *sash pockets*: sections of wood (which may be covered by layers of paint) held in place by screws or nails that, when removed, provide access to the sash weights. If your windows have no sash pockets, you'll have to remove one of the window casings to gain access to the sash weights.

Sash weights are made of either stone or cast iron. Iron weights will most likely be rusted. If so, remove the rust with a wire brush, then coat the weights with a rust-inhibiting paint. Stone sash weights frequently break; replacements (make sure you get the same size and weight) are usually plentiful at salvage yards. Some double-hung windows are controlled by a spring mechanism. If these break, replacements are available at hardware stores.

REPLACING SASH CORD Most sash cord is 1/4 inch in diameter. Use cotton cord for replacement, since it wears well and will not become brittle after it has been wet. Tie a single overhand knot at the very end of the rope and place it through the hole at the edge of the window. Thread the rope through the pulley at the top of the window channel and push the cord down into the sash pocket. Cut the cord so that when it is attached to the sash weight the weight will hang approximately 1-1/2 inches from the bottom of the window casement (when the window is at the top of the casement). This will allow the cord to stretch with the weight of the sash and will prevent the weight from banging against the bottom of the casement. Tie the sash cord at the end of the sash weight, using an overhand knot.

STICKING WINDOWS Double-hung sash windows that stick usually do so because paint buildup has slightly narrowed the window channels. If this is the case, sanding or stripping the paint will alleviate the problem. If the window still sticks—or if it is not painted—try lubricating the channel with paraffin or white graphite.

If the window is painted shut, try breaking the seal by inserting a putty knife between the window and the stop. If there is a serious paint buildup, you may have to use paint remover to unstick the window.

Refrain from painting either the window channels or the sides of the window if the wood is sound and has not weathered. Old, dry wood, however, or

wood exposed to the elements (unprotected windows on the south side of the house, in particular) should be protected with a thin coat of oil-based primer.

REBUILDING AND REPLACING WINDOWS Frequently, old windows come apart at the seams, and, over time, the corners come unglued. If the window is falling apart but the wood is sound, regluing and clamping it will suffice. Reinforcing the joint with dowels will help prevent the problem's recurrence.

Often, exposure to the elements causes the wood to rot. If the corner has rotted but the wood is sound 2 to 3 inches from the joint, a small metal L bracket will hold it in place. Using a router or a wood-carving knife, rout an L-shaped channel for the bracket, screw the bracket into the wood, then completely fill over the bracket with wood putty.

If the wood has rotted past the corner, you will probably have to replace the entire window. Check the salvage yards—and occasionally newspaper classified advertisements—for replacements. Because there is an unlimited number of window sizes, you may have a hard time finding the right one. Local lumber mills will custom-make windows; however, their prices are high ($30–$60 per window).

If you have to replace a window that has multiple panes, you can save money by having the lumber company use a single pane of glass and glue strips of wood to it to simulate *muntins*: the small bars of wood that divide the panes.

When you replace a window, make sure you measure the old one carefully, so you can duplicate it. Measure the height of the window at both sides (just in case it has warped) and at both the inside and outside; most double-hung sash windows are longer on the outside, since the exterior windowsill usually slopes downwards to allow rain water to run off of it. And, don't forget to measure the thickness of the wood, so that a replacement window will fit into the window channel.

REPLACING BROKEN WINDOWS

Before I moved into it, my once-derelict old house had been vacant for months and was the object of neighborhood target practice. One of the first renovation tasks I had to master was repairing broken windows, since cardboard does little to keep out winter rain and cold.

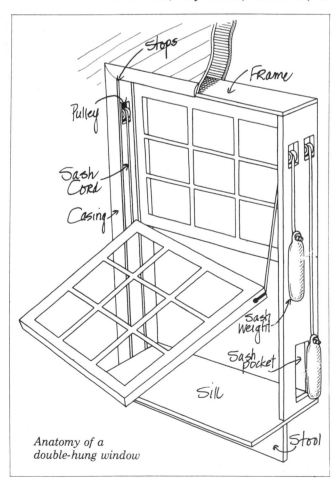

Anatomy of a double-hung window

● A pane of glass is held in place with glazier's points (1/8-inch triangular points of thin metal—most hardware stores carry them), then *stopped* with either wooden stops (small moldings) or window putty. If the window is held in with wooden stops, remove them as you would a molding (see Chapter 21), pull the points out with a pair of pliers, and remove the glass.

● If the window is puttied, first soften the putty with a propane torch. Don't expect the torch to melt the putty; if you hold the flame on the window that long it will scorch the wood. Use the lowest flame and merely touch it to the window—just enough so that you can pry up the old putty with a putty knife.

● After you remove the old putty, remove the glazier's points with a pair of needle-nosed pliers. Lightly sand the window opening, then apply a coat of linseed oil. After this has dried, prime the opening with oil-based primer. These last two steps are essential for a puttied window; otherwise the wood will leach the oil out of the new putty, which will then dry, crack, and fall out.

● The replacement pane of glass should be cut to dimensions that are 1/8 inch smaller than the size of the window opening. Place a 1/4-inch-wide bead of linseed oil window putty or glazier's adhesive all around the perimeter of the glass.

● Putty is much easier to work with if it is soft; take a large glob out of the can and work it with your hands, like modeling clay. If you first rub a little paint thinner on your hands, the putty won't stick to you.

● Stick the puttied window into the opening, puttied side down, pressing evenly on all sides until the putty oozes out the back of the window. Stick the glazier's points back in the window frame to hold the window in place securely.

● If the window is held by wooden stops, replace these as you would a fine-quality molding (see Chapter 21), using tiny finishing nails and a brad pusher.

REPUTTYING A WINDOW Reputtying a window is not difficult, but it is time-consuming, especially for the beginner. Don't try to do more than one window at a time until you've mastered the technique.

● To putty a window, soften a large lump of linseed oil putty in your hands (remember to coat those hands first with paint thinner). Rub the lump between the palms of your hand until it forms a "snake" about 1/2 inch in diameter. Lay it along the edge of the window.

● Hold a small putty knife with the edge of the blade at a 45-degree angle to the window frame edge. Run the knife in one continuous movement along the window frame from one corner to another. Repeat all along the perimeter of the window.

● After you've finished, dip the tip of your finger in paint thinner and run it along the puttied surface to smooth it.

● Putty is intended to be painted, but let it form a skin before you apply a brush.

STAINED GLASS

Stained glass is enjoying a revival of popularity, and modern-day glasswork, much of it boasting innovative theories of design and new types of glass, adorns many contemporary residences and businesses.

The Victorian era marked perhaps an even greater stained-glass renaissance, when it became popular after more than three centuries of disfavor. This was also the first time that stained glass escaped its sacred classification and was used in residences and in commercial establishments.

The use of colored, decorative glass dates back before the birth of Christ. By the twelfth century A.D., stained glass was a booming European industry, as witnessed by the magnificent windows in European cathedrals, which are unparalleled today. The fifteenth to nineteenth centuries, however, marked the dark ages for stained glass. Glass was still manufactured and windows were still built, but the craft relied heavily upon a technique known as glass painting, where an artist literally used the glass as a canvas. Windows became a tribute, not to the beauty of the glass or the skill of the glazier, but to the artistry of the painter.

The revival of interest in stained glass began in Europe and in America during the 1860s and went hand in hand with the Gothic Revival movement. The first residential stained glass appeared during this period, and these windows resembled copies of those in medieval churches. Old glass-making formulas were revived, and new and beautiful colors and textures of glass emerged. Designs, however, were still often painted or stenciled onto the windows. Many patterns were simple, featuring geometric backgrounds behind a single, painted rondel in the center of the window. *Jewels*—faceted of pieces of colored glass—were also used to decorate the windows.

Most window glass had to be imported into this country, at great expense, from Europe. Americans were not to be left behind, however, and in the late nineteenth century John La Farge developed an entirely new type of glass, called opalescent, that was uniquely American. It was the first opaque glass, and it had streaks of color running through it. The Europeans scoffed at it and called it ugly. Since opalescent glass resists all but the strongest light, however, it was perfectly suited for a then-new stained-glass form: the lampshade.

Stained-glass windows were a beautiful complement to the Queen Anne style of architecture, and an array of beautiful and complex symmetrical designs, known as Renaissance patterns, emerged during the latter part of the nineteenth century.

People updated their stained-glass windows to modernize their houses, just as they might change their decor. Stained-glass windows appeared everywhere—even in chimneys. They were commonly used above the window openings, in the centers of bay and oriel windows, beside the front door or in transoms and fanlights, and in bathrooms. The most elaborate windows were often placed along stairways and above stairway landings where they could be easily viewed.

Also popular in Queen Anne architecture, and especially in the more modest middle-class dwellings, were small squares of colored glass set around a rectangular window. These windows were commonly found either in the top section of a double-hung sash window or at the top of a door. Wood, instead of lead, was used to separate the pieces of glass.

In the late 1890s, the beautiful and elaborate stained-glass works of Louis Comfort Tiffany became popular. Although Tiffany's landscapes and other masterpieces were commissioned only for commercial establishments and the homes of the very wealthy, his works strongly influenced the entire stained-glass industry. He integrated opalescent glass into his patterns, and subsequent designs in the field of stained glass incorporated it. Tiffany popularized the use of landscape scenes for stained glass, often with one central person or animal. His studios also substituted copper foil and solder for

Stained-glass windows in the Spreckels Mansion in San Francisco were made in 1885, using John La Farge's "new" opalescent glass.

lead between the pieces of glass, which allowed smaller and more intricate designs.

At the turn of the century, the glass beveling machine was invented, and many of the fin de siècle and Colonial Revival houses featured transoms, fanlights, etc. of elaborately beveled pieces of clear plate glass.

With the end of the Victorian era, however, and the accompanying move towards simplicity of design, the fad for stained glass ended. True, Art Nouveau designs flourished briefly, and there were the wild geometric patterns of the Art Deco era, but the practice of using stained glass to adorn houses waned, not to revive until just this last decade.

REPAIRING OLD GLASS Whether you are fortunate and have an original stained-glass window in your house, or you just like antiques and decide to purchase a stained-glass piece, you may face the unfortunate necessity of repairing stained glass.

Except for trauma, most damage to stained glass occurs because the lead or solder joints have weakened with age or exposure to the elements. Temperature and humidity variations, excessive moisture, and atmospheric pollutants damage lead caming. Over the years, the lead oxidizes, becomes brittle, and cracks, usually at the joints where it is held together with solder. After this occurs, the section sags and buckles. This loosens the putty (which will have become brittle if it has not been renewed), then the glass becomes loose and can either fall out or buckle and crack.

Tiffany-style or copper foil windows or lamps (where the perimeter of each piece of glass is covered with copper foil, then soldered with one continuous joint) are immune from many of these problems. Heavy stress on certain sections of the piece might, however, pull the foil away from the glass. Some glass designs, such as concentric circles; parallel lines forming diamond, square, or rectangular patterns; and parallel-lined borders, especially at the bases, are more susceptible to damage than others.

Repairing damaged windows, lamps, and other stained-glass pieces is the most difficult, time-consuming, and generally frustrating aspect of working with stained glass. Many shops would rather not do repairs, and those that specialize charge high prices to make the labor-intensive job worthwhile.

Many people—friends, acquaintances, perhaps even yourself—do "a little glasswork." These are *not* the people to entrust with your stained glass repairs. Matching old stained-glass materials is often difficult. Finding the exact color of glass is usually possible, since color composition has been virtually unchanged for centuries. Matching textures is the real problem, since new methods of manufacturing glass produce slightly different effects than did the old. Old solder and lead caming darken with age, also, and these are difficult to match well.

With the recent popularity of stained glass, there are many repair shops from which you can choose. Check carefully before you leave your cherished piece with one, since poor repair work is unsightly and can cause further damage to a piece. Look at a sample of the shop's repair work and get several different estimates, not only of the price, but of the extent of work needed. Some repair people will insist that a window needs to be completely releaded, when the damage may not actually be that serious. An underestimation of the work required is just as bad, however, since the window probably will not look right after it is repaired, and it will probably have to be re-repaired.

If you have a window releaded, insist that the person doing the repair weave, lap, or tuck the lead at the seams, to give greater strength.

For more information about stained-glass repairs, contact the Restoration and Repair Committee of the Stained Glass Association of America, P.O. Box 376, Fishkill, NY 12524.

MAINTAINING STAINED GLASS Anyone who owns a stained-glass piece, old or new, should know how to maintain it. Leaded stained glass needs to be reputtied periodically to maintain water resistance and to keep the glass secure. Use metal-sash putty, and work it between the glass and the lead with your fingers.

A stained-glass window that is larger than 18 inches by 24 inches should be horizontally reinforced every 8 to 12 inches with brass or copper rods or flat iron. The rods can be bent and soldered into existing seams so that they are unnoticeable, but this should be handled only by an experienced professional. You can, however, install pieces of flat iron yourself. First, cut sections of 1/8-inch flat iron to the width of the window. (If the window is set into a wooden frame, you can notch the wood and install the steel into it. This is difficult, however, if the window is already installed.) Tack pairs of 2-inch-long 20-gauge copper wire to the lead or solder joints at 6-inch intervals all along the window. Stand the piece of iron perpendicular to the glass and twist the wires around the iron until it is snug against the window.

If you're installing the window in your house, don't put it in a southern exposure. Windows will buckle when exposed to a lot of sunlight.

An ancient controversy exists about whether or not to clean old glass. In Europe, stained glasswork crafted over seven hundred years ago had become dulled by centuries of exposure to acidic air that had been polluted by burning coal. The French developed special brushes made from glass fibers to clean the windows—only to find that after they were cleaned many people thought they looked sterile and lacked the luster of their dirty counterparts. On the other hand, since not many of us are fortunate enough to own thirteenth-century windows, and "modern" antiques seem to look more vibrant after they are cleaned, I'd opt for cleaning.

The best concoction to use for this is a paste of whiting (available at paint stores) and water. Scrub with a medium-bristle brush, then wash.

Floors

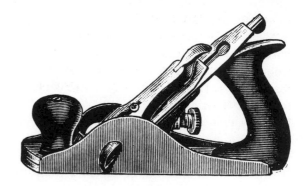

CHAPTER 23

WOODEN FLOORS

Refinishing the floors is really the last task you should undertake—after you patch, paint, plaster, and paper—so you will not have to worry that spills and dirt will spoil a new finish or stain the wood.

"UNFINISHING" METHODS The first step in refinishing a wooden floor is to "unfinish" it, either by scraping, stripping, or sanding. Shellac or single, flaking coats of paint or varnish can be scraped off using a flexible paint scraper, steel wool, and perhaps a small quantity of alcohol or acetone stripper. For multiple layers of paint, varnish, or urethane, sanding is the quickest and the preferred method for the majority of hardwood floors.

Power abrading, however, may grind away much of a softwood floor, weakening the planks and destroying the character that small nicks and bumps in the floor add. If you have softwood floors and can tolerate the mess of chemical strippers or are proficient with heat paint removers (see Chapter 20), this may be the best method. Beware: it is a mammoth job.

Stripping is probably best also for parquet and veneer hardwood floors, which a heavy-duty sander will easily wear through, or for floors that have already been sanded. Sanding with the grain of an intricate parquet floor is virtually impossible.

SANDING If sanding the floor is your choice, the first decision to make is whether to have it done professionally or do it yourself. Although sanding floors is not a difficult task (you can probably complete a 20-foot-square room in one day), much of the trick of floor sanding is developing a knack for using a drum sander, and few people have spare floors on which to practice. A drum sander is

heavy. One misstep, and you have permanently marred the surface of your floor. For this reason, I strongly suggest that you watch a professional sand a floor before you attempt the task yourself. It is even worth the money to hire someone to sand one of your rooms for you if you're going to be refinishing a large area of your house. A sympathetic pro may even share a few trade secrets with you.

If you opt for the do-it-yourself method, you will need both a small power sander (belt or disk) for the edges and corners of the room and a drum sander, which is available at most rental places for under $30 per day. There are two types of drum sanders. One type you must pull back on to disengage the belt; the other automatically lifts the belt from the floor when you turn it off. The latter is easier for the novice to operate. When renting a drum sander, have the rental agent verify that it is operable and in good condition. If the sander has been abused and the drum is dented or uneven, it could seriously gouge your floors. If you have a 220-volt outlet in your house, rent a 220-volt sander.

Remove all furniture, pictures, and other adornments (including curtains) from the room. This is important, not only to give clear working space, but to protect the furniture from the inevitable cloud of superfine sanding dust. This dust is extremely combustible, so take care in discarding it, and make sure you always wear a dust mask and ventilate the room well. (Also, make sure the drum sander you rent has a dust bag.)

Next, patch any cracks and large gouges (see page 118) in the floor. Renail loose floorboards (protruding nail heads will ruin your sanding belts) and replace any that are substantially damaged. Remove the shoe molding (the small molding, usually quarter-round, that covers the seam between the baseboard and floor) so that you can sand right up to the edge of the wall and avoid damaging the molding with the sander.

Start in the center of the floor with the drum sander and move outwards in a straight path, working in the direction that the floorboards run. If your sander gets off at even a slight angle to the boards, you will mar the wood. Do not stop moving the sander while it is turned on or you will gouge the wood.

To break up and lift the old finish off the floor, first sand with coarse sandpaper. Next, to remove scratches and marks left by the coarse paper, sand a second time with medium-grit paper. Finally, use fine sandpaper to remove scratch marks and leave a surface that's ready for finishing. Work the last step in soft-soled shoes to avoid scratching the floor.

Next, repeat the above steps at the very edges of the floor (where the drum sander won't reach) with the belt or disk sander. Again, work with the grain.

FINISHING THE FLOOR Although some people prefer to wax their hardwood floors, the most common method of finishing is to apply a coat of urethane. Urethane not only imparts a beautiful shine to hardwood floors, it lasts five to ten times longer than other finishes—plus, it protects the wood from dirt and dampness.

Those who shy away from urethane coatings for floors complain that urethane tends to yellow or wear off. Actually, when correctly applied over a compatible stain, urethane yellows very little— much less than a wax buildup. True, it does wear off, especially in high-traffic areas of the room, but it wears much slower than wax. To renew the urethane finish, just sand lightly and reapply the urethane over the existing coat.

If you want to stain the floor before you finish it, buy a product that will be compatible with the final finish. Urethane finishes will yellow, peel, bubble, or not even stick to an incompatible stain. A flooring dealer will carry specially formulated products for use under urethane on hardwood floors.

PAINTING FLOORS Early American floors, from the colonial era up to and including most of the Victorian period, were often made of softwood (usually pine or fir) that was painted to preserve the wood, to hide its nakedness, and to add color.

If you have a softwood floor that has been gouged, has wide spaces between the boards, or is badly spotted or stained, painting might be the most practical—and aesthetically pleasing—solution. Floors in poor condition often require extensive sanding and puttying, and the resultant surface would usually not look good with a natural finish anyway. Bleaching, which is often necessary to remove stains from wood, can weaken the boards and splinter and raise the grain.

Many early American floors were painted in solid colors. Sometimes, only a border was painted on a bare floor. When floor cloths, rags, hooked rugs, straw matting, and carpets came into use, these usually complemented designs painted onto a floor.

Among the most popular colors for painted floors were grays, dark greens, pumpkin yellows, and brick reds. Popular patterns, often rendered by itinerant painters, included geometric designs, scroll borders, and black and white checkered (known as *diamond*) patterns. Wooden floors were often painted to look like marble or tile, consistent with the Victorian penchant for making things look like what they were not. Simulated stair runners were even painted on stairways.

Several distinct types of painting were used to decorate Victorian-era floors, including spatter painting, also called *spatterdash*. Spatter painting is still a practical method of covering an otherwise unsightly floor, and it is also an authentic and colorful restoration technique.

Early spatter painting featured dark spots spattered on a gray background, but later examples show the reverse: dark floors spattered in two or more light colors, giving a cheerful and colorful aura to a room. Some typical early color schemes included copper brown with black, white, yellow, and green spatters; black with any color of spatters; blue with red, white, and yellow; gray with small spatters of black and white (known as *pepper and salt*—popular for New England halls and stairs).

To spatter paint, the background color is first applied to a prepared surface and allowed to dry. Dip a stiff-bristled brush (try a whisk broom) into one of the top coat colors. Flick your wrist, aiming the bristles towards the ground so they literally spatter flecks and droplets onto the floor. Practice first on sheets of newspaper, so you don't spatter the family dog. Be sure to protect the baseboards and walls at least 2 feet above the floor by taping newspaper to the walls. Spatter only one color at a time and let it dry thoroughly before spattering the next.

Stenciled floors reached their peak popularity after the American Revolution and were used widely until the mid-nineteenth century. After preparing the surface of your floor and painting the background color, stenciling floors is much like stenciling walls and ceilings (see page 147). Before diving in with a can of paint and a stencil, however, draw a scale model of the room and the design you want. Designs look much different on the floor than they do in your head.

When you've developed a design you like, mark it off on the floor with chalk and ruler. Then, tape the stencil in place and paint. Choose paints that are specifically formulated for floors: these usually contain polyurethane, are less slippery when wet, and are more durable. They are acrylic or epoxy resin. Deck paint, exterior porch paint, and marine paint are especially hard-wearing. Special paints are also available for concrete floors.

Before you start to paint, prepare the surface (see page 142). Repair any places that are gouged or cracked, and fill spaces between the floorboards. If floorboards are extremely worn or have especially large cracks, replace them (new floorboards are readily available at lumber stores). Set any nail heads that are protruding from the floor. Sand the floor smooth, and always prime puttied or bare wood surfaces before painting.

Just prior to painting, scrub the floor with a strong solution of trisodium phosphate (TSP) and warm water, followed by a clear-water rinse. Let the floor dry thoroughly before painting, especially if you are using oil-based paint. After you finish painting your floors, apply a coat of urethane to preserve your work of art.

SUBFLOORS

When adding a new floor, you should, in certain cases, install a subfloor first:
- If the old floor is rotted, treat the rot (page 71) and install a subfloor.
- If you are laying vinyl flooring over old tongue and groove, install a subfloor first to prevent the joints between the floorboards from showing through.

- If you plan to lay ceramic tile over a wood floor, a subfloor should be installed first to increase the rigidity of the surface.

Particle board is the most common and least expensive material used for subflooring. Plywood, however, is more rot resistant and is therefore better to use as subflooring in kitchens, bathrooms, or wherever there is water. Better yet, around toilets and sinks, invest some extra money and use lumber for the subfloor, which will be much more resistant to rot. (Also, treat with a wood preservative any wood that is near a water source.)

CERAMIC TILE

Throughout the Victorian era, elaborate decorative tiles (many of them hand painted) were used on walls, ceilings, fireplace mantels and hearths, and furniture. At the turn of the century ceramic tile first became popular for bathroom floors, because it is scrubbable and easily maintained.

Bathroom floor tiles were usually small (about 1 inch in diameter), and hexagonal or round. Most floors were white, although sometimes dark (usually black) accents, such as tiny circles or a striped border around the perimeter of a room, were used. These little tiles have recently regained popularity in modern construction and are readily available from ceramic tile supply stores.

REPLACING DAMAGED TILES Unless tiles are badly damaged, don't attempt to replace them. When you remove a damaged tile, you can easily ruin adjacent tiles or destroy the grout and mortar. In addition, colors of old tiles and grout are difficult to match, and repairs may look worse than do a few cracked tiles.

To remove ceramic tiles, you will need a cold chisel and a hammer. If the grout joints are sufficiently wide, chisel out the grout around the damaged tile, then wedge the chisel behind the tile and lever the tile out. If the grout joints are too small to permit this, you'll have to break the tile with the chisel and hammer.

Badly chipped or missing grout is replaced in the same manner as repointing masonry (page 57). Use an awl to dig out the old grout. To match grout that has grayed over the years, tint the new grout with pigment, which is available at paint stores.

ADDING A NEW TILE FLOOR If you want to install a ceramic tile floor in your house, first make sure that the surface is completely rigid, since even the slightest movement in the floor can crack both mortar and tiles. Even if there is no discernable give, to ensure that a wooden floor is as rigid as possible, install a 3/4-inch subfloor over the old, nailing it every 6 inches with ringshank or screw nails. To prevent the subfloor from drawing moisture from the tile grout and adhesive, seal it with a primer before you tile.

Laying ceramic tile is not difficult, but it is exacting. There are many how-to books that adequately explain the techniques, such as Sunset's *Remodeling With Tile* (Palo Alto, California: Lane Publishing Company, 1978), or Donald P. Brann's *How to Lay Ceramic Tile* (New York: Directions Simplified, 1975).

There are, however, certain considerations that the how-to books do not discuss. First, there are various ways to stick tile onto a floor. *Mortar,* also known as *thin set,* was the only method used until about twenty-five years ago, and many professionals still prefer this method. It may not be the best, however, for an old house, for if the house settles, the mortar bed will crack, and the cracks will transfer to the grout.

Also, many people—professional tile setters included— don't always realize that setting tiles in a bed of mortar adds hundreds of pounds to the weight of a floor, which might be excessive in an old house.

Mastic, a premixed thick glue, is inexpensive and easy to apply. Its adhering capacity has improved during the recent years. Professionals who use mastic claim it will give slightly, to accommodate house settling, and will not transfer stress to tile grout. Critics, on the other hand, maintain that because the mastic never completely hardens, its bond is not strong enough to sustain floor traffic.

A third product for tile setting is a *three-part epoxy,* which dries hard like mortar but will flex slightly with stress and does not add much weight to the floor. Epoxy is about 1-1/2 times as expensive as mastic; however, it may be the best treatment for an old house.

After the tile is laid, grout is forced between the joints. Use latex additive instead of water to mix the grout. This will provide an additional bit of flexibility to help the grout absorb any stress without cracking. It will also prevent the grout from drying and crumbling. To prevent moisture from seeping into the grout, seal it with a silicone sealer.

LINOLEUM

Purists scoff at using vinyl and other synthetics in renovation, insisting instead upon "authentic" materials. Many don't realize that linoleum was one of the most fashionable decorative treatments available at the turn of the century.

Linoleum was invented in 1867 in England by Frederick Walton (also the inventor of Lincrusta-Walton), who brought it to America when he visited the United States as a consultant to the Armstrong Cork Company (now Armstrong World Industries). The word *linoleum* comes from the Latin *linum* (meaning flax) and *oleum* (for oil). Basically, linoleum is a combination of linseed oil (which comes from flax) and gum, which is mixed with ground cork or sawdust, pressed onto burlap or canvas, and then forced through heated rollers and hung to dry.

Linoleum quickly gained favor as a more durable alternative to the painted and varnished oilcloths used to protect kitchen floors, and it was manufactured in a wide variety of patterns similar to many used today. The use of linoleum was generally limited to the kitchen, however, until the turn of the century.

After 1900, linoleum became a popular treatment for other rooms of the house. Patterns became more subtle, in keeping with the tenets of the Arts and Crafts Movement, and solid colors appeared. In 1909, the Armstrong Cork Company entered the linoleum business and mounted an intensive advertising campaign to promote the use of linoleum in every room of the house. Linoleum "rugs"— large sheets of linoleum laid in the centers of rooms—appeared, and linoleum borders were manufactured for use in conjunction with carpeting.

The Armstrong Company ceased producing linoleum in 1974 in favor of vinyl, a plastic floor covering, which is more resilient and easier to care for.

Siding

Siding—or *cladding,* as it is also known—is the exterior covering of the house. Siding not only serves a decorative purpose, it acts as insulation, helps keep water from running into the walls, and may even add strength to the structure.

Except for stucco and masonry, siding for Victorian-era homes was made of wood. Asbestos or asphalt shingles or aluminum siding is often used for replacement, but these are among the paramount no-nos in the renovation field. Not only are they unauthentic, they often look unsightly.

HOW SIDING IS APPLIED

Siding can be nailed directly to the house studs or to an underlayment of wood sheathing and building paper, depending on the type of siding used and how the house is constructed. Large, interlocking horizontal boards are usually the only type of siding used without sheathing. Wood shingles have little tensile strength, and are always nailed over a type of sheathing.

Sheathing may be plywood, fiberboard (which offers better insulation but is less resistant to moisture), or boards. Diagonal sheathing boards (usually 5/16 to 7/8 inch thick) were often used in balloon-frame construction (page 46). These serve the same purpose as let-ins, adding some strength to the structure and helping to prevent the studs from raking.

If sheathing needs replacing, use a good-quality sanded exterior plywood. Local code requirements may specify types and grades. Before the siding is applied, the sheathing should be covered with building paper, which retains heat within the wall and inhibits moisture seepage. Building paper is usually coated with one of several materials (often rosin or asphalt) and comes in rolls 30 inches or more wide and 500 feet long. Code requirements usually specify the weight and composition to be used with different types of siding.

TYPES OF WOOD SIDING

Basically, there are three types of wood siding: vertical, horizontal, and shingles.

VERTICAL SIDING The most common type of vertical siding used in Victorian-era homes is *board and batten.* Sheets of wood are nailed to the house studs, and the joints where the sheets meet are covered with *battens*: strips of molding about 1/2 by 1 inch. Other, less common types of vertical siding are *batten and board* (the boards sit on top of the battens) and *board and board* (utilizing boards 3 or more inches wide).

HORIZONTAL SIDING The most common types of horizontal siding are *bevel siding* and *drop siding.*

Beveled siding consists of boards that are tapered or beveled so that each board is thinner on the upper edge than on the lower. The boards are nailed over sheathing, starting from the bottom and working upwards, in courses that overlap at least 1 inch. Each board is affixed independently, and the nails should not penetrate the board beneath it. Bevel siding boards less than 8 inches wide are known as *clapboards*; those 8 inches wide or more are known as *Colonial* or *bungalow* siding.

Drop siding, which is manufactured in a variety of styles, always has either *tongue and groove* or *ship-lap* joints. Drop siding is stronger than other types of siding and may be nailed directly to the studs, without any sheathing. Perhaps the most common type of drop siding used in Victorian-era homes is ship-lap that is 9 inches wide and grooved once or twice along its length to give the appearance of several smaller boards.

SHINGLES Wood shingles used for siding are commonly made of cedar, cypress, or redwood and are applied over tight wood sheathing and waterproof building paper. Lightweight shingles are usually used for siding, though shakes are sometimes used.

Wood shingles were always used as siding on Shingle style homes and were also common on Craftsman and bungalow houses. Often cut in decorative patterns, wood shingles were mixed with masonry and other types of siding on Queen Anne–style houses as well.

Rectangular shingles are readily available at lumber stores. Decorative shingles, marketed under the trade name Fancy Cuts, are manufactured by the Shakertown Corporation, Winlock, WA 98596. Patterns include half-cove, diagonal, square, fish-scale, octagon, hexagon, arrow, diamond, and round; they cost about $52 per carton (a carton covers 33 feet of 10-inch exposure).

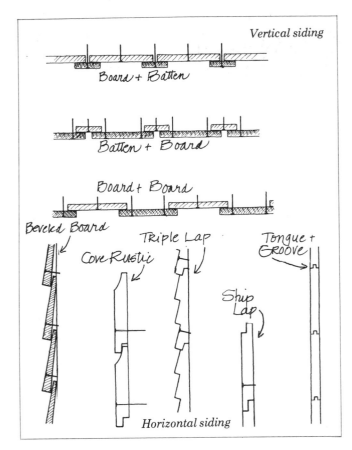

REPAIRING SIDING

Before you replace any type of siding, check your local building code requirements, which may specify type and number of nails and sheathing requirements.

Vertical siding is usually easy to remove, because the nails holding the siding to the house are usually accessible, and you can work a prybar underneath the battens to remove them as you would remove moldings (page 103). Where the trim or casings cover the siding, you may not be able to reach the nails. Try loosening the battens at the end opposite the trim. Then, twist the batten to loosen the nail and cut the nail with bolt cutters, a hacksaw, or a reciprocating saw. You can also remove the trim.

When you replace vertical siding, caulk the joints before you cover them with the battens to help keep moisture from the walls, and also caulk the backs of the battens.

Wood shingle siding is repaired and replaced in the same manner as wood shingle roofing (see page 63).

Beveled siding is usually easy to remove, since each board is nailed individually to the sheathing.

Slip a pry bar underneath the board directly above the one you want to remove and loosen it slightly. Then, pry up the board you want to remove until you can either reach behind the board and cut the nails or until the nails pop away from the sheathing.

Replacement bevel siding is readily available at most lumber yards; simply slip a new board into place and renail it and the board above it.

The best advice I can give about removing old siding is *don't*, if you can avoid it. Drop siding is difficult to remove, and you will probably break more boards trying to remove a damaged one. There are so many pattern variations that finding a duplicate of your siding will be difficult. And drop siding is hard to replace without a patch showing.

Minor cracks in drop siding can be repaired while the siding is in place, if there is sheathing underneath it. Use a strong, waterproof glue (such as Resorcinal). Carefully force the glue into the crack and between the siding and the sheathing. Have one person wedge a pry bar underneath the siding and lever it into place. When the crack closes, have another person nail it into place. Fill and sand the area so the crack does not show.

Several different techniques can be used to

remove wood drop siding. If there is no sheathing, and if you are removing the lath and plaster inside the house, the easiest way (especially if you want to remove a large amount of siding), is to hit it from the back, using a hammer and block of wood (page 104).

If there is sheathing covering the studs, or if you do not have access to the back of the siding, the next best bet is to remove the nails holding the siding in place. A nail puller is best for this, but a cat's paw will also work. Removing the nails leaves nasty holes that will have to be patched, but this is preferable to breaking the siding, which can easily happen if you pry the boards. Once the nails are out, gently lift the board directly above the one you want to remove, and the latter board should fall right out. If you need to remove more than one board, the others should now come out easily. Remember that the farther you have to pry the siding, the greater the possibility that it will split.

You can also cut away the siding, using a reciprocating saw, a jigsaw, or a circular saw. If the siding is applied without sheathing, make your cuts at a location (such as at the center of a stud) where you will be able to renail the siding. You can also cut right next to a stud, then nail a board to the stud and affix the new siding to that board.

Try to stagger your cuts so that you do not cut more than one board at a single place—otherwise, when you replace the siding there will be an obvious and unsightly seam that will require extensive patching and sanding.

REPLACEMENT SIDING

Many companies manufacture siding, which is readily available at lumberyards. Obtaining vertical siding and beveled siding is usually no problem, but finding drop siding to match yours can be a problem, since each manufacturer, it seems, makes it just a little bit differently: perhaps the grooves are in slightly different places, or the faces of the boards are different from yours. Chances are that you will be unable to find replacement drop siding at a lumber store and will have to rely on salvage sources, custom milling, or your wits.

Some homes built at the same time in a particular area might have identical siding, so check your neighbors. You could find some leftover siding in an outbuilding, lining a closet (this is common; often it is turned over), or even a few boards stuck in an attic.

You may also be able to find replacement siding at a salvage yard. Salvage siding is in high demand, however, and can fetch exorbitant prices, so make sure, before you choose this option, that it will be financially worthwhile. Consult page 44 for tips on purchasing salvage materials.

You can always have replacement siding custom milled, but this could cost more than totally replacing the siding. A major component of custom milling prices is a charge for "setting up" the milling machines to create a particular pattern, so if you know someone else who needs the same siding, you can save money by combining your orders.

If none of the above options seem viable, there are several tricks you can try:

● If you can find siding that is very similar to yours but does not exactly match, use the new boards and totally re-side one side of your house. Cover the corners where the two types meet with a small molding, and the difference will be virtually undetectable.

● If you are missing only a board or two, and if there is sheathing underneath the siding, you may be able to create a mock siding, using thin pieces of molding affixed to a piece of plywood. If done carefully, this can be indistinguishable from the original siding.

● If you are missing several boards, try using a different type of siding (the plainer the better) for the first course or two above the foundation.

Make sure, when you replace drop siding, that you put the correct side up. Ship-lap is designed to be applied so that the overlapping board is on top, to keep water from running inside the walls. Tongue and groove siding also has a front and a back. Although the two sides may appear identical, one side of the groove is usually slightly larger, and the spaces between the grooves and the top of the siding may vary. You can force the wrong sides together, but they will never look exactly right.

Also, apply replacement siding starting at the foundation of the house and working upwards. Be sure to measure accurately: the last piece must fit exactly or there will be a gap in the siding.

Paint

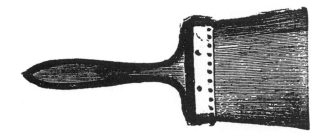

CHAPTER 25

COLOR THEORY

Many color schemes are chosen entirely by intuition. There are, however, reasons why certain colors and color schemes look good in certain situations; these make up what is known as color theory. There are several different color theories. The following is perhaps the simplest and most common.

There are three *primary* colors—red, yellow, and blue—which combine in different proportions to form all the colors in the universe. Combining equal parts of two primary colors yields the *secondary* colors: orange (red + yellow), green (blue + yellow), and violet (red + blue). If a secondary color is mixed with one of the primary colors that comprise it, one of the six *tertiary* colors (red-orange, yellow-orange, yellow-green, blue-green, blue-violet, and red-violet) result. These twelve colors, also known as *hues*, form the *color wheel*.

Colors close to each other on the color wheel are known as *harmonious* or *analogous* hues; those on opposite sides (red and green, for example) are called *complementary* colors. Analogous colors will blend together; complementary colors will contrast.

Colors on the top half of the color wheel (ranging from red-violet to yellow) are known as *warm* colors. They literally absorb more light than do their counterparts on the bottom half of the wheel, and can actually raise the temperature of a chilly room.

The *cool* colors—violet to yellow-green on the color wheel—are restful. They absorb less light than warm colors and can lower the temperature in a hot room by several degrees.

In addition to the color wheel hues, there are the *neutrals:* white, black, and gray (a mixture of white and black). The *lightness* or *darkness* denotes how much white or black is added to a particular hue. A *tint* is a mixture of white with a hue (which lightens the hue); a *pastel* is a tint with a large proportion of white. A *shade* is a hue that is darkened by the addition of black. A *tone* is a further mixture: either a tint with black or a shade with white.

The terms *saturation, intensity,* and *chroma* describe a color's brightness, which is controlled by the amount of gray added to the hue. *Muted* colors have large proportions of gray in them; those with little or no gray are *vibrant*. Differences in lightness and saturation of the same color are known as *degrees. Monochromatic,* or *tone-on-tone,* treatments utilize varying degrees of a single color for a color scheme.

HOW COLORS WORK

Because they reflect or absorb light differently, different colors and different color schemes can be used to create visual effects that can disguise or accentuate certain features of a room or structure—or can be used to create different moods.

● Certain colors reflect light and recede from the eye. Other colors absorb light and advance in one's vision. Painting a room with a color that recedes will make the room appear large; painting it with a color that advances will shrink it in the mind's eye.

COLORS THAT RECEDE	COLORS THAT ADVANCE
pale colors	dark colors
cool colors	bright colors
	warm colors

Thus, a light-colored object placed next to an identical object that is dark colored will appear farther away than the dark-colored object.

● To make a high ceiling appear lower (closer), or to make a trim stand out, paint ceiling or trim darker or bolder colors than the main color; or, if the main color is cool, paint the ceiling or trim with

a warm color. (Note: The Victorians loved those tall ceilings and, to make them appear even loftier, often painted them lighter colors than the walls.)
● Warm colors create a cheery atmosphere, making a room or building inviting. Too much warm color, however, can create a hot, restless atmosphere.
● Cool colors are relaxing, but too much cool color appears cold and uninviting.
● Neutrals, light shades, and tints create a tranquil atmosphere, but, in the wrong place or used excessively, can be boring. Bold, vibrant colors are inspiring and exciting, but can provoke restlessness.
● Most people find that the "nature" colors—greens, yellows, and browns—are easier to live with than are reds, blues, and violets.
● Use of bold, complementary colors near each other makes the eye jump back and forth from one color to another. This is an effective way to break up large, monotonous spaces (such as huge, boxy rooms) but can be too much for a small area.

VICTORIAN COLORS

The Victorians commonly used very complex colors. Most of these were extremely muted—never by the addition of gray or black to the paint, but by the addition of a color's complement. These grayed tones—also known as *saddened* colors—could be used together in virtually any combination. This is how Victorian color schemes could use complementary colors together without offending the eye.

CHOOSING A COLOR SCHEME

● Consider first those aspects of the setting that are permanent or semipermanent: colors of furniture or wood trim or, for exteriors, colors of shrubbery and nearby structures.
● Neutral monochromatic color schemes (such as creams and beiges) are usually the most versatile for interior color schemes. These can be combined with an accent color or colors to create a particular mood. Then, when you tire of the accent color or want to change the aura of the room, you can change the accent pieces to create a totally different impression.
● Neutrals will contrast with colors unless a small amount of the color is combined with the white, black, or gray. Whites with a bluish or greenish cast, for example, look best with cool colors. Pinkish gray blends well with maroon; bluish white will clash with orange. Even beiges and creams

blend best when a minute amount of the accompanying color is added to them.
● Don't forget to consider the effects of colors of adjacent buildings or adjoining rooms when choosing a color scheme.
● If you enjoy bold treatments, don't be afraid of nontraditional color combinations. Photographs in Terence Conran's *The House Book* (New York: Crown Publishers, 1974, pp. 132–44) illustrate how this can be done successfully.
● Always take paint color chips (and other samples, too) home before you make a choice. Colors will appear differently under different types of lighting and in different surroundings.
● The choice of an interior color scheme involves not only paint, but curtains, wallpaper, floor and trim treatment, and furniture. As such, pattern and texture become important considerations. A thorough treatment of this can be found in an interior design handbook. Among the best of these is Ray and Sarah Faulkner's *Inside Today's Home* (New York: Holt, Rinehart, and Winston, 1975).

THE EXTERIOR COLOR SCHEME

Unfortunately, there were no color photographs during the Victorian era, and little art depicting house exteriors. Colors, however, ranged from white with forest-green trim (Greek Revivals) to vibrant multicolor schemes (Queen Annes, Stick-Eastlakes), to muted browns (Shingle and Craftsman styles) and stark whites (Colonial Revivals). For a discussion of exterior and interior colors popular during the Victorian era, see pages 13–14.

To gain ideas for exterior color schemes, look at completed renovation projects in your area and peruse the many picture books of Victorian houses. A paint store dealer is another good source. The Athenaeum Library of Nineteenth-Century America's *Exterior Decoration,* a reprint of the F. W. DeVoe Company's idea book for Victorian-era exteriors, is another good source.

Queen Annes and West Coast Stick-Eastlake houses lend themselves to exterior schemes of three, four, or even five colors. If you choose to use a variety of colors, make sure that you consider the relationships between each two colors used next to each other, and that you decide which parts of the house you want to stand out.

Although personal preferences may differ radically, generally the most interesting parts of a Victorian house are the trims: window and door casings, porches, balusters and stairways, porticos, brackets, etc. To make these stand out from the rest of the house, paint them colors that will advance in your vision.

A common formula for house exteriors utilizes three colors: light, dark, and medium. Paint the main body of the house in the medium color. Paint the trim that comes in contact with this color with the dark color. Since the trim is darker than the main body of the house, it will stand out. Use the light color to highlight carvings or other accents in the trim. This will contrast with the dark color to make the decorative accents stand out.

Many people choose to add a fourth, even darker color for the window sash, which lends visual prominence to the windows.

Even if you use several colors, try to keep them simple, since too much activity on a surface will tire the eye.

Don't forget, also, when choosing an exterior color scheme, to consider which direction the house faces and how much sun it will receive. Painting a house that faces south or west with a warm, dark color will make it look like a hot box.

Authentic exterior colors used during the Victorian era are being produced under the name Heritage Colors by the Sherwin Williams Paint Company, 101 Prospect Avenue, Cleveland, OH 44115.

CHOOSING PAINT

Paint is basically a pigment thinned with solvents (oil-based) or water (latex), to which is added other chemicals that help it to bind, and increase its durability, spreadibility, etc. During the past, when oils were scarce (such as during World War I), milk was used as a base for paints; other old paint was lead based, but this has been outlawed.

Oil-based paint penetrates and forms a strong bond with the surface to which it is applied, and it dries to form a hard, usually scrubbable surface. Brushes and spills must be cleaned with mineral spirits, which add to the time and expense of painting with oil-based paint.

Note: "Oil-based" paint sold in California has been reformulated, using resins instead of oil, to comply with environmental protection regulations. The state of New York is considering adopting similar standards.

Latex paints, which have been available since the 1940s, do not penetrate surfaces, but are easier to use than oil-based paint because they are water soluble. Latex paint will not stick to a surface that is dirty, chipping or peeling, or glossy, however.

Most interior and exterior household paint is sold in flat, semigloss, and gloss enamels, all available in oil base or latex. Gloss paints have more resins in them than do flat paints and therefore provide harder finishes that are usually more resistant to dirt and scrubbing.

Normally, gloss and semigloss paints are used for bathroom and kitchen walls, trims, and other surfaces that require scrubbing. However, many old walls have a surface that is uneven, where cracks have been patched. This *rise and fall*, as it is known, tends to stand out more under a glossy surface, and therefore flat paints might be the better choice for old walls that have been patched many times.

If you are painting an exterior, the paint must seal and protect the house from water and sun as well as be decorative. Buy paint specifically formulated for exterior use. This will hold up longer and provide greater protection.

The type of paint you use depends upon the condition of the surface, including the types and colors and quality of previous coats of paint, what kind of preparation was done for this and previous coats, the condition of the old paint, and the type of weather the surface (especially exteriors) will be exposed to.

Since there are so many different possibilities, which vary in different climates, the only way to choose the right type of paint is to take a sample of the surface with all its layers of paint—perhaps a molding that you can dislodge easily, or a piece of plaster—to a good paint store and let an expert make the determination.

HIRING AN EXPERT

Painting is not difficult for even the novice do-it-yourselfer; however, you may want to hire a professional with an airless sprayer. Spraying is almost a necessity for exteriors, but renting an airless sprayer can cost as much as hiring a professional. Make sure that whomever you hire will prepare the surface properly. Many professionals do not.

TOOLS

Brushing is the most time-consuming method of painting, but, unless you have a paint sprayer, it is the only way to paint trim and siding. Brushes are manufactured with different types of synthetic and natural bristles for different types of paint, and in different widths for trim and flat surfaces. Wall brushes are flat and range from 3 to 6 inches wide. Sash and trim brushes, 1-1/2 to 3 inches wide, are available with flat bristles or bristles cut on the diagonal (for fine work). Buy the right brush for the type of paint you are using and for the surface you are painting. Some people buy inexpensive paint brushes and then throw them away, rather than cleaning them. *Don't* buy cheap brushes—they shed their bristles into the paint.

Rollers are the most popular method for painting large flat surfaces such as interior walls and ceilings. Rollers come in nap lengths from 3/8 inch to 1-1/4 inches; the shorter nap is for smooth surfaces, the longer for rough surfaces.

Rollers also come in different types of materials: lambswool is used only with oil-based paints and will mat when used with latex. Mohair rollers, which can be used with both oil-based and latex paints, have a short nap and are therefore best for smooth surfaces. Acrylic fiber rollers may be used for both rough and smooth surfaces, and for both oil- and water-based paints. Polyester rollers also may be used with both oil- and water-based paints. These have the softest nap and minimize the bubble formation that latex paint causes on smooth surfaces.

The beauty of plaster walls is their perfectly smooth surface, which is difficult to maintain when painting with a roller, especially when using latex paint. Even if you use a roller with a very thin nap, there will be some sort of bubble formation or stippled effect. Perhaps the best type of roller to use on plaster surfaces is a *high-leveling roller,* which is designed to leave little or no stipple.

Better yet, to achieve a smooth surface without bubbles or stipple, use paint pads: flat pieces of napped cloth that fit into a handle, are dipped into paint, and are then dragged across the wall. A set of paint pads costs around $10. They apply paint much slower than does a roller.

Paint may also be sprayed with a compressor and paint pot. A good quality pot costs about $50; make sure you buy one that is compatible with your compressor. Since the compressor vaporizes the paint, this method creates a lot of overspray, and therefore is unsuited for interior painting. It also uses a lot of paint.

Airless sprayers, perhaps the best method for exterior painting, can apply between 3/8 to 1 gallon of paint per minute. Unlike the compressor/paint pot method the sprayer sits in the paint (no thinning or decanting), and a siphoning action forces the paint through a hose and out the spray nozzle. Airless sprayers are readily available at rental yards, but they can cost as much as $100 per day to rent. If you have little experience, rent a small model, which is best for interiors anyway and won't deliver the paint too fast for you to handle.

PREPARATION

Within the last twenty years or so, paint has developed to the extent that most varieties on the market today are of decent quality. Now paint failure is usually caused, not by poor-quality paint, but by inadequate and improper surface preparation, which will prohibit the paint from sticking. Probably everyone has heard horror stories of the person who returns to his/her freshly painted room only to find the newly applied coat of paint sagging or hanging in ribbons. In an old house, this problem is compounded. If previous owners did not properly prepare the surfaces, problems can exist several layers down and can transfer to the surface.

Since exterior surfaces are seen from a much greater distance than interior walls, they don't have to be prepared as meticulously as do interior surfaces. Even though they don't have to be as smooth, however, make sure they are adequately cleaned and rid of poor surface conditions so the paint will adhere. Proper preparation and application of exterior paint is important, not only for aesthetic reasons, but to protect the wood from sun and water damage.

PROBLEM SURFACES

Problems the old-home owner frequently encounters include chipping and peeling paint, chalking or lime deposits, alligatoring, mold and mildew.

CHIPPING AND PEELING Chipping paint may occur if the surface underneath was chalky, dirty, or damp when the paint was applied. Paint that peels off in sheets or ribbons is often latex that was applied over a poorly prepared oil-based coat of paint.

What can you do about peeling, chipping paint? One professional painter says "Just paint over it," and many people do; but the surface will appear uneven and ugly, and the paint will continue to peel or chip. Some people maintain you can cover chipping paint with a skim coat of plaster or joint compound. This has never worked for me—the chipping just seems to transfer even through the joint compound or plaster.

The upshot is that nothing can stick chipping and peeling paint back onto the wall. Therefore, you need to get as much of it off the wall as possible before you paint.

If the chipping or peeling is occuring on a wooden surface, you can use heat or chemicals and strip the paint off. If it occurs on plaster or drywall, your only recourse (short of replacing the entire wall) is to chip it all off.

First, wash down the walls with a mixture of 1/2 cup TSP and 1 gallon of hot water, using a nylon or natural-bristle brush. This will remove much of the loose paint. Experiment with wire brushes, flexible putty knives, paint scrapers, even your fingernails, to get as much as possible of that peeling and flaking paint to come off the walls. I have chipped paint until I was standing in piles of the stuff.

You will probably not be able to chip all the paint off the walls, and the places where you have chipped will show up as indentations in the wall. These places you will have to *feather in*: sand down the edges so they will blend with the surrounding area. The Rockwell Bloc Sander (page 33) is a great tool for this.

ALLIGATORING Most common on exterior wood, alligatoring occurs when the top of a paint coat dries too quickly, forming a skin on the outside and trapping moisture on the inside. When this skin dries it cracks in tiny lines resembling an alligator's skin. All traces of alligatoring should be removed, either by sanding or with heat or chemical strippers, since it will always work its way to the surface through any number of layers of paint.

MOLD AND MILDEW Black, brown, or white mold and mildew spots grow where there is excessive moisture. When treating mold and mildew, first eliminate the moisture, otherwise the fungus will most likely recur. (If you see signs of mold and mildew on your exterior or interior walls or woodwork, check the area also for dry rot, see Chapter 14). Inside, mold and mildew often occur in basements, laundry areas, and bathrooms that have poor ventilation; outside they grow where the house comes in contact with damp earth, or where water sits on wood.

To remove mold and mildew, first scrub the area well, using a nylon or natural-bristle brush and a mixture of 1/2 cup TSP mixed with 1/4 cup household bleach or mildewcide (available at hardware and paint stores). After the surface dries, thoroughly sand the area until all traces of fungus are gone. Wash again. To prevent fungal growth, add a mildew preventative (available at paint stores) directly to the paint.

WALLPAPER Always remove wallpaper before you paint a surface. If you do not, the seams will usually show through the paint, colors may bleed even through primer to the top coat, and the paper may peel off. To remove wallpaper, you can either rent a wallpaper steamer or saturate the paper with a mixture of equal parts antifreeze and warm water.

CHALKING AND LIME DEPOSITS Powdery (chalking) or granular white (lime) deposits on plaster walls occur when the lime reacts with the paint, probably as the result of inferior paint used on previous coats. These are removed by scrubbing the wall with 1/2 cup TSP mixed with a gallon of hot water. To prevent the recurrence of chalking and lime deposits, use an alkyd primer and an oil-based paint.

FILLING AND CLEANING

Follow instructions for patching plaster (Chapter 19) or for patching wood (Chapter 20), whichever is appropriate. Don't use joint compound to patch walls, or when you wash them down prior to painting, you will wash away the patch, since joint compound is water soluble. You can mix white glue with primer to fill nail holes in wood (see page 118). Also, for exteriors, make sure you use exterior fillers that are specially formulated to withstand exposure to the weather and to dirt.

Even if you have washed the surface several times already, make sure you give it a thorough cleansing just before you paint, using a sponge and a mixture of 1/4 cup TSP per gallon of hot water. Follow with a warm rinse.

Cleaning is an especially important facet of paint preparation on exterior surfaces, which come in contact with a great array of dirt, grime, soot, leaves, and tree and bird droppings.

The common method for preparing exterior surfaces is a high-pressure water blaster, which attaches to a common garden hose and delivers high water pressure to clean the building and remove loose paint. High-pressure water blasters cost between $1,500 and $3,000 but are readily available at rental yards. Some adjust so they deliver water in a wider pattern and therefore deliver less force; these are probably best on old houses.

The problem with high-pressure water cleaning of old buildings is that the old wood or masonry may be deteriorated or porous, and high-pressure water could damage it—or could destroy decorative wood trim—and could dislodge fillers from cracks and holes. The only way to determine if this is going to happen is to try a test patch on your house. Generally, avoid using high-pressure water if:

- wood is especially dry or cracked.
- all the paint is gone from the wood. The total force of the water will go into the wood.
- the wood appears soft or spongy, or there is any other evidence of dry rot or termite damage.
- putty or fillers are loose. Putty or fillers, especially in dry wood, tend to shrink away from the edges of the hole and can be dislodged by high water pressure.

THE IMPORTANCE OF PRIMER

Before the top coat is applied, most surfaces in an old house should be given an undercoat of paint known as *primer*, which serves two basic purposes: First, since primer has no resins in it, it dries with a porous (not a hard) finish, so that the top coat adheres well to it. Second, it seals the surface. This protects the surface from the elements, and prevents

the surface from soaking up the top coat of paint, thus reducing the number of top coats you will have to apply. It prevents wood from leaching oils from wood fillers, and inhibits dyes, stains, and problems in previous coats of paint from transfering to the surface and marring the new top coat. Metal primers also inhibit rust.

There are two types of primers commonly used on walls and woodwork; both types are compatible with and may be used under water or oil-based top coats.

Alkyd primer, which is oil-based, is formulated especially for use on plaster walls, although it is also effective on wood and drywall. It prevents such chemical reactions as chalking and lime deposits from transferring to the surface; and although nothing can stick peeling and flaking paint back onto a wall, alkyd primer is helpful in preventing further chipping and peeling.

PVA (polyvinyl acetate acrylic) sealer is a water-based primer that is primarily used on wallboard to prevent it from soaking up paint. Although PVA sealer offers the advantage of cleanup with soap and water, if you have any concern about the paint adhering, or there are problems with old coats of paint, use an alkyd sealer.

Tint the primer the same color as the top coat of paint, and you may be able to avoid having to apply extra coats of the top color. Many paint stores will do this free of charge if you purchase the primer and the top coat at the same time.

PAINTING TIPS

- Start from the top and work down.
- Paint the trim last.
- A smoother appearance will be achieved by several light coats rather than one heavy coat.
- Do not dip brushes or paint pads more than one third of the way into the paint, to minimize dripping.
- If you are using a roller, roll in a V pattern—in one direction, then across in the other direction—to cover more evenly.
- If you are using oil-based paints, you can store brushes, rollers, and pads wrapped in plastic bags overnight in the freezer to avoid the time and expense of daily cleanup.
- When using an airless sprayer, make sure you keep the filters clean, for the hoses and nozzles clog easily.

Embellishments

Stenciling

Stenciling denotes any method of decorating that uses a brush or other implement to apply color onto a surface through shapes cut from an impervious material.

There are two common types of stenciling: *Japan paint stenciling,* the most prevalent, applies paint over the stencil, which is placed on the material to be decorated. *Bronze powder stenciling* utilizes bronze, aluminum, gold, or silver metallic powders that are rubbed through cut-outs in stencils onto a varnished surface that is still tacky enough for them to adhere to.

Stencil designs may be multicolored and intricate, involving the use of many different cut-outs and various layers of color. They may also be simple: the "single stencil" uses only one application of color.

Another use of stencils is to *pounce* large, non-repeating designs onto a wall or other surface. The design is outlined by holes punched in the stencil. The stencil is held against a wall, then a bag filled with charcoal (the pounce) is applied to it. The stenciler then paints directly over the places on the wall where the charcoal has left color.

Although there is no surviving evidence, stenciling is thought to have originated as early as 2500 B.C. in Egypt (where it purportedly adorned mummy caskets) or 3000 B.C. in China. The earliest known stencil patterns, which date to approximately 500 A.D. and are preserved in the Caves of the Thousand Buddhas in China, were executed on toughened paper and outlined by thousands of tiny pinpricks.

Stenciling was first seen in America in the early seventeenth century, in homes of the wealthy who could afford the highly fashionable stenciled wallpaper manufactured in France. Just prior to the revolution, however, stenciling became a common fashion in the colonies and adorned floors, wall coverings, floor coverings, boxes, screens, trays, and coverlets. After plaster was developed, stenciling was most often done directly on walls and ceilings.

VICTORIAN STENCILING

Stenciling really had its heyday during the Victorian era. Uses ranged from a simple design in the corners of a ceiling to elaborate blends of different patterns covering all the walls, the ceiling, and the woodwork in a room. Designs often reflected the use of a particular room: scenes of socializing were depicted in the parlor, for example, or fruit designs in the dining room. Oriental motifs and pounced murals were also popular. During the Eastlake period, geometrics became fashionable as stencil patterns. Among these were *diaper* patterns: elaborate repeating designs that interlaced with each other and were often done in gold leaf.

Stenciling was often done by itinerant artists who roamed from town to town. Their tools were simple and inexpensive: a few brushes, some milk paints or oil pigments, and stencils made of paper (coated with shellac or oil) or perhaps leather. Among the most famous of these roaming stencilers were George Lord, John Taalman, Travers Holland, and Moses Eaton; Eaton is especially renowned for his beautiful and still-copied pineapple and bell designs.

High-priced decorators, such as Louis Comfort Tiffany (son of the wealthy founder of Tiffany Company), custom designed and painted stencils and other "artistic interiors" for the nation's prominent citizens. These patterns, which featured intricate borders on the frieze of the wall or around the edges of a ceiling, were later reproduced by the thousands and revived to immense popularity in the 1920s and 1930s.

Towards the end of the ninettenth century, inexpensive, machine-made wallpaper was developed. This ultimately replaced stenciling, but, for a number of years, the two decorative forms coexisted. Stenciling in a frieze, for example, would complement wallpaper on the main portion of a wall—the hand-painted design usually echoing some part of the print in the paper.

Perhaps the most popular location for a stencil was the frieze of a wall: the area just below the ceiling and above the cove. Stenciling was also common on the *wipe line*: a border that was painted directly above a wainscot or dado. The housekeeper would eventually get a dirty smear on the wall from dusting the molding that capped the wood paneling. To camouflage this dirt, a 2- to 4-inch line was painted directly above the molding. Designs were often stenciled on this line, which was glazed with a dull varnish, so it could be scrubbed.

Today, most stenciling in Victorian homes has been covered with layers of paint, but in many homes the original patterns can be detected and copied (see Chapter 4). Don't expect to unearth a masterpiece, however. Most designs, if you can find them, will have to be traced, then repainted, since time, layers of paint, and paint remover can easily eradicate a stencil.

DOING YOUR OWN

If you decide to do your own stenciling (it's not difficult), I can't recommend enough Adele Bishop and Cile Lord's book *The Art of Decorative Stenciling* (New York: Penguin Books, 1978), which describes every aspect of the art, from cutting stencils to keying your pattern so it will repeat evenly.

The authors, unfortunately, do not address the specifics of reproduction stenciling in old homes. Make sure you prepare the surfaces well for painting (see Chapter 25); it would be heartbreaking to spend so much time and effort to stencil a room only to have the paint underneath chip and crack. Always prime the surface before you stencil, using a good, oil-based primer.

Although the Lord-Bishop book discusses various materials that are suitable for stencils, you can also make your own stencil paper: Boil manila folders in linseed oil for fifteen minutes, then let them dry for at least twenty-four hours.

There are many sources of stencil design inspiration. Look at wallpaper books, especially those that feature antique reproductions. Several books illustrate actual stencil patterns. These include *Early American Stencils on Walls and Furniture* by Janet Waring; *Art Nouveau Cut and Use Stencils* by JoAnne C. Day; *Victorian Stencils for Design and Decoration* by Edmund V. Gillon, Jr.; and *Victorian Cut and Use Stencils* by Carol B. Grafton (all from Dover Publications, 180 Varick Street, New York, NY 10014).

The decorative stenciling pattern in this Sacramento, California, home came from a pattern in an old paint book. The owners did the stenciling themselves with no prior experience and at a cost considerably less than for wallpaper.

Wallpaper

CHAPTER 27

VICTORIAN WALLPAPER

THE MACHINE AGE MAKES WALLPAPERS AFFORD-ABLE Before 1840, nearly all of the world's wallpaper came from France, where it was hand printed using blocks and sheets of paper to produce a very limited line of patterns. This was an expensive process, and only the very wealthy could afford it.

Although France dominated the decorative arts at this time, England possessed superior industrial technology, and in 1837 (the same year that Queen Victoria was crowned), the world's first wallpaper machine was patented in England. This machine, which resembled a miniature Ferris wheel, was a combination of rollers, stencils, and brushes that could apply as many as twenty-four different colors to a continuous roll of paper.

Technology had also developed new, less costly paper-making processes, using inexpensive straw and wood pulp in place of costly linen and cotton rags.

Overnight, the cost of wallpaper plummeted. By the end of the nineteenth century, wallpapers were selling for less than one half of the price that they had commanded fifty years earlier.

DECLINE OF THE FRENCH INFLUENCE IN PATTERNS Early nineteenth-century patterns were heavily influenced by French design traditions and often featured scroll patterns and realistic-looking flowers and foliage. Among the most popular designs were large, open roses, and the early French-inspired patterns and their English counterparts are often collectively referred to as *cabbage rose* designs. In the manner of *trompe d'oeil,* many patterns were elaborately shaded to resemble curtains, carvings, masonry, columns, and arches.

England began to mass produce wallpapers in the 1830s but did not become the leader in commercial wallpaper design until the 1870s. By then, however, Britain had become the trend setter in the decorative arts and exported many wallpaper patterns to countries around the world, including the United States.

Whereas earlier patterns used vertical boundaries, delineated by stripes, fake columns, rows of flowers, etc. to break up wall space, in the mid-Victorian era English patterns evolved into coordinated sets of *companion* papers to divide the wall horizontally: a wide *frieze* at cornice level; a *dado* in the lower portion of the wall, about 22 inches from the top of the baseboard; and the center *fill,* or *screen,* portion. Paper manufacturers also supplied narrow border papers to put between the companion papers in rooms that had no chair railings or frieze/picture moldings.

The dado patterns were often the boldest and darkest in a set of wallpapers. Fill papers were slightly lighter, and those for friezes and ceilings were the lightest yet. The only exception to this was a brief fad in England for dark ceiling papers that would visually shrink the room. Ceiling paper was nearly always directionless, to avoid carrying the eye to any particular area of a room.

THE WALLPAPER CRAZE The development of affordable wallpapers coincided with the young middle class's hunger for anything that gave the semblance of wealth and culture, and wallpaper had traditionally been a hallmark of affluence. This created, in the 1870s and 1880s, a wallpaper mania. Virtually every room in every house was wallpapered. Companies issued new patterns each season, and some homeowners changed their wallpaper annually.

Wallpaper became a sign of domesticity and culture. Stores in major American cities featured a bewildering variety of thousands of patterned papers in myriad styles, produced in America or imported from Japan and Europe. On the frontier, wallpaper was one of the first items that the general store would stock; even new settlements would stock as many as 250 patterns.

Much of the middle-class wallpaper trade occurred through mail order. Catalog advertisements, usually printed in black and white, gave only a list of available colors and guaranteed that companion papers would coordinate. Unfortunately, many of these mail order papers were hideous, and for every tasteful treatment that graced walls and ceilings of middle- and upper-class homes, there were five distasteful ones.

A fad for metallic copper on wallpapers peaked during the 1890s, although copper, gilt, and mica highlights, especially on frieze and ceiling papers, were common from the 1850s through the early twentieth century. When treated with metallics, papers were usually also embossed so that they would shine when viewed from any direction.

At the very height of the wallpaper craze, someone discovered that two popular shades of green wallpaper pigment contained arsenic, and this paper was subquently blamed for a host of illnesses and even deaths. Controversy arose over whether arsenic poisoning could occur by merely sitting or dining in a room with green paper and whether other colors might cause poisoning as well. Wallpaper manufacturers quickly removed the culprit green tones from the market and ran advertisements insisting that their papers were "non-arsenical."

As germ-consciousness expanded at the end of the century, papers were printed with oil-based, non-water-soluble paints that were advertised as scrubbable or sanitary.

WALLPAPER AS IMITATION The upper-upper class continued to use fabrics as wall coverings, so wallpapers continued to imitate damasks, silks, velvets, and satins. The first *flocked* wallpapers—with bits of fabric glued into the pattern—were also developed. Ultra-thin veneers were glued to certain papers that, after installation, were varnished to resemble wood. Imitation leather wallpapers also came on the market. One of the most popular and authentic looking of these was *leather paper*, made using a process that originated in Japan: heavy paper stock was embossed while still wet, then often pounded with hammers, then glued to a cloth or waterproof backing.

In 1877, Frederick Walton, an Englishman instrumental in the development of linoleum, introduced the ultimate in imitations: *Lincrusta-Walton*, a wall covering made of linseed oil and flax that was actually a type of linoleum. Lincrusta could be made to appear like carved wood, embossed leather,

An early wallpaper machine, from Scientific American, *July 24, 1880*

Above: *Typical companion papers.* Right: *Lincrusta-Walton.* Below: *Typical catalog-supplied machined papers were often garish and florid.*

or even cast plaster. It was painted, highlighted with metallics, and grained or varnished. Often it was almost indistinguishable from the real thing. Lincrusta-Walton was so popular that many companies manufactured imitation Lincrusta. These brands, which were made of everything from cork to rubber to wood fiber, included Corticine, Salamander, and Lignomur. One of these imitations, Anaglypta, a heavy paper that was embossed while wet, became extremely popular and eventually took the place of Lincrusta-Walton.

THE AESTHETICS AND WILLIAM MORRIS During the late 1870s, the Aesthetic/Arts and Crafts Movement, which had been brewing in England for several decades, came to the fashion forefront. The Aesthetics favored the use of natural materials and simple, flat, unshaded designs. Popular wallpaper designers of the Aesthetic Movement were Walter Crane, a children's book illustrator who designed (among other patterns) a series of nursery rhyme wallpapers for children's rooms; C.F.A. Voysey, whose work is characterized by flocks of "Voysey birds" flying across the wallpapers; the eccentric botanist, Dr. Christopher Dresser, whose fantastic designs presaged the Art Deco era eighty years later; and the American Louis Comfort Tiffany of stained-glass fame.

At first, the Aesthetic Movement was popular with the intelligentsia and the rich. Aesthetic proponents believed that the masses should be educated in what they considered "good taste," and they chose the wallpaper industry as a vehicle for this. As the Aesthetic papers became popular, however, they rose in price and became too expensive for the middle class to afford.

Allied with the Aesthetic Movement, although a phenomenon in his own right, was William Morris, who influenced all the decorative arts. Morris designed many papers of his own, but his ideas and teachings were so far-reaching that the term "Morris paper" is applied to a genre of flat, intricate floral designs that cover the entire surface of the paper, repeating not on a vertical or horizontal axis, but on a curve.

Although many people, especially Americans, kept buying traditional, realistic-looking "cabbage rose" wallpapers, gradually tastes began to change on both sides of the Atlantic. By the late 1890s, the Aesthetic principles had become well entrenched in America's wallpaper industry.

As the use of natural wood became increasingly popular at the turn of the century, natural wood dadoes began to replace dado papers. During the late nineteenth and early twentieth centuries, papers were combined with natural wood. Airbrushed patterns were popular, and traditional companion papers were replaced by new, innovative combinations. One of these was the *crown frieze,* wherein the frieze paper "crowned" the pattern in the fill paper, such as a frieze printed with blossoms to accompany a fill paper printed with flower stalks. Children's papers, many of them patterned after Crane's designs, were also popular.

World War I rang the death knell for the art wallpapers. Shortages of raw materials drove production costs sky-high, forcing many of the smaller companies that produced art papers out of business or into the hands of large conglomerates that cared only for maximizing profits—not for maintaining wallpaper as an art form. Since that time, wallpaper has never regained its prominence in interior decoration.

REPLICATING OLD WALLPAPERS

Some old-house owners are lucky: the old wallpaper is still in place, or there is a partial roll stored away in the attic. Even if this is not true for you, you may be able to uncover a scrap of old wallpaper underneath multiple layers of old paint and paper; techniques for doing this are described on pages 25-26.

You may unearth a scrap of wallpaper and discover that the colors are drab and ugly. Chances are that these are not the original colors. Some pigments, known as *fugitive colors,* lose their tone over time and with exposure to the elements. Certain colors on some papers may deteriorate in as short a time span as six months.

If you examine scraps of old wallpaper under a microscope or a strong magnifying glass you may be able to find traces of the original colors that have been caught in tiny cracks. Other likely places to check for original colors are under moldings, behind fireplace mantels, and in closets.

Most companies that replicate old wallpapers (see below) require that you have a full repeat of the pattern. Bradbury and Bradbury, however, will attempt to reconstruct the pattern from just a scrap using original nineteenth-century pattern books. They will also date the paper for you.

CHOOSING WALLPAPER PATTERNS

Although many Victorians chose wallpaper to fit fashion and not necessarily good taste, you should try to choose a wallpaper that harmonizes with the architecture of your house. Unless your home is truly a mansion, you should remember also that most reproduction papers on the market are copies of expensive, high-quality papers originally pur-

chased by the very wealthy. Chances are that none of them would have been used in a middle-class house.

Papers designed for Gothic Revival houses often had angular lines and abstract designs suggestive of the medieval era. Renaissance Revival papers, which were characteristically bold floral patterns, are best suited for Italianate and Mansard-style houses. The natural, flat patterns (including Dresser and Morris designs) of Arts and Crafts designs are historically correct for homes built in the late 1870s and thereafter. Since the Aesthetic Movement and Victorian-era architecture in general were both influenced by Gothic design, these papers will be compatible with virtually any Victorian decor.

Many wallpaper stores know little about Victorian-era decoration, and may therefore unwittingly recommend a totally inappropriate wallpaper for your house. If you choose to consult someone about wallpapers, make sure that person is a specialist in Victorian-era design—not just in wallpapers. A good resource book on Victorian wallpaper is Catherine Lynn's *Wallpaper in America* (New York: Norton, 1980).

Designs from Dr. Christopher Dresser's Modern Ornamentation *(1886)*

SOURCES OF REPRODUCTION WALLPAPERS

BRADBURY AND BRADBURY, P.O. Box 155, Benicia CA 94501 (707) 746-1900
This is the only company listed that exists solely to reproduce Victorian-era wallpapers—and the only company that welcomes queries from and will work directly with home owners. Bradbury and Bradbury offers, for $24 to $75 per roll, a series of hand-screened reproduction patterns by such designers as Morris, Dresser, Pugin, and Voysey. The company welcomes custom orders (prices vary), will analyze and date old wallpapers, and will replicate papers from salvage samples.

BRUNSCHWIG AND FILS, 410 East Sixty-second Street, New York, NY 10021 (212) 838-7878
This company offers hand-screened reproductions of eighteenth- and nineteenth-century wallpapers; costs range from $25 to $100 per roll.

SCALAMANDRE, 950 Third Avenue, New York, NY 10022 (212) 361-8500
This company carries an award-winning line of hand-screened reproduction wallpapers and fabrics from the eighteenth and nineteenth centuries. Wallpapers cost $25 to $100 per roll.

SCHUMACHER, 919 Third Avenue, New York, NY 10022 (212) 644-5900
The Schumacher Company offers a complete line of wallpapers, including one book that features machine-made Victorian-era patterns, which range from $16 to $26 per roll. Hand-screened companion border prints are also available for $3 to $11 per yard. In addition, Schumacher manufactures a reproduction Anaglypta, which is available in several patterns.

ZINA STUDIOS, 85 Purdy Avenue, Portchester, NY 10573 (914)937-5661
This company manufactures reproduction wallpapers from a variety of periods in American history; papers cost between $30 and $50 per roll. Custom orders, at varying prices, are also taken.

PREPARATION FOR WALLPAPERING

Preparing your walls and ceilings for papering is done in basically the same manner as preparation for painting (see Chapter 25) and is as important.

Although wallpaper was traditionally used to hide cracks in plaster, you really should patch the cracks *before* you paper. Also, remove old wallpaper, peeling paint, etc. and make sure the surface is sanded smooth.

To remove acoustic "cottage cheese" from ceilings, spray warm water onto the surface. This will soften the acoustic material; you can then scrape it off.

If walls or ceilings have been textured, you should restore the smooth surface before you paper. Using a wide-bladed putty knife, apply a thin coat of joint compound to the wall. Sand lightly.

A coat of *wallpaper sizing* is commonly applied to walls and ceilings before wallpapering. This aids the adhesion of wallpaper paste and keeps colors underneath from bleeding through to the surface. On old surfaces, however, you should prime the walls with an alkyd primer instead of using wallpaper sizing—this provides even better adhesion.

HIRING A PAPERHANGER

Techniques for hanging wallpaper are explained well enough even for the beginner to grasp in wallpaper dealers' handouts and simple do-it-yourself handbooks. Working with modern papers is usually easy. Most of the time, they are prepasted, strippable, scrubbable, and beat-upable. Reproduction wallpapers, however, are none of the above, and may require more patience to hang. At a cost of up to $100 per roll, do you want to take the chance of ruining any? Also, applying paper to a Victorian-era house—in bay alcoves, around window and door easings, over coved ceilings and walls that may not be true—can be a nightmare for even an experienced paperhanger.

A professional will not only be more likely to do a good job and not ruin your paper, but s/he may be able to suggest patterns that might hide surface flaws (such as large cracks and rise and fall) in the walls and ceilings and that will harmonize with the configuration of the walls in your house.

Lighting

Lighting, primarily gas, but, towards the turn of the century a combination of gas and electricity, was an important element of Victorian decor. It was not uncommon for a parlor, for example, to have a ceiling chandelier, alcove lights, wall sconces, table and floor lamps, and indirect beam lighting; as many as twenty different fixtures might have graced a single room, providing almost infinite possibilities for atmosphere. The room could be brightly illuminated to display all the fancy objets d'art for a large party, or it could be dimly lit by a small table lamp and serve as the setting for a romantic tryst.

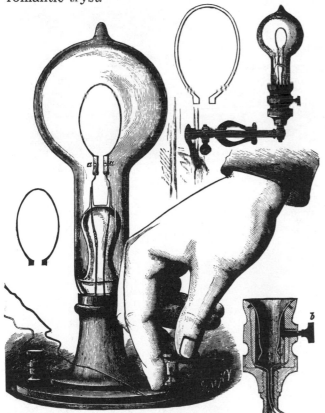

Edison's "Marvelous Incandescent Lamp,"
from the Gem Cyclopedia of World Knowledge *(1896)*

Victorian light fixtures came in many different styles and materials: iron, white metal, oxidized copper, bronze, and ormolu (a rough metal resembling gold). European fixtures were nearly always cast in large sections; American lights were composed of small, detachable pieces. The Europeans also used ormolu extensively, whereas American manufacturers utilized it primarily for highlighting.

Most early light fixtures had glass shades (usually etched or stained glass) to diminish the glare of electric bulbs or hide the naked kerosene or gas flame. Lights with many prisms, characteristically equated with the Victorian period, were actually quite rare and enjoyed only brief popularity during the High Victorian period.

How to tell whether your fixtures were originally gas: Gas lights always have their jets pointed upwards. Also, there had to be a way of supplying the gas to the light, so fixtures were suspended from the ceilings by the supply pipes. You might be able to spot gas pipes running in your ceiling or attic.

If your house was originally built without electricity, you will notice evidence of its addition, such as floorboards that have been lifted (and possibly cut), then replaced, or beams that have been cut to accommodate wires.

If some of the original fixtures are still left in your house, you may have a real find. Many Victorian light fixtures were made of solid brass. Check the fixture with a magnet: if it's nonmagnetic, it is probably brass. Take it to your local brass plater to have it polished. You can also disassemble the fixture, soak the brass parts in Mr. Clean until all the paint, finish, or tarnish is removed (this may take only a few hours or up to several days, depending upon the coatings), then buff with Brasso (available at hardware and antiques stores) or SemiChrome Polish (find this at an auto parts store). If the light has actually been plated with another metal, you will have to have it commercially stripped.

There are many old and reproduction light fixtures available (see Appendix C). Authentic glass shades are harder to come by; originals can cost more than $50 apiece (authentic Tiffany shades are porcelain).

Lighting can make a room warm and cozy, open and airy, crisply efficient, or rich and romantic. Try augmenting the central lighting fixtures in your rooms with small accent lights as the Victorians did. Kerosene wall sconces, for example, are authentic and add versatility to a room.

I have seen several homes that have been completely restored to their original states, including the original kerosene lighting. This is a lovely and authentic touch—but you can't see a thing. Sylvania and General Electric both manufacture candle-style flicker lights that give a flamelike appearance but cast much more light. Uncoated reproductions of the earliest electric lights are also available, but these emit a harsh glare.

Typical light fixtures

CHAPTER 29

Curtains

The Victorian-era house owner has an almost unlimited choice for recreating authentic window treatments: simple to ornate, opaque to transparent, inexpensive to outrageously exorbitant. The Victorians used every type of material, from lightweight organzas and silks to heavy brocades and stiff paper for shades. In some of the more formal rooms, particularly parlors, owners might have combined four or five treatments on a single window, allowing them to vary the incoming light almost infinitely. In other rooms, particularly where privacy was not a factor (such as kitchens), they might have used only a simple valance. As today, the choice was dictated by personal preference, the decor of a room, and the family's lifestyle.

The tops of the windows were often hidden by cornices, lambrequins, and/or valances; and many of these were elaborately painted, carved, or gilded. Perhaps the simplest type of curtains were *jabots*: pieces of cloth, slightly shorter in the middle than at the edges, that were tacked in a fixed position to the edges of the window, usually underneath a valance, lambrequin, or cornice.

What were *not* seen in the Victorian home were today's popular pinch-pleated draperies running the entire length of a wall.

Most rooms, with the exception of the kitchen, had some sort of heavy drape, which had originally derived from the ancient bedhangings that protected sleepers from drafts. These draperies were elaborate and rich, were usually made of velvet or brocade that matched the valance or lambrequin, and were decorated with festoons, tassles, or ribbons. With the exception of jabots, drapes were rectangular pieces of lined fabric that hung from large rods, usually of wood but sometimes made from cast iron. They were often hand-drawn and hung by either rings or loops of matching material to the floor or the window sill. They were frequently tied back on either side of the window with a braided rope, a chain, or a piece of matching fabric. Fabrics were expensive, and to display their wealth (real or pretended) people would hang their rich brocades and velvets so they "puddled" onto the floor.

Another treatment featured a single, heavy drape, drawn back to one side of the window. This is effective when there are two windows on one wall and the drapes are drawn back to opposing sides.

Beneath the heavy drapes were often curtains made of lace—the Victorians loved it—which were also simple and hand-drawn. Most Victorian-era homeowners insisted upon an opaque covering over windows in rooms where people gathered or slept, especially in the city, where closely built houses offered little privacy. This covering was usually a shade, and during the mid-Victorian period, they were often painted or elaborately decorated. Oriental and landscape motifs were popular, as were repeating stenciled designs.

Another popular window treatment that afforded both light and privacy was the *glass curtain*: a thin drape, often made of net or organdy, that went under the drapes and lace curtain, actually touching the window glass.

MAKING VICTORIAN WINDOW TREATMENTS

Solids, stripes, and patterns of virtually every type and color were used for curtains in Victorian-era homes, so that today's old-home owner can probably find suitable reproduction fabrics at local stores. Many companies manufacture reproduction fabrics. Check the *Old-House Journal Catalog* for sources.

CORNICE BOARDS Lambrequins, cornices, and some valances are attached to a wooden cornice board, which is 1 inch by 6 inches and runs the length between the outer edges of the window casing. Attach this board to the window top, using small shelf brackets and good-sized (at least 3/4 inch long) wood screws. Make sure the board is level before tightening it in place.

LAMBREQUINS A *lambrequin* is a small drapery hanging from a shelf and used to cover the upper part of a window or doorway. It is almost always stiffened with heavy interfacing or wires, and so differs from a valance, which is free hanging. A lambrequin is generally made of heavy cloth, cut to a scalloped or scroll-shaped pattern, then tacked onto the cornice board. Make sure you hem or otherwise finish the edges. If you affix the lambrequin to the cornice board with large hooks and eyes, it can be easily removed for cleaning.

CORNICES A wooden cornice, also tacked to the cornice board, literally encases the curtain in a wooden frame at the top of the window. The cornice is usually constructed from a combination of wooden moldings (see page 122) and mitered at the corners. In the wealthiest homes, cornices were carved wood or cast plaster.

VALANCES Another popular treatment, dating from the beginning of the eighteenth century, is the *valance*, which can be used in combination with draperies and/or curtains or by itself over a window that you do not want to otherwise cover, adding a simple finishing touch without blocking the light or the view.

A simple valance can be made from a rectangular piece of fabric 6 or 8 eight inches long and approximately 1-1/2 times as wide as the window casing. The top is folded and sewn, then a small-diameter rod is pushed through, gathering the fabric.

A *swag valance* looks more ornate but is even easier to make. A large rectangular piece of fabric is tacked to the window casing, to the cornice board, or to rings or hooks at the top of the window casing. The center of this fabric is swagged across the top of the window; the ends fall gracefully into jabots on either side of the window.

An *Austrian valance* is more formal and is always attached to a cornice board. A lightweight fabric is used, gathered tightly at the ends of the cornice board and in two or three places across the swag.

Constructing a cornice board (below right): (A) Attach shelf brackets to the window casing; (B) Attach a piece of 1-inch lumber to the brackets; (C) Nail pieces of 1-inch lumber to the front and sides of the first piece, forming a box. Cover it with cloth. If you wish to leave the valance uncovered, you can use decorative moldings instead of the lumber.

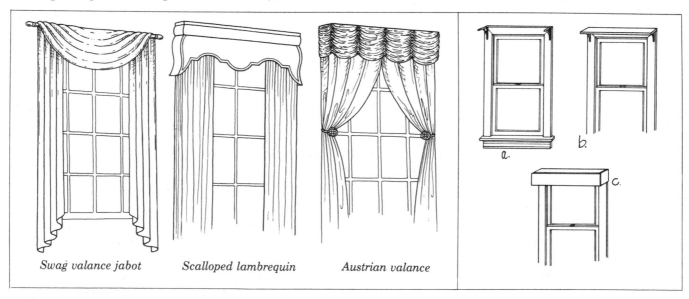

Swag valance jabot Scalloped lambrequin Austrian valance

a. b. c.

CHAPTER 30

The Garden

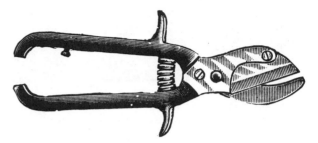

VICTORIAN GARDENS

The first gardens in the American colonies contained only food-producing plants necessary for the settlers' subsistence. Only when the settlements started to thrive could attention and energy be devoted to cultivating ornamental plants, among the first of which were white flowers for weddings. The popularity of these flower gardens grew steadily, and by the beginning of the nineteenth century, the ornamental garden had become separate from—and received equal status and care with—the vegetable garden.

Much of the Victorian-era landscape fashion emanated from British landscape architect (and author of the popular *Cottage Residences*) Andrew Jackson Downing. Downing stated that the house and its surroundings should be compatible, and that the lines of the garden should echo the lines of the house. Tall, conical conifers, he suggested, were perfect complements for a Gothic Revival house.

The Victorian garden was a whimsical fantasy world of geometrically shaped flower beds, mazes, fountains, cast-iron statues, and shrubbery trained to resemble objects or animals (a practice known as *topiary*). The landscape invited visitors, with pathways for strolling and benches and gazebos for private trysts, and always a beckoning driveway leading to a prominent front porch.

Victorian gardens required constant attention, often by a staff of gardeners. Lawns were immaculately groomed (although they were usually kept 3 to 4 inches high), hedges were pruned severely, and trees were even tied together and pruned to form "natural" arches.

Like the Victorian parlor, the High Victorian garden was designed to impress others with the wealth, worldliness, and culture of the owners. One favorite pastime in Victorian-era cities was the evening stroll to view the neighbors' gardens. In the city, especially, yards were oriented so they were easily seen from the street. Although most yards were fenced, wide-spaced wrought iron or wooden pickets under 3 feet high were commonly used.

Expanded travel brought new plant specimens for the garden from all over the world: azaleas from Japan, for example, bulbs from Holland, tropicals from Africa and South America. The transcontinental railroad system could bring mail order plants and seeds to virtually any point in the country, giving nearly everyone access to new plant arrivals. The "keep up with the Joneses" attitude inspired collectors to display almost every plant they could get in their yards. Victorian gardens soon became living display cases that flaunted "one of everything" and were as much of a hodgepodge as the Queen Anne–style houses they frequently adorned. Avid collectors stuck their acquisitions here and there in the yard, often destroying the carefully planned symmetry of the landscaping.

The typical Victorian-era house—even a small dwelling or a home in the city—was self-contained, with its own smokehouse, pump house, fruit trees, and vegetable garden. Outbuildings were often miniature replicas of the main house or of one of its prominent architectural features, such as a turret. Paths led to gazebos, many made of logs (or concrete molded to resemble logs) or of wood lath. The cutting and kitchen gardens, considered unsightly, were set apart from the ornamental gardens and walkways. Other popular garden treatments included redwood tubs filled with plants, hanging baskets of flowers, and cast-iron urns.

Training a tree as topiary for an entrance gate, from The Art of Beautifying Suburban Home Grounds *(1870), by Frank J. Scott.*

The lady of the house often planned or actually worked in the garden herself. Tips and a column on gardening and plants were regular features in early issues of such magazines as the *Ladies' Home Journal.*

Towards the end of the nineteenth century, as the cities and their middle-class populations grew, the yard sizes became smaller. Land values escalated and many lots were split to accommodate additional dwellings. Frequently, the original house was moved from the center of a lot to one of the corners of the parcel, ruining many beautiful Victorian gardens.

The middle-class Victorian Italianate row, Stick, and Stick-Eastlake houses, mass produced at the end of the nineteenth century, had postage-stamp–sized yards. Each home had its own small garden, however, complete with vegetables, and a token planting strip in front of the house. These tiny ornamental gardens, known as *parlor gardens,* were usually located underneath the parlor bay window where visitors to the house could enjoy the fragrance and color.

During this time, Luther Burbank and others were breeding new varieties of flowers, fruits, and vegetables; those that appeared on the market were eagerly bought and placed among collections in Victorian gardens.

Interior plants were also popular during the Victorian era, and nearly every room of the house had at least one house plant. Large mansions frequently had a special room—the *conservatory*—placed on a southern exposure just for plants, and conservatories often featured fountains or aviaries. Popular indoor plants included palms, philodendrons, ferns, rubber plants, bamboo, and for the ardent horticulturist, orchids.

The social changes that occurred at the end of the Victorian era and that spawned the Art Move-

ment and the Craftsman, Shingle, and bungalow houses also caused dramatic changes in residential landscaping. Gardens were now designed to blend with nature and to need less care. Labor had become expensive, so few families could afford gardeners. Characteristic treatments included natural vines, untrimmed hedges, and unpruned shrubs and trees. Nasturtiums were a favorite plant. For the first time, also, gardens offered privacy, hiding the houses behind fences and walls, the latter often made from natural river rock.

OLD-GARDEN PROBLEMS

If you're lucky, there will be more of a legacy left in your old-house garden than a dumpster full of debris. This is entirely possible, for many trees and bushes are capable of surviving hundreds of years.

THAT MONSTER PLANT If you have original plantings in your yard, chances are they're much larger than the person who planned them ever envisioned. What might have originally been intended as an accent bush may now be the largest thing in the yard, creating problems of its own. That lovely little flowering bush that a former owner planted for viewing from the parlor bay window, for example, may very well have grown up to obscure not only the view from inside but the light coming into the

A typical gazebo. "Log" railings were often cast of concrete. From The Art of Beautifying Suburban Home Grounds.

room. Assess whether this darkens the room inordinately; if so, consider cutting the bush back or removing it.

Plants that had been placed against a wall originally may have grown out away from the house, becoming twisted and unsightly. The only solution to this, short of removing the plant, is pruning. Many evergreens, such as junipers and yews, can be cut back severely, but they will grow back slowly and remain unsightly for years. Instead, cut away all the old, woody growth all around the plant. Then, keep pruning the new growth at the top and front, forcing the plant to send its new shoots to the back, so eventually the plant will fill in flush against the wall. The tree or bush will probably not look its best for a few years, but at least you will avoid the ravaged appearance that severe pruning causes.

Victorian garden layout was extremely symmetrical, and a house was often flanked by two identical plants or trees. Over the years, one of the pair may have died off, leaving the remaining one to stick out like a sore thumb. For an authentic restoration, remove the remaining plant and replace it with two new specimens. To avoid removing the remaining plant, try balancing it visually with something particularly striking, such as a bush with bright foliage, or a fountain or flower bed that will catch the eye. Although not strictly authentic, this treatment will restore some symmetry to the garden.

If you are tempted to plan your entire garden around a heritage bush or tree, have a horticulturist examine it to make sure it is healthy and will live a while longer.

NO PRIVACY Even though all but the Victorian city row houses originally had good-sized yards, over the years these yards were often divided to accommodate additional homes. This leaves most old-house owners in the city with an oversized house on an undersized lot. There is really nothing you can do about this. Even heritage trees won't hide a 40-foot-high house. The house was intended to be prominent; you should therefore, as the Victorians did, achieve privacy with a combination of window coverings (see Chapter 29).

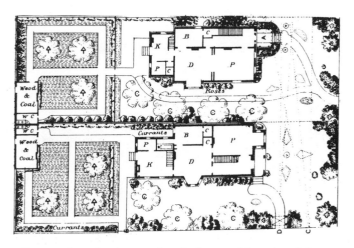

Suggested garden layouts for city houses (above) *and for a large lot* (below), *from* The Art of Beautifying Suburban Home Grounds.

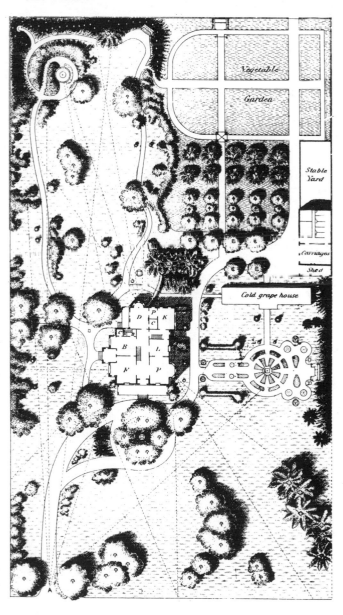

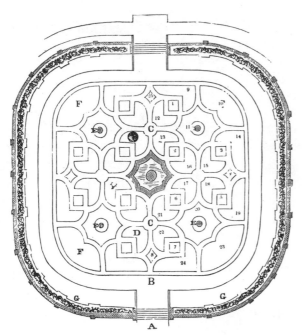

A flower bed from Andrew Jackson Downing's Cottage Residences. *Each area is planted with flowers of a different color.*

VICTORIAN-ERA GARDEN PLANTS

FLOWERS Azalea, bachelor's button, balsam, calendula, calceolaria, Canterbury bells, China aster, Chinese lantern plant, chrysanthemum, crocus, dahlia, delphinium, dianthus, forget-me-not, fuchsia, geranium, grape hyacinth, heliotrope, larkspur, lily of the valley, lupine, marigold, money plant, morning glory, narcissus, nasturtium, peony, poppy, rhododendron, rose, salvia, snapdragon, sweet violet, sweet william, tulip, zinnia.

TREES Catalpa, citrus, cypress, dogwood, fir, ginkgo, horse chestnut, loquat, magnolia, mulberry, olive, palm, poplar, tree of heaven, weeping willow, witch hazel, yew.

BUSHES Boxwood, citrus, flowering quince, hawthorne, holly, jasmine, lilac, oleander, rose of Sharon, spice bush, verbena, vinca.

VINES Clematis, English ivy, grape, honeysuckle, trumpet vine, wisteria.

HERBS Anise, basil, caraway, catnip, chamomile, chives, dill, garlic, lavender, marjoram, parsley, peppermint, rue, sage, savory, spearmint, tansy, tarragon, and thyme.

PLANNING YOUR GARDEN

There are several books available that discuss planning and planting gardens for Victorian homes. One of the best is *Victorian Gardens for Victorian Homes,* a reprint published by the American Life Foundation of Frank J. Scott's 1870 edition of *The Art of Beautifying Suburban Home Grounds.* Scott describes functions of the garden and considerations when planning a yard, and he suggests garden layouts for country houses, city dwellings, and even city row houses.

Another good source is Rudi and Joy Favretti's *Landscapes and Gardens for Historic Buildings,* although its orientation is as much towards commercial landscaping as residential gardens. This book is published by and available from the American Association for State and Local History, 1400 Eighth Avenue South, Nashville, TN 37203.

Old varieties of plants are widely available from mail order sources. Remember that many times old species bear only a slight resemblance to modern, multihybridized varieties. For example, modern flowers—most notably camellias, roses, and fuchsias—have longer blooming seasons, may last longer after being cut, have more petals, and are available in more exciting colors. Old varieties, on the other hand, are delightful in their own right. They often have strong fragrances that their modern counterparts lack, and the flowers may be more delicate.

SOURCES

Carroll Gardens
Westminster, MA 21157
(plants)

Lamb Nurseries
101 Sharp Avenue
Spokane, WA 99202
(perennials)

Nichols Garden Nursery
1190 North Pacific Hwy
Albany, OR 97321
(seeds and plants)

Park Seed Company
Greenwood, SC 29647
(seeds)

Tillotson's Roses
Brown's Valley Road
Watsonville, CA 95076
(roses)

Thompson and Morgan
P.O. Box 100
Farmingdale, NJ 07727
(seeds)

Wayside Gardens
Hodges, SC 29653
(flowers)

White Flower Farm
Litchfield, CT 06759
(flowers)

CHAPTER 31

Victorian Christmas Traditions

Christmas during the Victorian era was a delightful mixture of old customs and new, evolving traditions. The Christmas tree had, long before, shed its pagan origin (its evergreenness had been worshipped as spiritual magic by the Germans) and was accepted as a major component of the Christian yuletide celebration. The tree sported candles (which were lit during a special ceremony on Christmas Eve) until the advent of electricity. A Nativity scene was invariably found beneath its boughs, and decorations were a variety of handmade and edible baubles.

A wealth of goodies—candied fruit, painted and gilded nuts, strings of popcorn and cranberries and dried apples, candy, and cookies—earned the evergreen the nickname "sugar tree." Cookies were especially popular and were shaped with tin cutters (new fashions developed each year) to resemble toys, religious symbols, animals, and flowers. These yummy decorations tantalized the children until the twelfth night of Christmas (Jan-

uary 5), when all but a few (which were saved from year to year) were eagerly gobbled.

A variation of the evergreen is the Victorian snow tree, which originated when thrifty families kept their Christmas trees year after year. Trees were often kept up until spring, then were taken down and stored to dry. The following year, the tree was stripped of its needles, and the branches were wrapped in cotton to simulate the look of new-fallen snow on bare branches. Additional "snow" was provided by shaking mica flakes over the tree after glue had been sparingly applied to the branches.

The first Christmas tree ornaments—glass icicles and heavy glass bulbs—were brought to America by German immigrants. The first commercially manufactured ornaments were made by the Germans in 1880 from tin, wax, glass, and fabric. Small color pictures of Victorian Christmas scenes were added to commercially manufactured ornaments at the end of the nineteenth century. Most families purchased only one or two ornaments per year. In the late 1800s, when merchant F. W. Woolworth was presented with an opportunity to sell glass ornaments in his store, he laughed. He did agree to take a few decorations on consignment to see if they would sell. Mr. Woolworth sold $25 worth that Christmas in less than two days, marking the beginning of a new trend in tree decoration.

One of the earliest Victorian Christmas traditions was that of writing long "news" letters to friends and relatives, filling them in on the past year's events. The tradition of sending Christmas cards, as we know them, during the holiday season is only a century old in America. Louis Pranz, an exile to America from the German uprisings of 1848, is considered the father of the American Christmas card. He developed a multicolor lithographic printing process and created colorful cards that he exported to England for Christmas in 1874. They were so well received in Great Britain that the following year he introduced a few in America, and within a decade he was printing five million Christmas cards annually. The themes of his cards were often religious but also featured Santa Claus, reindeer, Christmas trees, or stars. Cards received from family and friends were displayed on tables and fireplace mantels in Victorian parlors, along with elaborate arrangements and evergreen wreaths of flowers, holly berries, and mistletoe.

Another tradition that was popular during the Victorian era was the Christmas garden, called a *putz*. Like many other Christmas traditions, the putz was brought to this country by German immigrants. Originally, it consisted solely of a manger scene, but with each passing year it became more elaborate. In its heyday, the putz was a whimsical fantasyland, complete with snow-covered villages constructed of heavy paper, cardboard, wood, or iron. Mountains, lakes, miniature animals (made of celluloid clay), trains and other mechanical toys added character and vitality to the model villages. The putz was usually surrounded by a tiny wooden or wrought-iron fence.

Today, the Christmas garden has been replaced by stacks of presents. With a little imagination, however, a putz of original materials can be constructed from scraps at minimal expense. White sheets or tablecloths spread over boxes and wadded paper create the terrain. Moss rocks, branches and dried weeds are another major ingredient in the garden, which is dotted with small ponds and lakes formed by tiny mirrors. Small figures, including Santa Claus with his sleigh and reindeer, complete the scene. Once it's all in place, a snowstorm of mica flakes is poured over all.

PART VII

The People With Money

Financing

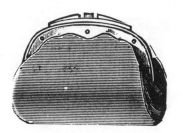

In addition to any emotional impulses prompting you to buy an old home, you should also consider a prospective renovation project from a purely financial standpoint—after all, you won't have much pride of ownership left if the bank repossesses your house.

HOW MUCH WILL IT COST?

This, in one sense, is an absurd question, since no one answer can address the virtually infinite number of situations that can exist. Each project will be unique; each house is different and requires different repairs; material and labor costs vary geographically and can fluctuate each week; and owners possess varying levels of skills and different renovation philosophies.

If your house needs no structural work, and if the plumbing, heating, and electrical systems are adequate, you probably *can* complete an entire renovation for under $10,000. On the other hand, I've known people who have spent over $100,000 just *decorating* an older house.

Financial problems with old houses come, usually not from high budgets, but from those jolting surprises (hey, this is supposed to cost $500, not $5,000!) that often occur. If you don't want any rude awakenings, give careful thought to the following:
● If you are hiring anyone on an hourly basis, have at least a rough agreement on a price ceiling. Labor is perhaps the most costly item in house renovation and, if you don't watch it, can quickly blow your budget.
● Allow enough leeway in your budget to cover price increases. Most granting agencies and lending institutions require a concrete, approved budget before they issue funds. Unfortunately, the red tape involved may drag the approval process out over several months. Price increases often occur during the time lapse between application for and disbursal of funds. Some agencies have no leeway in this case, and you may be stuck. However, you have a better chance of being able to augment the budget if you present your arguments in concrete figures. Show the exact cost calculations on your original budget. Review material and labor costs every week or so to stay on top of price fluctuations. If there are any increases, notify the agency immediately and request a budget increase. Again, provide concrete estimates.
● Be careful when you hire a contractor; see Chapter 6.
● Keep the purse strings under your own control. Someone else (consultant, supervising contractor, etc.) who has the authority to spend your money may very well not care about cutting costs.

COST ESTIMATIONS

Assess the following carefully before you buy the house, since these may make the project too costly a venture:

STRUCTURAL PROBLEMS (see Chapters 9 and 10) include moving houses, replacing foundations, jacking up buildings. These are all extremely expensive undertakings (maybe thousands of dollars), so obtain some bids.

DRY ROT AND TERMITE WORK A structural pest report should always be reviewed when the house is in escrow. Remember that this only gives an indication of needed work and may not indicate damage.

CUSTOM MILLWORK Is a lot of the decorative trim missing or ruined? Have stairway balusters rotted? Having these milled can cost a fortune.

EXPENSIVE ITEMS These include plumbing, electrical, and heating systems, and the roof. These frequently need replacing in an old house; each can cost thousands of dollars. You should, however, be able to make a fairly accurate assessment of the conditions of these systems before you purchase the house.

OBTAINING FINANCING

Lenders' attitudes towards financing older homes and rehabilitation projects have undergone a recent, dramatic change. As little as three years ago, most institutions would not loan money on homes that needed rehabilitating, especially those in core city areas. Today, lenders recognize older homes, even those needing extensive rehabilitation, as worthy credit risks. Although tight money and high interest rates paint a bleak picture for virtually anyone buying a house in today's market, if you can qualify for a loan to purchase a new tract house, you can most likely obtain financing on an older home. This is primarily due to the success of so many rehabilitation projects.

An even more dramatic change—one that tips the scales in favor of older homes—is the current willingness on the part of many lenders to appraise an old house at its "after work completed" value— i.e., lenders will consider what the house will be worth after rehabilitation is completed and loan against that figure instead of its current (usually much lower) fair market value. This, known as the *purchase/rehabilitation loan program*, is one way to obtain capital funds for rehabilitation.

For example, you purchase an old house for $50,000, making a down payment of $30,000 cash. You plan an extensive rehabilitation that will cost $30,000 and will raise the value of the house to more than $90,000. Under the purchase/rehabilitation loan program, the lending institution will probably be willing to lend you at least $50,000; of this $20,000 goes to escrow to complete the purchase; the remaining $30,000 is "held back" in an impound account and disbursed as stages of the renovation work are completed.

The Federal Home Loan Bank Board backs the purchase/rehabilitation loan program through the Federal National Mortgage Association (FNMA or "Fannie Mae") urban loan program. The FNMA will buy 100 percent of a purchase/rehabilitation loan, if the lending institution services the loan and oversees the rehabilitation.

Each institution has its own conditions for purchase/rehabilitation loans. Most require that rehabilitation be conducted by a licensed contractor and be completed within twelve months of purchase. Most also insist that applicants submit detailed building diagrams or architect's plans.

Some secondary lending institutions also offer purchase/rehabilitation loans, but most second-mortgage brokers usually require a 20 to 25 percent *equity cushion*—i.e., they will only loan on 75 to 80 percent of a house's value after rehabilitation.

THOUGHTS FOR CUTTING COSTS

PHILOSOPHY How you approach your renovation project can make a significant difference in the cost. Labor is probably the biggest cost in a renovation project, so if you do the work yourself, obviously you will save money. Committing yourself to exact period restoration may also be expensive, especially if you insist on custom-made reproductions.

CONSULTATION SERVICES This is another potentially expensive element of house renovation, which may or may not be worthwhile. One friend of mine, for example, invested over $17,000 in consultant fees—before he ever touched his house. If you are going to move walls and change the structure, an architect can be valuable. If all you need is house plans, hire a draftsperson for about one-fourth the cost.

In most areas, there are historic-house consultants and interior designers who specialize in decorating old houses. If you don't know how your house should look and money is no object, these people can provide valuable information. If all you want is advice, consult your historical society or state historic preservation office. Often these agencies employ preservation architects who can help you at no charge. If you do not know about your house, another great *free* resource is the local library.

MATERIALS Salvage items can be costly or cheap, depending on where and how you locate them. If you want to save money, stay away from the big (especially mail order) companies, which charge top dollar. If you're patient, you can probably find a lot of things you need at thrift stores, flea markets, demolition sites, and through newspaper advertisements.

Avoid paying retail prices for building materials. If you are working with a contractor, make sure s/he is charging you his or her contractor's prices. Hardware and other building supply stores often give discounts to owner/builders. If you've been patronizing a store that won't, find a new source. Also, you can frequently find special prices on building materials through newspaper classified advertisements.

EXTRA COSTS

NICKEL AND DIME ITEMS These include sandpaper, paint scrapers, paint and lacquer thinner, gloves, dust masks, paint brushes, drill bits—things you don't normally consider, but that can add up to hundreds of dollars before you know it.

THOSE IRRESISTIBLE FIXTURES Leave some room in your budget for surprise finds: special hardware, a period light, some old stained glass.

RENOVATION ON A SHOESTRING

Ideally, everyone undertaking an old-house renovation should have enough money to finish the project. The reality, however, especially for young couples, is that purchasing the house often takes all available resources. Many people, therefore, are forced to do their renovations on a shoestring—completing each task as they can squeeze together enough money.

Don't attempt a renovation project unless you have enough money to take care of major dry rot, plumbing, electrical, roof, and heating problems, and to ensure that your house is secure against the elements and intruders. You can forget the wallpaper, the new floors, and the lace curtains, but you can't forget the roof. If you don't have enough money to take care of these problems, you probably should avoid a renovation project.

Keep a list of tasks you can do that cost little money, so the renovation does not come to a standstill when funds are scarce.

THE ULTIMATE QUESTION

Will the project be financially worthwhile?

One of the paramount things to consider in purchasing any piece of real estate is the location. Although real estate appreciation has slowed, you still should choose a house in an area that is being improved or at least maintained. Don't invest tens or even hundreds of thousands of dollars in a renovation project unless the area has homes of comparable value. In the right area, every dollar you put into an old house can increase its value five or tenfold. In other neighborhoods, a house will never command over a certain price, no matter how much money you put into it.

Overextending yourself financially can turn even a seemingly worthwhile investment into a disaster. The tragedies in the field of home rehabilitation (and any other speculative venture) are those people who get themselves in too deep financially to get out if they have to. Remember, also, that the current slow real estate market makes it more difficult to get out if you decide you don't want to or cannot continue a project.

Insurance

Essentially, there is no such thing as an uninsurable house. Certain companies have stricter criteria than others and may refuse to insure homes they consider too great a risk; but there are programs available to insure even the worst firetrap.

Unfortunately, many insurance companies prefer to insure the suburban middle-class tract house because it is relatively new, is like all the others in its subdivision, and has a predictable loss rate and a predictable rebuilding cost.

The older house is different; it may pose unknown fire risks and may be costly to replace; it doesn't fit the average loss/replacement formula. Therefore many insurance companies refuse to insure homes that are over a certain age, usually thirty years. Other companies, especially those based in urban areas (where there is a sizable percentage of Victorian-era homes) or on the East Coast (where Victorian-era homes are young compared to Colonials!) offer excellent coverage at reasonable rates.

HOMEOWNERS INSURANCE CRITERIA

Virtually every company that offers homeowners insurance for older houses requires that the house conform to certain standards. Before they will agree to insure the home, a company representative will inspect the electrical, heating, and plumbing systems. In addition to examining these systems, which are considered the primary causes of homeowners insurance losses, the company will usually conduct an overall assessment of the premises to determine if fire or other hazards exist.

IF YOU DON'T QUALIFY

Most companies will provide limited fire insurance for homes that are not (in the eyes of the industry) acceptable risks for homeowners insurance. Such policies do not generally include liability coverage or coverage for theft of personal property.

Some homes pose such high risks that companies will not even insure them under fire policies. Under the federally mandated *FAIR* plan (an acronym for "Fair Access to Insurance Requirements"), however, even those homes can be insured. Designed specifically for run-down houses in urban core areas, the FAIR plan mandates each private company to provide insurance (in a quantity proportionate to its share of the statewide insurance market) for otherwise uninsurable homes.

THE ADEQUATE COVERAGE DILEMMA

Homes may be insured on an *actual cash value* or *replacement cost* basis. Actual cash value is the depreciated value of the property at the time of the loss.

Most homeowners policies offer, and most agents recommend, a *replacement cost option*, whereby for a few additional dollars, everything will be replaced in the event of a loss. Companies that offer this option warn that lost items will be replaced with those of "like kind and quality," and will not necessarily be *duplicated*. Talk with a company representative before you take the coverage, to ensure that you and the company agree on the definition of "like kind and quality."

A house must be insured to a certain percentage (usually 80 percent) of the total cost of rebuilding in order to receive full coverage if a loss occurs. A homeowner who opts for the replacement cost option may be required to insure his/her home to an even higher percentage of its value.

If the house is under-insured and a loss occurs (even a partial one), the insurance company will pay a settlement proportionate to the percentage of insurance coverage carried. For example: If a house insured for replacement cost is worth $100,000 but is only insured for $70,000 (70 percent of value), in case of loss, the insurance company's liability is limited to from 70 to 80 percent of the cost of replacing the damaged portion.

Herein lies the old-house Catch 22: Under the actual cash value basis, if you apply depreciation to a Victorian-era home, its actual cash value will be extremely low. Replacement cost insurance on the other hand could be prohibitively expensive. Also, how do you replace the irreplaceable elements of your house?

Some companies recognize this dilemma and are beginning to offer specialized insurance alternatives. For those who are seeking the most comprehensive coverage, some companies offer a special replacement cost program whereby custom building techniques and features are recognized and covered. Fireman's Fund, for example, offers a "Prestige-Plus" plan, which includes full-cost replacement coverage, even if the cost of replacing the structure exceeds the policy limits. The policy also covers extra rebuilding costs necessary to bring the structure up to current building code requirements.

For those who cannot afford the high cost of premiums to insure a house, other companies are experimenting with insuring houses to their market value only.

TIPS FOR ENSURING THAT YOU'RE INSURED

● Maintain frequent communication with your insurance broker. When you finish a portion of your renovation, you should increase the amount of coverage to reflect the house's increased value.
● Watch construction costs. If they rise, so does the cost of rebuilding your house, and you could need more insurance.
● Some companies have specialized programs that guarantee replacement, even if it costs more than you're insured for.

WORKERS' COMPENSATION

When you hire people who are not licensed professionals to work on your house, in most cases you are required to purchase special workers' compensation insurance to cover any accidents that may occur while the job is in progress.

Most homeowners policies include a liability provision that will provide a maximum of $1,000 worth of medical payments if you are legally liable for accidents to visitors on your property—including friends who hurt themselves while volunteering their labor on a one-time basis only. Such liability generally excludes anyone you pay to do any work.

If you hire people to work on your house, check with an insurance agent about requirements for workers' compensation insurance. Depending upon where you live, you, as an employer, can secure coverage through private insurance companies or a special state workers' compensation fund. Cost of the policy depends upon how much you pay the worker(s) and how hazardous is the work performed.

A licensed independent contractor is responsible for carrying workers' compensation to cover his/her employees.

Government Programs

CHAPTER 34

THE NATIONAL PRESERVATION ACT

To date, the bulk of federal money for historic preservation has come under the auspices of the National Historic Preservation Act of 1966. This law, provisions of which have been extended through 1987, created the nation's historic preservation program. Among other provisions, it establishes the National Register of Historic Places and authorizes the appropriation of federal funds for acquiring and preserving historic resources. The program is administered by the National Park Service of the federal Department of the Interior.

To be eligible for any of the funds, a state must designate a state historic preservation officer and must have a federally approved preservation plan.

When first established, the Historic Preservation Act authorized a $2 million appropriation for historic preservation. This allowance has been raised (through 1987) to a maximum of $150 million annually, although the federal government has never appropriated the full amount. In 1979–80, it appropriated the highest amount ever: $55 million. Only $24 million was appropriated for fiscal year 1980–81, however. This cut—over 65 percent—is even larger than it appears, for more states have met the criteria for participation in the program and are vying for the money.

Money given to the states is specifically allocated for historic resource surveys, planning, demonstration projects, and information about professional preservation techniques. A percentage—which varies from state to state—of the allocation is given to the direct grant-in-aid program (see below) for selected properties on the National Register of Historic Places.

In addition, amendments made in November 1980 to the Historic Preservation Act specify that at least 10 percent of each state's apportionment be given directly to local governments certified by the secretary of the interior. No money has been budgeted for this yet, however.

The availability of government funds is diminishing. Veteran old-home owners tell tales of 3 percent loans, of rehabilitation grants and preservation stipends. Today, virtually all government rehabilitation subsidy programs (except the grant-in-aid program) are defunct. Not only have the economy and curbs on federal spending forced cutbacks, but, as the preservation movement grows, there is increasing competition for the few remaining dollars.

Home renovators seeking financial assistance should be exploring sources other than government grants or loans. On the East Coast, there are many private and corporate endowments; on the West Coast, this resource is virtually undeveloped. Check the magazine *Foundation News* (published bimonthly by the Council on Foundations, 888 Seventh Avenue, New York, NY 10019) for ideas.

NATIONAL REGISTER DESIGNATION

The National Register of Historic Places is a list of places officially recognized and protected by the United States Department of the Interior. Properties listed on the National Register are exclusively eligible for many benefits, including grants, loans, tax relief, and legal protection against defacement or demolition. National Register designation may be given to single sites, to a specific area, or to a group of resources. In addition, local governments may designate historically significant districts that, when certified by the secretary of the interior, will qualify for the benefits.

A house, to be included on the National Register, must be of local, state, or national importance and must meet one or more of the following federal criteria:

1. Be associated with events that have made a significant contribution to the broad patterns of our history; or 2. Be associated with the lives of persons significant in our past; or 3. Embody the distinctive characteristics of a type, period, or method of construction, or represent the work of a master, or possess high artistic values, or represent a significant and distinguishable entity whose components may lack individual distinction; or 4. Have yielded, or be likely to yield, information important in pre-history or history.[7]

Anyone may nominate a building or other resource for National Register inclusion, even if that person does not own the property (although a property will not be listed if the owner objects). Applications, which are available from the state historic preservation officers, must be completed in accordance with the federal requirements set forth in *How to Complete National Register Forms,* which is available from any federal bookstore (usually located in federal office buildings in large cities). There are people who make their living applying, in behalf of owners of historic properties, for National Register status. Local preservation and historical societies can probably put you in touch with these consultants, who can be a valuable resource.

Completed National Register applications are submitted to and reviewed by the state historic preservation officer, who makes the nominations (which are generally accepted) to the National Register staff in Washington, D.C.

THE HISTORIC PRESERVATION GRANT-IN-AID PROGRAM

One distinct advantage of placing your house on the National Register of Historic Places is that you become eligible for a National Historic Preservation Act grant-in-aid. Although funds are scarce and becoming scarcer, you could be lucky and receive a grant to purchase or rehabilitate your house. (Provisions of this grant program, and therefore of this discussion, also apply to grants from foundations and other sources.)

Your state historic preservation officer can provide you with specific information about the grant-in-aid program in your state, including application forms, and can tell you how many projects in your state will receive grants. You should, however, be aware of the following provisions of the program:

● The federal government will rarely pay for work until it is completed, and you must complete the project within thirty-three months.

● You will have to keep strict accounts of all your expenditures. The project is subject at any time to an audit by the state historic preservation officer—and you will probably be audited before you receive final payment. The state officer, in turn, is heavily audited by the federal government every three years.

● That portion of the property that is renovated with the use of federal funds must be open to the public at least twelve days a year.

The recipient also has to match the amount of money given by the federal government. The matching amount you provide may be via labor equity: donated labor or materials or tools from yourself and people you know. Even if you elect to provide your half in sweat, when you receive the grant you will have to post cash for the matching funds.

Another problem is valuing the labor in labor equity. If you earn your living as a licensed contractor, you can value your labor according to what you normally charge. If not, you can only charge the prevailing minimum journeyman wage for each task you perform. One engineer friend of mine, who normally charges $50 per hour, could only claim $3.18 per hour labor equity for hours on hours of wood stripping.

There is, however, a flip side to this coin. The same engineer, for example, could value, at her customary $50 per hour, any engineering she had to do for the grant application.

There are many things you can include in your costs that are often overlooked: the labor involved in preparing the grant application, the rental value of any tools loaned to you, any time donated by friends and professionals. If you buy your local plumber a cup of coffee and s/he spends two hours explaining to you how to repair that leaky bathtub drain, you can tally those hours (at the customary rate) in addition to tallying the hours you spend fixing the drain (at the lower journeyman's rate).

DO YOU REALLY WANT THAT GRANT OR LOAN?

Before you complete a grant or loan application, seriously consider the consequences of actually receiving one. Although having money is always nice, and I certainly don't want to deprecate the folks in the preservation agencies (they've saved many neighborhoods and helped many people), there are certain ramifications of working with bureaucratic agencies. What appears at first to be a boon may, in fact, be a boondoggle— with more headaches than it is worth.

With most grants and loans, the work has to go out to bid, and you are required to hire the lowest bidder. This may or may not be the person *you* want to do the work, and you lose the option of hiring your friend the contractor who, on the spur of the moment, decides to do the work on weekends and charge you only a fraction of what the lowest bid is.

In addition, if you receive more than $10,000 through a government source, you are required to adhere to federal affirmative action standards. Although the objective of ensuring equal employment opportunities for minorities, women, and handicapped persons is laudable, such restrictions might prohibit you from hiring your friend, the carpenter whose work you like best, etc. Even if this poses no problem for you, you will have to fill out forms and more forms attesting your compliance with affirmative action.

Everything you do to your house will be collected, inspected, neglected, dissected, or rejected by a

host of bureaucratic agencies. Not only will you have well- and ill-wishers and inspectors crawling around your house, these various approvals take time—you could find yourself waiting for months just to have the color of your house okayed!

Obviously, the extent of this bureaucratic red tape will vary in different areas. In some places, the regulatory agencies should be applauded for their role in saving old neighborhoods. Approvals may also be no problem in some areas, especially if you are familiar with the people with whom you will be dealing. If you are not, contact them before you apply for the grant or loan. This will give you an opportunity to determine whether they will be allies or foes. And, if they are helpful, they could assist you in securing that funding.

APPLYING FOR A GRANT OR LOAN

Grant writing is an art of sorts. Although this is a task you can do yourself, here are a few guidelines:
● If you do not feel confident about your writing skills, hire a professional writer who has experience with grants.
● Make sure you answer any questions asked on the application. If you paraphrase a question in your answer, you will reassure the person reviewing your application that you have addressed the issue.
● Make sure your application is complete—it will not receive any attention if it is not.
● Have the application professionally typed. Appearances do count, despite what anyone tells you.
● Remember that you will probably be competing against many other applicants—perhaps even thousands. Just because you love your house is no reason why anyone should give you special status or money for rehabilitation. Why is the house significant? Is it the only one left of its kind? Is it linked to any significant person or event of the past? Research your house thoroughly. Even if it is

not historically significant, if you can provide some interesting information or anecdotes, you might catch the interest of those who review the applications.
● Carefully review the secretary of the interior's *Standards for Rehabilitation and Guidelines for Rehabilitating Historic Buildings* (Appendix B). These standards are the bible of both governmental agencies and private groups.

If you would like more information on grants and grant writing, contact the Grantsmanship Center at 1031 South Grand Avenue, Los Angeles, CA 90015; or 719 Eighth Street SE, Third Floor, Washington, D.C. 20003. They also publish a bimonthly magazine, *The Grantsmanship News.*

TAX INCENTIVES

The sweeping changes that went into effect January 1, 1982, under the Tax Recovery Act of 1981 broadly favor the holding of any commercial real estate, most notably by allowing investors to depreciate income-producing properties over a fifteen- rather than a thirty-year period. The Tax Act also contains provisions designed to encourage the rehabilitation of older structures, although it repeals many of the attractive tax incentives enacted by the Tax Reform Acts of 1976 and 1978.

Basically, the new law creates a three-tiered *investment tax credit* for capital expenditures incurred in rehabilitating buildings over thirty years old. An investment tax credit (ITC) is subtracted from any tax liability due, unlike deductions, which are subtracted from gross income before taxes are calculated. One dollar of investment tax credit can—for certain tax brackets—equal three dollars of deductions.

Capital expenditures, in this context, include renovation, restoration, and reconstruction costs that extend or preserve the life of existing structures.

An investment tax credit of 15 percent is allowed for rehabilitation of structures thirty to forty years old; 20 percent for structures at least forty years old; and 25 percent for structures more than forty years old that are either on the National Register of Historic Places or are designated as significant structures within a certified historic district (pages 169-170). Lessees with lease terms of at least fifteen years are also eligible for the credit.

To qualify for the investment credit, rehabilitation must meet certain tests:
● Seventy-five percent of the original exterior walls must remain as exterior walls after the rehabilitation is completed.
● The renovation must be completed within twenty-four months, unless an architect's plan calling for a longer period was completed prior to January 1, 1982, in which case a period of up to sixty months will be allowed for completion.
● Rehabilitation must be certified by the secretary of the interior as consistent with the building or the district where the building is located. (What this certification entails is not yet known and may vary from state to state.)
● The building must undergo a *substantial rehabilitation*: rehabilitation expenditures must equal the greater of either $5,000 or the *basis* (original purchase price plus any capital improvements undertaken before rehabilitation) of the property (including both land and structures). This substantial rehabilitation test severely limits eligibility for the tax credit. The secretary of the interior's office concedes that one third of the rehabilitation projects it has knowledge of would not meet the substantial rehabilitation test. (Preservationists are seeking amendments to strike this provision from the law, but so far they have been unsuccessful.)

The substantial rehabilitation test also discriminates against new owners of property. Consider a person who has owned a commercial building for many years and has depreciated it to nothing. The building has a fair market value of $500,000, and now needs $200,000 worth of renovation work. If the owner chooses to keep the building and do the work, s/he can qualify for an investment credit; a new owner, however, could not.

The investment credit system is designed to discourage speculative selling of historic properties, since premature sales can result in complete or partial tax recapture of the investment credit:

YEARS HELD	PERCENT OF RECAPTURE
Less than one	100 percent
One to two	80 percent
Two to three	60 percent
Three to four	40 percent
Four to five	20 percent
Longer than five years	none

Although this new tax act creates enormous incentives for large commercial real estate investors to enter the field of historic preservation—and may very well result in the renovation of derelict buildings that can be bought cheaply (at a low basis) and that need substantial renovation, it does repeal benefits for other people who enjoyed advantages under the Tax Reform Acts of 1976 and 1978.

One such group consists of owners of income-producing properties located on the National Register or in certified Historic Districts, who could previously amortize capital expenditures over a sixty-month period. This is no longer the case. Also, a 10 percent investment tax credit was allowed for any capital rehabilitation expenditures for commercial nonresidential properties twenty years and older. If these buildings do not meet the "substantial rehabilitation" test, or if they are between twenty and thirty years old, they will be denied benefits.

If a rehabilitation is already in progress and it qualifies in 1982 for the new tax credits under the Tax Recovery Act of 1981, the new guidelines and benefits will apply. If not, a 10 percent credit, if applicable, will be allowed. *No* rapid amortization of any expenditures incurred January 1, 1982, or thereafter will be allowed, however.

The above is only a sketch of the new tax laws favoring historic preservation. For more information, including changes in the guidelines, consult a tax attorney, an accountant, or a financial counselor.

THE NEW TAX LAW AND HISTORIC PRESERVATION

The 25 percent investment tax credit for rehabilitation of National Register and Historic District properties is additionally attractive because, unlike the 15 and 20 percent ITCs, the 25-percent credit is not subject to the *adjustment to basis* rule of the new tax law. This rule requires that any 15 or 20 percent tax credits taken for rehabilitation be subtracted from the total rehabilitation costs in computing the amount of the rehabilitation that can be depreciated as part of the basis of the property.

EXAMPLE A forty-year-old building costs $150,000; rehabilitation costs $200,000; all other criteria for the new tax credit are met:

BUILDING ON NATIONAL REGISTER
OR WITHIN A CERTIFIED HISTORIC DISTRICT

$ 150,000 (depreciable basis: cost)
+200,000 (rehabilitation costs)
− 50,000 (25 percent tax credit)
_____

$300,000 ($23,334 per year under
a fifteen-year cost recovery schedule)

BUILDING NOT ON NATIONAL REGISTER
OR WITHIN A CERTIFIED HISTORIC DISTRICT

$150,000 (depreciable basis: cost)
+200,000 (rehabilitation)
− 40,000 (20 percent tax credit)
_____

$310,000 ($20,667 per year under
a fifteen-year cost recovery schedule)

Thus, the difference the first year is nearly $13,000 and for the following fourteen years is $3,000.

CONSERVATION EASEMENTS

One provision of the Tax Reform Act of 1976 that has been retained is that of *conservation easements.* These are transfers to charitable organizations or governmental entities of partial interests in property for the preservation, public education, and enjoyment of historically important land areas and structures. They guarantee the protection of the land or structure donated.

Transfers that qualify under this provision include building facade easements, land easements, and archeological site easements. Donation of easements will obviously affect the future use and disposition of the property.

Easements may be given for a specific period of time (*term easements*) or for perpetuity (*gift easements).* Gift easements may result in reduced income, gift, estate, or real property taxes for the donor.

Anyone can give a conservation easement. The value of the easement should be determined by a competent property appraiser, who will calculate the worth of the property before and after the gift of the easement. The decrease in value of the property created by the gift will be used in determining any tax deductions.

For more information, contact your state historic preservation officer.

Appendixes

Some Renovation Experiences

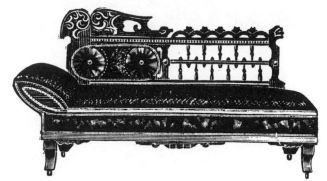

Following are several chronicles of old-house renovation experiences (some of the names have been changed to protect the owners' privacy). Each owner/renovator has a different house, a different approach, a different budget, and a different set of skills. The one thing that all these projects have in common is that they were all successful. I have spared you the tales of the failures: those houses that needed too much work; the projects that ended in divorces; the friend who had just purchased his dream house when it was destroyed by a fire; those people who cannot afford to complete their houses yet cannot afford to sell them.

But take heart; there are a lot of successes. Read on . . .

DO-IT-YOURSELF RENOVATION ON A LIMITED BUDGET IN RURAL ALABAMA

BY ALICE JOHNSON

I enjoy living in an older house. I guess it gives me a heritage, a sense of history and roots. You don't get that with a new house.

In 1975, after I saved enough money for a down payment on a house, I approached several realtors with the idea that I wanted to buy and fix up a house at least seventy-five years old. This was before renovation had become popular in my area, and some of the realtors scoffed at my ideas. One realtor, however, knew what I wanted. She drove me around several different towns close to where I work and helped me locate an "up and coming" neighborhood: where I could afford to buy a house, and where putting money and effort into fixing it up would pay off.

I found several houses I liked, although none of them were on the market. The realtor was very helpful, though, and she approached the owners to see if they would sell. One of them said yes, and, after only a few weeks of looking, I had found my home: a small (1,800 square feet) Gothic Revival cottage built around 1875.

I checked the house out carefully before I made an offer. The inside was a mess: brilliant orange paint on the walls, a miserable kitchen and bath, urine-soaked carpets in the living room, and fir floors that were cracked and warped. The back porch had rotted away, and the paint on the outside of the house had worn away to the wood. Structurally, however, the house was in good shape; and the plumbing and wiring had been redone about twenty years earlier. The sellers put a new roof on the house and paid to fix $300 worth of dry rot in the foundation.

I was able to secure an 8-3/4 percent loan to buy the house, but since I had to pay over $10,000 in down payment and closing costs, when I moved into the house I had very little money.

I did have several years of experience. I had redone a forty-year-old parsonage and a twenty-five-year-old yacht with my ex-husband. I had learned, during these projects, how to hang wallpaper and how to do minor plumbing and electrical repairs, wood stripping and refinishing, carpet laying, stained glass repair, ceramic tile laying, painting, and dry rot work. Because I enjoy the work—and also to keep costs down—I was determined to do as much of the renovation on my house as possible.

I had no commitment to restoring the house to its original condition or floor plan. First, it was hard to determine exactly what the house had been. I could tell, by marks on the floor, that some previous owner had torn out a hallway and combined the front and rear parlors, but I liked the large living room that this created. A bathroom and kitchen had also been added onto the back of the house, probably when the house was first plumbed. I decided to combine the current kitchen with the original one to form a large, country-style kitchen.

Since I already knew what I wanted to do to the house, I did not consult an architect or contractor. I did, however, draw scale plans of the house (this helped me estimate material needs) and devised a general plan of action: I would work on the entire house, starting with demolition, then framing, minor plumbing and electrical work, Sheetrock and plaster, ceramic tile, woodwork, painting and papering, floors, and decorative items (light fixtures, stained glass, curtains, and shutters).

The first month I spent just tearing things out. I got rid of the rotted porch, the wall between the original kitchen and the added kitchen, the smelly old carpets, plastic curtains, etc. Although it was good to see those things go, I found I was living amidst a shambles—and not coping with it very well. I could not find anything, my temper was short, I had to live out of boxes, everything was covered with a layer of plaster dust. In short, I was not enjoying living in my house.

I realized that I had to rethink my idea of working on the entire house at one time. If I was going to live in the house while I worked on it, I needed some place where I could go to escape the mess. So, I chose to finish the master bedroom first. I patched the walls, painted the trim, rewired the light fixtures, wallpapered, laid a new carpet, and installed curtains.

What a great little sanctuary it was! Not only could I escape the mess of the rest of the house, but my little bedroom served as a constant inspiration to me: this is what the whole house would look like some day!

This plan of action worked so well that I decided to finish the house room by room. Next, I reconstructed the back porch. This served several purposes. Since the weather was nice, I used my new porch for entertaining friends—and for organizing tools and materials. Also, since the kitchen and bathroom—which both required a lot of work—were at the back of the house, the new porch gave me good access for working on these rooms.

The porch was a major expenditure: the wood itself cost over $1,000. I was able to cut some costs, though. I reused the old staircase, which was still in good condition, and moved it from one side of the house to the other. I made my own sawn wood balusters (147 of them!), using 3/8-inch redwood siding and a scroll jigsaw. To buy this many balusters or to have them made would have probably cost me as much as the entire porch.

Although most of the items I needed for my house were available through mail order catalogs (such as the *Old-House Journal Catalog*), I saved a lot of money by hunting for them in junk stores, garage sales, and newspaper advertisements. For example, I scrounged around the scrap bins at a molding manufacturer's plant and found decorative moldings for only 4¢ a foot. I found an old pull-chain toilet for $50 at a barn sale—reproduction models cost as much as $600. My boyfriend's parents gave me an old carved door that had sat in their garage for many years. And the man at the paint store gave me the name of a retired floor layer who, because he loved old houses (and knew mine in particular) laid three new hardwood floors in my house for less than $1,000—and even let me work with him.

I also saved money by buying materials on sale—even if I wasn't ready to use them yet. I purchased the paint and wallpaper, for example, at a 1¢ sale—even though I did not use them for nearly a year.

Except for the floors, I was able to avoid paying anything for labor. Many of my friends volunteered or traded their time. My brother and his roommate needed a place to stay while they attended a nearby university. I traded them room and board in exchange for help after school and on weekends. Although they had no construction experience, they did a lot of tearing out, cleaning, and wood stripping.

I also have a friend who is a contractor, and he helped me build my porch, and frame in and hang Sheetrock. In exchange, I helped him decorate a house and made him a quilt.

The only problem with this approach is that I had to schedule some of my projects around my friends' availability. One friend, for example, who is a professional painter, offered to lend me his airless paint sprayer while he was on vacation. Although I was stripping the wood in the kitchen at the time, I stopped everything to paint the outside of the house.

And, although I had budgeted well and even saved money on the major expenditures, I was amazed at how much money I had to spend on those little nickel and dime items: paint scrapers, sandpaper, wood filler, etc.

The entire rehabilitation project took me a little less than two years—working religiously after work and on weekends, and even using my lunch hours to seek out and purchase materials.

In 1975, when I bought my house and first started tearing it up, many of the people I knew said I was crazy. At times, I thought they might be right. But today, even many of the skeptics are buying old houses to fix up, and they only wish they'd started several years earlier, when prices and interest rates weren't so far out of sight.

BUDGET SUMMARY

Size of house: approximately 1,800 square feet
Total cost of rehabilitation (interior and exterior): $10,000

INTERIOR
Building materials:

Plaster	$ 50
Drywall	150
Electrical supplies	50
Plumbing supplies	30
2x4 fir studs for framing	100
S4S baseboards	100
Decorative moldings	50
Tile (kitchen counter, living room hearth)	350
	$880
Wallpaper (all rooms)	700
Paint (all rooms)	350
	$1,050

Floors:

Carpet (2 bedrooms, bath)	$ 900
Hardwood (oak) flooring, installed	1,000
	$1,900

Fixtures:

Kitchen sink	$50
Wedgewood gas cook stove	75
Pull-chain toilet	50
Door hardware	30
Franklin fireplace (later replaced)	75
Shutters (living room, one bedroom)	150
Curtain material (all rooms)	100
Brass (stripping and buffing)	80
	$530

EXTERIOR

Back porch—wood	$1,000
Paint	400
Topsoil	200
Plants	300
Fence	400
	$2,300

Miscellaneous: joint compound, paint stripper, wood filler, linseed oil, stain, varnish, sandpaper, wallpaper sizing, nails, razor and paint scrapers, etc.
$3,000

Building permit and inspection fees: $100

RENOVATING A FAMILY HEIRLOOM IN CALIFORNIA

BY RICK STEVENSON

My house, an eclectic Victorian in Sacramento, California, was built by my great-grandfather, a German immigrant, between 1887 and 1890. After his death in 1914, my great-aunt lived in the house. She loved cats and owned many of them, and when she died in 1969, she left the house to the Society for the Prevention of Cruelty to Animals (SPCA). Her will specified that the house was to be used as an animal hospital, and that it was to be maintained "in the Victorian style."

The building was unsuited, according to code and zoning requirements, for an animal hospital, and the SPCA, without consulting my family, gave it to the Baptist church. The church, located adjacent to the house, had unsuccessfully attempted to purchase the house from my great-aunt years earlier.

The church had planned to raze the house and erect senior citizens' quarters . . . then President Nixon vetoed the federal funds that would have financed the new construction. So the church rented out the house. It was not maintained well and gradually deteriorated until 1973, when the church put it on the market.

I became aware that the house was for sale and learned about its dilapidated condition. Convinced that neither the SPCA nor the Baptist church was meeting the provisions of my great-aunt's will, I sued, just before the deadline of the statute of limitations, in my mother's name, greatly surprising her (she was out of town).

Community support for preserving Sacramento's old buildings was just awakening at this time. The city had recently passed an ordinance protecting its significant structures—including my house. And, in 1975, a financial settlement restored title to the house to our family.

I know a lot about my house from my mother's memories and from records, receipts, and notes stuffed into a big, leather trunk that had once been in the house. These, as well as the different construction techniques and materials, indicate that a kitchen and an upstairs bathroom were added to the house between 1908 and 1910. In the 1930s, my great-grandmother broke her hip, and a hand-operated elevator, which still works, was installed for her. Otherwise, the original exterior walls of the house are intact; the old outhouse still stands in the back yard, and has been expanded into a wash house and woodshed.

Since this house is really my greatest heirloom, and since I plan to live in it for a long time, I am doing a thorough, first-class renovation that has taken literally years. Luckily, I have another place to live while the project is being completed. I am hiring professionals to do most of the jobs, but I am working alongside them.

My first renovation task was to take care of the structural problems in the house. The mortar in the brick foundation had crumbled and had to be repaired and repointed. The joists and studs on one side of the house had nearly rotted away, and the only thing holding it together was the siding.

The old mortar in both chimneys had also deteriorated. Instead of repointing it, I installed a chimney flue. This is more expensive, but it protects against chimney fires. (One of my friends recently lost his old house in a chimney fire.) I also had both fireboxes (originally built for coal fires) enlarged and rebuilt to accommodate large wood fires.

With the exception of the septic tank, which is cast iron and in good working condition, I had to replace all the mechanical systems in the house. I completely redid the supply system in the house.

One of the first things to go was the old two-wire 30-ampere service (dated 1927), which was replaced with a 200-ampere service, with each circuit having sufficient amperage to carry any electrical load I could ever dream of putting onto it.

I had intended to preserve all of the old plaster inside the house, and I therefore had the electrical circuits fished inside of the walls and ceilings. Unfortunately, much of the plaster had pulled away from the lath and had to be removed. If I had known this before the electrical work was done, I would have removed the plaster before the wire was run, and the electrical work probably would have cost much less.

There was no way to run modern heating ducting between the floors without adding either a chase along one of the walls or a soffit in the ceiling. Since neither of these options was acceptable, I installed two electric heat pumps: one in the basement to service the first floor; the other in the attic for the second floor.

The unusual decorative shingles and siding were encrusted with many layers of paint, so I had the exterior completely stripped and sanded. The house will be repainted this summer when the wood dries out thoroughly.

Although the structural and mechanical tasks are completed, I still have most of the interior and the finish work to do. The house will have a modern kitchen, complete with microwave oven and dishwasher. I am planning authentic period restorations for other parts of the house, including the original outhouse and the upstairs bathroom. The clawfoot bathtub is still in place. I invested $500 in an embossed, antique toilet bowl that is marked "Sacramento"—a true museum piece that will probably cost an

additional $150 to restore to working condition.

The original light fixtures were stolen from the house before I started work. I purchased a couple of old lights and was lucky enough to buy several boxes of lamp parts from a friend. Old lamps are like tinker toys: it's easy to put together or repair one, or even to convert a gas lamp to electric.

For the rest of the interior I plan to use a lot of reproduction wallpapers. I'll probably install linoleum in the kitchen and replace or renovate the original tongue and groove fir floors in the rest of the house.

One of the things I have discovered during this project is that many so-called "professionals" do poor work, and I insist upon the best. I used three different electricians before I found one that did the job properly. I also hired a highly recommended carpenter to build some cabinets, and I was unhappy with what he produced. So, I purchased a radial arm saw, enrolled in a carpentry class at the local junior college, and am going to make my own cabinets. The result will be what *I* want, and the money I'll save will pay for the saw.

Although I paid well under the market price for the house, I did have to pay the attorneys, and I had no money for a renovation project. I applied for a 312 loan (a low-cost federal rehabilitation program that no longer exists) under the Department of Housing and Urban Development (HUD). I requested $27,000 (the maximum available) and was granted $26,130. At 3 percent per annum for twenty years, my house payment is $188 per month!

Formal approval of the loan took more than two years. Once it went through, the local administrator for HUD kept changing the loan rules: what receipts they would accept for reimbursement, how they would disburse the money, what type of records had to be kept. Inflation was bad, too, and by the time the money came through, many of the bids I had received were out of date, and the work ended up costing thousands more than I had originally planned.

Of course, the HUD loan is not sufficient to cover the entire rehabilitation. I have paid additional thousands of dollars from my pocket for the project, and I recently secured a $10,000 second mortgage to enable me to finish the project. (I had no problem qualifying for the loan, since the house, in its current unfinished state, appraised at $142,000.

Although I have no exact figures, the basic budget for this project is:

Foundation work/dry rot repair	$2,000
Scaffolding rental	1,000
Fireplaces (rebuilding and relining)	1,000
Exterior stripping and sanding	6,500
Electrical	3,500
Plumbing	1,500
Heating and air conditioning	3,500
Bathroom fixtures	1,000
Kitchen fixtures	2,000
Cabinets	1,000
	$23,000

Projected future costs:

Paint exterior	$2,500
Linoleum	700
Sand and finish floors	1,000
Interior walls	7,000
Finish interior (paint, paper, moldings)	5,000
	$16,200

Miscellaneous costs: building permits, supplies, light fixtures, hardware $5,000

Total renovation costs: approximately $44,200

A COUNTRY HOUSE IN ILLINOIS BECOMES A WAY OF LIFE
BY HARRY AND JOAN SAMUELS

My wife, Joanie, and I never really thought we would get involved in old-house renovation. We really love antiques and old houses, and we have several friends who are redoing Victorians in the city. But we're not city people; I want nothing to do with urban pollution, noise, traffic, and crime.

The first time we saw our house was in 1976, when we were coming home from an upstate business trip, driving through this open, lush farmland dotted with mature trees. We saw a "for sale" sign at the end of a large driveway that was flanked by large walnut trees, and, on a whim, we drove up to the house.

Well, it looked like the old haunted house on the hill in a B-grade horror movie. It's made out of stone in the Gothic Revival style, with tall gables and fancy gingerbread, and it was sitting amidst the overgrown remains of a formal garden.

We contacted the selling agent and discovered that the house was involved in a probate controversy, and that it had been vacant for two years. We made an offer; because of the probate, nearly two more years elapsed before the escrow closed.

The house had originally been owned by a wealthy industrial executive, who had it built in 1869 as a summer retreat for his family. It had stayed in the original family until we bought it. One of the heirs showed us scores of old photographs. It had been redecorated many times—especially in the nineteenth century—since I guess the family wanted to add all the newest inventions and fashions. There were pictures of the parlor with four different patterns of wallpaper and types of furnishings—and of the servants standing proudly in front of the new electric range.

Structurally, the house was in good condition, with the exception of an addition in the rear (where a bathroom and service porch had been constructed in about 1892), which had settled considerably. The mortar in the masonry had also deteriorated and needed to be repointed. We decided to hire professionals to do these jobs, since they were major undertakings. The rest of the work we did ourselves. At first, we kept our house in the city, visiting and working on our "country manor" on the weekends.

The electrical system had been updated in 1950 or 1960 to accommodate 240-volt appliances, and all the circuits were run in conduit. We also had the gas convection heater checked, and it was pronounced in good health.

The septic tank and cast-iron waste drain system were in good shape. Last spring, I replaced one of the lines leading from the house to the septic tank. The galvanized supply lines, however, were so badly corroded that there was almost no water pressure. I replaced these with new copper pipes.

The house had its original slate roof, which was in good condition (according to the termite report done as a part of the escrow). There were a few missing tiles that I decided to replace myself. I had never done any roofing before; everyone assured me it was easy. The pitch of the roof was so steep, and I was so timid, that I insisted upon renting a lifeline. Slate tiles can be slippery, and I slipped and sprained my ankle. The lifeline probably saved my life.

Our friends had told us glowing tales of government loans and subsidies that were readily available for old-house renovation. However, by the time that escrow closed on our house, much of these funds had dried up. Also, whereas there were a host of programs, advisors, etc. to help people fix up old houses in the city (under the auspices of urban redevelopment), there is virtually no assistance for the rural dweller.

Although we had hoped for some financial assistance, we had really not counted upon it, and we figured we could purchase materials as we could afford them.

What we had *not* counted upon was Joanie becoming pregnant, which occurred about two months after we bought the house. We were delighted (both our sons are adopted)—but that meant that she would have to leave her job and we could not afford to support two houses.

We loved the country house too much to consider abandoning the project, and ultimately we decided to sell the house in town. Although we would have to live in the country house while we were redoing it, we would be able to get away from the city for good and we could also have some capital funds with which to complete the renovation.

At first, it was fun to live and work in the house. We had picnics amidst the construction, and I enjoyed coming home from work and spending a few hours on the house. The boys, who were twelve and fourteen at the time, loved living and going to school in the country. When the first snows fell, the house looked like a fairy palace, with icicles hanging from the gingerbread.

But, by the middle of winter, the fun and novelty had worn off—and we hit the low point of the project. Although the old gas heater worked, it would only adequately heat a few rooms of the house. One of the fireplaces smoked too badly to use. Our daughter, who was born in December, had to sleep with us to stay warm. We were working on the kitchen at that time, and we had to do all the cooking on a tiny camping stove.

Somehow, we survived the winter, and springtime not only brought sunshine and flowers, but we cleared a major hurdle: we finished the kitchen. When we first started on the house, the kitchen was a 1950s-vintage disaster, decorated in a hideous turquoise, pink, and gray motif. Joanie and I both enjoy cooking, and we wanted a modern fully equipped kitchen—but we wanted it to blend well with the old house.

First, we stripped the turquoise paint from the cabinets. We used chemical remover at the onset but hated it, especially the mess and the noxious fumes (I hadn't moved to the clean air of the country to be asphixiated by wood stripper). I saw an advertisement in the *Old-House Journal* for an electric heat stripping gun and decided to give it a try. It worked great, cost less than chemical removers, and was easy to use (in fact, my sons became so good at wood stripping that they started a summer business working in friends' old houses).

Underneath the paint, the cabinets were plain pine, but, after a lot of sanding and replacing the chrome handles with iron hardware, they gave the kitchen an old, rustic appearance. Several companies manufacture kitchen appliances with removable fronts, and we were able to put matching pine fronts on the refrigerator and dishwasher. We also added an antique pine table, a butcher block island with a hanging pot rack, and a stenciled frieze.

The rear parlor had been converted to a bedroom at about the turn of the century for the son of the original owner, who had lost both his legs in the Spanish-American war and could no longer climb the stairs to his room. We chose to turn this room into a study. We stripped the paint from the woodwork and added bookshelves. For this, I built simple cabinets and embellished them with moldings that matched the door and window casings.

One large expense that we had not anticipated was a milling charge to replace some of the exterior window casings, which had fallen off the house while it stood vacant.

Before the next winter came, we had the smoking fireplace rebuilt and added perimeter, closed water heating systems to several of the rooms. These were easy for Joanie and me to install, are energy efficient, and keep us toasty warm during the cold months.

Most of the plaster in the house was intact, except in the back of the house where the structural work and plumbing were done. None of the original light fixtures remained; we found replacements at antiques stores.

One of our friends is an interior decorator who specializes in old houses, and she showed us some reproduction wallpapers and fabrics. They were so beautiful that we had to have them, even though they more than doubled our interior decoration budget.

In retrospect, the only mistake I believe I made on the house was to sand the hardwood floors myself. I saved a lot of money; renting the drum sander cost only $100; having the floors sanded would have cost about $900. However, although most people do not notice, I can detect marks on the floor that were left by the sander.

We finished the house last spring (1981), and we are now tackling and attempting to restore the old garden. Many of the plants are rare specimens that we had never heard of. We're going to restore the flower beds, the walks that wind through the grounds, and the gazebo that is now just a pile of rotted boards.

The entire project to date has cost about $23,000. which can be roughly divided as follows:

Structural repair	$3,000
Repointing masonry	5,000
Plumbing	
New supply lines	1,000
New waste line to septic tank	200
Rebuild fireplace	500
Add new heating (perimeter water system)	1,500
Repair exterior trim (milling charge)	900
Light fixtures	1,100
Pull-chain toilet for bathroom	500
Paint	500
Wallpaper and curtains	6,000
Cabinets for study (wood and moldings)	1,100
Miscellaneous	2,000
	$23,300

THE SECRETARY OF THE INTERIOR'S

Standards For Rehabilitation

AND GUIDELINES FOR REHABILITATING
HISTORIC BUILDINGS

The material in this appendix has been reprinted from The Secretary of the Interior's Standards for Rehabilitation and Guidelines for Rehabilitating Historic Buildings, *published by the National Park Service, U.S. Department of the Interior (1980).*

The Standards for Rehabilitation *contains the criteria that the federal government uses to determine if rehabilitations qualify for loans, grants, and tax advantages (see Chapters 32 and 34). Many local preservation agencies, advocacy groups, and even renovation "how-to" manuals have incorporated these standards, and they are generally highly regarded.*

The standards are currently undergoing a major revision, which should be completed before the end of 1982, although scarce federal funds may preclude publication of the revised standards. In the new version, the ten goals for rehabilitation will remain intact; the specific guidelines that follow are being expanded.

The current edition of the standards is available in limited quantities from the State Historic Preservation Officers (see Appendix C).

STANDARDS FOR REHABILITATION

Rehabilitation means the process of returning a property to a state of utility, through repair or alteration, which makes possible an efficient contemporary use while preserving those portions and features of the property which are significant to its historic, architectural, and cultural values.

The following "Standards for Rehabilitation" shall be used by the Secretary of the Interior when determining if a rehabilitation project qualifies as "certified rehabilitation" pursuant to the Tax Reform Act of 1976 and the Revenue Act of 1978. These standards are a section of the Secretary's "Standards for Historic Preservation Projects" and appear in Title 36 of the Code of Federal Regulations, Part 67.

1. Every reasonable effort shall be made to provide a compatible use for a property which requires minimal alteration of the building, structure, or site and its environment, or to use a property for its originally intended purpose.
2. The distinguishing original qualities or character of a building, structure, or site and its environment shall not be destroyed. The removal or alteration of any historic material or distinctive architectural features should be avoided when possible.
3. All buildings, structures, and sites shall be recognized as products of their own time. Alterations that have no historical basis and which seek to create an earlier appearance shall be discouraged.
4. Changes which may have taken place in the course of time are evidence of the history and development of a building, structure, or site and its environment. These changes may have acquired significance in their own right, and this significance shall be recognized and respected.
5. Distinctive stylistic features or examples of skilled craftsmanship which characterize a building, structure, or site shall be treated with sensitivity.
6. Deteriorated architectural features shall be repaired rather than replaced, wherever possible. In the event replacement is necessary, the new material should match the material being replaced in composition, design, color, texture, and other visual qualities. Repair or replacement of missing architectural features should be based on accurate duplications of features, substantiated by historic, physical, or pictorial evidence rather than on conjectural designs or the availability of different architectural elements from other buildings or structures.
7. The surface cleaning of structures shall be undertaken with the gentlest means possible. Sandblasting and other cleaning methods that will damage the historic building materials shall not be undertaken.
8. Every reasonable effort shall be made to protect and preserve archeological resources affected by, or adjacent to any project.
9. Contemporary design for alterations and additions to existing properties shall not be discouraged when such alterations and additions do not destroy significant historical, architectural or cultural material, and such design is compatible with the size, scale, color, material, and character of the property, neighborhood or environment.
10. Wherever possible, new additions or alterations to structures shall be done in such a manner that if such additions or alterations were to be removed in the future, the essential form and integrity of the structure would be unimpaired.

GUIDELINES FOR APPLYING THE STANDARDS FOR REHABILITATION

The following guidelines are designed to help individual property owners formulate plans for the rehabilitation, preservation, and continued use of historic buildings consistent with the intent of the Secretary of the Interior's "Standards for Rehabilitation." The guidelines pertain to buildings of all occupancy and construction types, sizes, and materials. They apply to permanent and temporary construction on the exterior and interior of historic buildings as well as new attached or adjacent construction.

Techniques, treatments, and methods consistent with the Secretary's "Standards for Rehabilitation" are listed [under] "recommended".... Not all recommendations listed under a treatment will apply to each project proposal. Rehabilitation approaches, materials, and methods which may adversely affect a building's architectural and historic qualities are listed [under] "not recommended".... Every effort will be made to update and expand the guidelines as additional techniques and treatments become known.

Specific information on rehabilitation and preservation technology may be obtained by writing to the Technical Preservation Services Division, Heritage Conservation and Recreation Service, U.S. Department of the Interior, Washington, D.C. 20243, or the appropriate State Historic Preservation Officer. Advice should also be sought from qualified professionals, including architects, architectural historians, and archeologists skilled in the preservation, restoration, and rehabilitation of old buildings.

THE ENVIRONMENT

RECOMMENDED
● Retaining distinctive features such as the size, scale, mass, color, and materials of buildings, including roofs, porches, and stairways that give a neighborhood its distinguishing character.
● Retaining landscape features such as parks, gardens, street lights, signs, benches, walkways, streets, alleys and building setbacks that have traditionally linked buildings to their environment.
● Using new plant materials, fencing, walkways, street lights, signs, and benches that are compatible with the character of the neighborhood in size, scale, material and color.

NOT RECOMMENDED
● Introducing new construction into neighborhoods that is incompatible with the character of the district because of size, scale, color, and materials.
● Destroying the relationship of buildings and their environment by widening existing streets, changing paving material, or by introducing inappropriately located new streets and parking lots that are incompatible with the character of the neighborhood.
● Introducing signs, street lighting, benches, new plant materials, fencing,

walkways and paving materials that are out of scale or are inappropriate to the neighborhood.

BUILDING SITE

RECOMMENDED
● Identifying plants, trees, fencing, walkways, outbuildings, and other elements that might be an important part of the property's history and development.
● Retaining plants, trees, fencing, walkways, street lights, signs, and benches that reflect the property's history and development.
● Basing decisions for new site work on actual knowledge of the past appearance of the property found in photographs, drawings, newspapers, and tax records. If changes are made they should be carefully evaluated in light of the past appearance of the site.
● Providing proper site and roof drainage to assure that water does not splash against building or foundation walls, nor drain toward the building.

NOT RECOMMENDED
● Making changes to the appearance of the site by removing old plants, trees, fencing, walkways, outbuildings, and other elements before evaluating their importance in the property's history and development.
● Leaving plant materials and trees in close proximity to the building that may be causing deterioration of the historic fabric.

ARCHEOLOGICAL FEATURES

RECOMMENDED
● Leaving known archeological resources intact.
● Minimizing disturbance of terrain around the structure, thus reducing the possibility of destroying unknown archeological resources.
● Arranging for an archeological survey of all terrain that must be disturbed during the rehabilitation program. The survey should be conducted by a professional archeologist.

NOT RECOMMENDED
● Installing underground utilities, pavements, and other modern features that disturb archeological resources.
● Introducing heavy machinery or equipment into areas where their presence may disturb archeological resources.

BUILDING: STRUCTURAL SYSTEMS

RECOMMENDED
● Recognizing the special problems inherent in the structural systems of historic buildings, especially where there are visible signs of cracking, deflection, or failure.
● Undertaking stabilization and repair of weakened structural members and systems.
● Utilizing early mechanical systems, including plumbing and early lighting fixtures, where possible.

NOT RECOMMENDED
● Disturbing existing foundations with new excavations that undermine the structural stability of the building.
● Leaving known structural problems untreated that will cause continuing deterioration and will shorten the life of the structure.

BUILDING: EXTERIOR FEATURES

RECOMMENDED*
● Retaining original masonry and mortar, whenever possible, without the application of any surface treatment.
● Repointing only those mortar joints where there is evidence of moisture problems or when sufficient mortar is missing to allow water to stand in the mortar joint.
● Duplicating old mortar in composition, color, and texture.
● Duplicating old mortar in joint size, method of application, and joint profile.
● Repairing stucco with a stucco mixture that duplicates the original as closely as possible in appearance and texture.
● Cleaning masonry only when necessary to halt deterioration or to remove graffiti and stains and always with the gentlest method possible, such as low pressure water and soft natural bristle brushes.
● Repairing or replacing where necessary deteriorated material with new material that duplicates the old as closely as possible.

*For more information consult Preservation Briefs 1: "The Cleaning and Waterproof Coating of Masonry Buildings" and Preservation Briefs 2: "Repointing Mortar Joints in Historic Brick Buildings" (Washington, D.C.: Heritage Conservation and Recreation Service, 1975 and 1976). Both are available from the Government Printing Office or State Historic Preservation Officers.

- Replacing missing significant architectural features, such as cornices, brackets, railings, and shutters.
- Retaining the original or early color and texture of masonry surfaces, including early signage wherever possible. Brick or stone surfaces may have been painted or whitewashed for practical and aesthetic reasons.

NOT RECOMMENDED

- Applying waterproof or water repellent coatings or surface consolidation treatments unless required to solve a specific technical problem that has been studied and identified. Coatings are frequently unnecessary, expensive, and can accelerate deterioration of the masonry.
- Repointing mortar joints that do not need repointing. Using electric saws and hammers to remove mortar can seriously damage the adjacent brick.
- Repointing with mortar of high Portland cement content can often create a bond that is stronger than the building material. This can cause deterioration as a result of the differing coefficient of expansion and the differing porosity of the material and the mortar.
- Repointing with mortar joints of a differing size or joint profile, texture or color.
- Sandblasting, including dry and wet grit and other abrasives, brick or stone surfaces; this method of cleaning erodes the surface of the material and accelerates deterioration. Using chemical cleaning products that would have an adverse chemical reaction with the masonry materials, i.e., acid on limestone or marble.
- Applying new material which is inappropriate or was unavailable when the building was constructed, such as artificial brick siding, artificial cast stone or brick veneer.
- Removing architectural features such as cornices, brackets, railings, shutters, window architraves, and doorway pediments.
- Removing paint from masonry surfaces indiscriminately. This may subject the building to damage and change its appearance.

WOOD:
Clapboard, weatherboard, shingles and other wooden siding

RECOMMENDED

- Retaining and preserving significant architectural features, wherever possible.
- Repairing or replacing, where necessary, deteriorated material that duplicates in size, shape, and texture the old as closely as possible.

NOT RECOMMENDED

- Removing architectural features such as siding, cornices, brackets, window architraves, and doorway pediments. These are, in most cases, an essential part of a building's character and appearance that illustrate the continuity of growth and change.
- Resurfacing frame buildings with new material that is inappropriate or was unavailable when the building was constructed such as artificial stone, brick veneer, asbestos or asphalt shingles, and plastic or aluminum siding. Such material can also contribute to the deterioration of the structure from moisture and insects.

ARCHITECTURAL METALS:
Cast iron, steel, pressed tin, aluminum and zinc

RECOMMENDED

- Retaining original material, whenever possible.
- Cleaning when necessary with the appropriate method. Metals should be cleaned by methods that do not abrade the surface.

NOT RECOMMENDED

- Removing architectural features that are an essential part of a building's character and appearance, illustrating the continuity of growth and change.
- Exposing metals which were intended to be protected from the environment. Do not use cleaning methods which alter the color, texture, and tone of the metal.

ROOFS AND ROOFING

RECOMMENDED

- Preserving the original roof shape.
- Retaining the original roofing material, whenever possible.
- Providing adequate roof drainage and insuring that the roofing materials provide a weathertight covering for the structure.
- Replacing deteriorated roof coverings with new material that matches the old in composition, size, shape, color, and texture.
- Preserving or replacing where necessary, all architectural features that give the roof its essential character, such as dormer windows, cupolas, cornices, brackets, chimneys, cresting, and weather vanes.

NOT RECOMMENDED

- Changing the essential character of the roof by adding inappropriate features such as dormer windows, vents, or skylights.
- Applying new roofing material that is inappropriate to the style and period of the building and neighborhood.
- Replacing deteriorated roof coverings with new materials that differ to such an extent from the old in composition, size, shape, color, and texture that the appearance of the building is altered.
- Stripping the roof of architectural features important to its character.

WINDOWS AND DOORS

RECOMMENDED

- Retaining and repairing window and door openings, frames, sash, glass, doors, lintels, sills, pediments, architraves, hardware, awnings and shutters where they contribute to the architectural and historic character of the building.
- Improving the thermal performance of existing windows and doors through adding or replacing weather-stripping and adding storm windows and doors which are compatible with the character of the building and which do not damage window or door frames.
- Replacing missing or irreparable windows on significant facades with new windows that match the original in material, size, general muntin and mullion proportion and configuration, and reflective qualities of the glass.

NOT RECOMMENDED

- Introducing or changing the location or size of windows, doors, and other openings that alter the architectural and historic character of the building.
- Replacing window and door features on significant facades with historically and architecturally incompatible materials such as anodized aluminum, mirrored or tinted glass.
- Removing window and door features that can be repaired where such features contribute to the historic and architectural character of the building.
- Changing the size or arrangement of window panes, muntins, and rails

where they contribute to the architectural and historic character of the building.

● Installing on significant facades shutters, screens, blinds, security grills, and awnings which are historically inappropriate and which detract from the character of the building.

● Installing new exterior storm windows and doors which are inappropriate in size or color, which are inoperable, or which require removal of original windows and doors.

● Installing interior storm windows that allow moisture to accumulate and damage the window.

● Replacing sash which contribute to the character of a building with those that are incompatible in size, configuration, and reflective qualities or which alter the setback relationship between window and wall.

● Installing heating/air conditioning units in the window frames when the sash and frames may be damaged. Window installations should be considered only when all other viable heating/cooling systems would result in significant damage to historic materials.

STOREFRONTS

RECOMMENDED

● Retaining and repairing existing storefronts including windows, sash, doors, transoms, signage, and decorative features where such features contribute to the architectural and historic character of the building.

● Where original or early storefronts no longer exist or are too deteriorated to save, retaining the commercial character of the building through 1) contemporary design which is compatible with the scale, design, materials, color, and texture of the historic buildings; or 2) an accurate restoration of the storefront based on historical research and physical evidence.

NOT RECOMMENDED

● Introducing a storefront or new design element on the ground floor, such as an arcade, which alters the architectural and historic character of the building and its relationship with the street or its setting or which causes destruction of significant historic fabric.

● Using materials which detract from the historic or architectural character of the building, such as mirrored glass.

● Altering the entrance through a significant storefront.

ENTRANCES, PORCHES, AND STEPS

RECOMMENDED

● Retaining porches and steps that are appropriate to the building and its development. Porches or additions reflecting later architectural styles are often important to the building's historical integrity and, wherever possible, should be retained.

● Repairing or replacing, where necessary deteriorated architectural features of wood, iron, cast iron, terra cotta, tile, and brick.

NOT RECOMMENDED

● Removing or altering porches and steps that are appropriate to the building's development and style.

● Stripping porches and steps or original material and architectural features, such as hand rails, balusters, columns, brackets, and roof decoration of wood, iron, cast iron, terra cotta, tile and brick.

● Enclosing porches and steps in a manner that destroys their intended appearance.

EXTERIOR FINISHES

RECOMMENDED

● Discovering the historic paint colors and finishes of the structure and repainting with those colors to illustrate the distinctive character of the property.

NOT RECOMMENDED

● Removing paint and finishes down to the bare surface; strong paint strippers whether chemical or mechanical can permanently damage the surface. Also, stripping obliterates evidence of the historical paint finishes.

● Repainting with colors that cannot be documented through research and investigation to be appropriate to the building and neighborhood.

BUILDING: INTERIOR FEATURES

RECOMMENDED

● Retaining original material, architectural features, and hardware, whenever possible, such as stairs, elevators, hand rails, balusters, ornamental columns, cornices, baseboards, doors, doorways, windows, mantelpieces, paneling, lighting fixtures, parquet or mosaic flooring.

● Repairing or replacing, where necessary, deteriorated material with new material that duplicates the old as closely as possible.

● Retaining original plaster, whenever possible.

● Discovering and retaining original paint colors, wallpapers and other decorative motifs or, where necessary, replacing them with colors, wallpapers or decorative motifs based on the original.

● Where required by code, enclosing an important interior stairway in such a way as to retain its character. In many cases glazed fire-rated walls may be used.

● Retaining the basic plan of a building, the relationship and size of rooms, corridors, and other spaces.

NOT RECOMMENDED

● Removing original material, architectural features, and hardware, except where essential for safety or efficiency.

● Replacing interior doors and transoms without investigating alternative fire protection measures or possible code variances.

● Installing new decorative material and paneling which destroys significant architectural features or was unavailable when the building was constructed, such as vinyl plastic or imitation wood wall and floor coverings, except in utility areas such as bathrooms and kitchens.

● Removing plaster to expose brick to give the wall an appearance it never had.

● Changing the texture and patina of exposed wooden architectural features (including structural members) and masonry surfaces through sandblasting or use of other abrasive techniques to remove paint, discoloration and plaster, except in certain industrial or warehouse buildings where the interior masonry or plaster surfaces do not have significant design, detailing, tooling, or finish; and where wooden architectural features are not finished, molded, beaded, or worked by hand.

● Enclosing important stairways with ordinary fire-rated construction which destroys the architectural character of the stair and the space.

● Altering the basic plan of a building by demolishing principal walls, partitions, and stairways.

NEW CONSTRUCTION

RECOMMENDED

- Keeping new additions and adjacent new construction to a minimum, making them compatible in scale, building materials, and texture.
- Designing new work to be compatible in materials, size, color, and texture with the earlier building and the neighborhood.
- Using contemporary designs compatible with the character and mood of the building or the neighborhood.
- Protecting architectural details and features that contribute to the character of the building.
- Placing television antennae and mechanical equipment, such as air conditioners, in an inconspicuous location.

NOT RECOMMENDED

- Designing new work which is incompatible with the earlier building and the neighborhood in materials, size, scale, and texture.
- Imitating an earlier style or period of architecture in new additions, except in rare cases where a contemporary design would detract from the architectural unity of an ensemble or group. Especially avoid imitating an earlier style of architecture in new additions that have a completely contemporary function such as a drive-in bank or garage.
- Adding new height to the building that changes the scale and character of the building. Additions in height should not be visible when viewing the principal facades.
- Adding new floors or removing existing floors that destroy important architectural details, features and spaces of the building.
- Placing television antennae and mechanical equipment, such as air conditioners, where they can be seen from the street.

MECHANICAL SYSTEMS

HEATING, AIR CONDITIONING, ELECTRICAL, PLUMBING, FIRE PROTECTION

RECOMMENDED

- Installing necessary mechanical systems in areas and spaces that will require the least possible alteration to the structural integrity and physical appearance of the building.
- Utilizing early mechanical systems, including plumbing and early lighting fixtures, where possible.
- Installing the vertical runs of ducts, pipes, and cables in closets, service rooms, and wall cavities.
- Insuring adequate ventilation of attics, crawlspaces, and cellars to prevent moisture problems.
- Installing thermal insulation in attics and in unheated cellars and crawlspaces to conserve energy.

NOT RECOMMENDED

- Causing unnecessary damage to the plan, materials, and appearance of the building when installing mechanical systems.
- Attaching exterior electrical and telephone cables to the principal elevations of the building.
- Installing vertical runs of ducts, pipes, and cables in places where they will be a visual intrusion.
- Concealing or "making invisible" mechanical equipment in historic walls or ceilings. Frequently this concealment requires the removal of historic fabric.
- Installing "dropped" acoustical ceilings to hide mechanical equipment. This destroys the proportions and character of the rooms.
- Installing foam, glass fiber, or cellulose insulation into wall cavities of either wooden or masonry construction. This has been found to cause moisture problems when there is no adequate moisture barrier.

SAFETY AND CODE REQUIREMENTS

RECOMMENDED

- Complying with code requirements in such a manner that the essential character of a building is preserved intact.
- Working with local code officials to investigate alternative life safety measures that preserve the architectural integrity of the building.
- Investigating variances for historic properties allowed under some local codes.
- Installing adequate fire prevention equipment in a manner that does minimal damage to the appearance or fabric of a property.
- Adding new stairways and elevators that do not alter existing exit facilities or other important architectural features and spaces of the building.

NOT RECOMMENDED

- Adding new stairways and elevators that alter existing exit facilities or important architectural features and spaces of the building.

Resources

Following is a list of major nationwide organizations and publications in the area of historic preservation. It is in no way intended to be exhaustive. There are literally hundreds of regional organizations, and these groups are growing as fast as the burgeoning preservation movement. Many of these local organizations are excellent sources of information, especially about policies, programs, and events in your particular area. Check them out!

NATIONAL ADVOCACY ORGANIZATIONS

ADVISORY COUNCIL ON
HISTORIC PRESERVATION
1522 K Street NW
Washington, D.C. 20005

AMERICA THE BEAUTIFUL FUND
219 Shoreham Bldg. NW
Washington, D.C. 20005

AMERICAN ASSOCIATION
OF STATE AND LOCAL HISTORY
1400 Eighth Avenue S.
Nashville, TN 37203

AMERICAN INSTITUTE
OF ARCHITECTS COMMITTEE
ON HISTORIC RESOURCES
1735 New York Avenue NW
Washington, D.C. 20006

ASSOCIATION FOR
PRESERVATION TECHNOLOGY
P.O. Box 2487, Station D
Ottawa, Ontario, KIP 5W6, Canada

ATHENAEUM OF PHILADELPHIA
219 South Sixth Street
Philadelphia, PA 19106

BROWNSTONE REVIVAL
COMMITTEE
230 Park Avenue
New York, NY 10017

CONSERVATION FOUNDATION
717 Massachusetts Avenue NW
Washington, D.C. 20036

DIRECTOR,
NATIONAL PARK SERVICE
U.S. Department of the Interior
Washington, D.C. 20240

MUSEUM
FOR THE BUILDING ARTS
The Pension Building
440 G Street NW
Washington, D.C. 20243

NATIONAL ASSOCIATION
OF HOUSING AND
REDEVELOPMENT OFFICIALS
2600 Virginia Avenue NW
Washington, D.C. 20037

NATIONAL ASSOCIATION OF
STATE HISTORIC
PRESERVATION OFFICERS
Suite 500, 1522 K Street NW
Washington, D.C. 20005

NATIONAL CENTER
FOR PRESERVATION LAW
2101 L Street NW
Washington, D.C. 20036

NATIONAL COUNCIL
FOR PRESERVATION EDUCATION
Middle Tennessee University
Murfreesboro, TN 37132

NATIONAL PARKS AND
CONSERVATION ASSOCIATION
1701 Eighteenth Street NW
Washington, D.C. 20009

NATIONAL TRUST
FOR HISTORIC PRESERVATION
748 Jackson Place NW
Washington, D.C. 20006
*(NATIONAL HEADQUARTERS
AND MID-ATLANTIC FIELD OFFICE)*

Midwest Regional Office
407 South Dearborn Street, Suite 710
Chicago, IL 60605

New England Field Service Office
141 Cambridge Street
Boston, MA 02114

Southern Field Office
456 King Street
Charleston, SC 29403

Southwest/Plains Field Office
903 Colcord Building
Oklahoma City, OK 73102

Western Regional Office
681 Market Street, Suite 859
San Francisco, CA 94105

PRESERVATION ACTION
1914 Sunderland Place NW
Washington, D.C. 20006

PRESERVATION LAW
2101 L Street NW
Washington, D.C. 20037

PRESERVATION
RESOURCE CENTER
Lake Shore Road
Essex, NY 12936

SOCIETY FOR
ARCHITECTURAL HISTORIANS
1700 Walnut Street, Suite 716
Philadelphia, PA 19103

SOCIETY FOR THE STUDY
OF ARCHITECTURE IN CANADA
P.O. Box 2935, Station D
Ottawa K1P 5W9, Canada

VICTORIAN SOCIETY IN AMERICA
219 South Sixth Street
Philadelphia, PA 19106

BOOKS AND PAMPHLETS

THE AMERICAN ASSOCIATION FOR STATE AND LOCAL HISTORY
AASLH is a major publisher of professional literature for local historians and historical organizations. For a copy of their catalog, write:

Catalog Order Department
American Association for
   State and Local History
1400 Eighth Avenue S
Nashville, TN 37203

THE ATHENAEUM OF PHILADELPHIA
The Athenaeum has published over a dozen books on historic architecture and culture. For a list of these, write:

The Athenaeum of Philadelphia
219 South Sixth Street
Philadelphia, PA 19106

NATIONAL TRUST FOR HISTORIC PRESERVATION
Publishes books and pamphlets under the auspices of the Preservation Press.

U.S. GOVERNMENT
One of the best sources of information on old-house renovation are documents printed by the U.S. government. The government publishes literally millions of books and leaflets. Unfortunately, due to cutbacks, there is no centralized bibliography. To obtain a list of publications, you must contact each individual government department. Those that publish information about old houses include:

Department of Agriculture
Department of Housing and Urban
   Development
National Park Service (including
   Technical Preservation Services)
Department of Commerce

SOURCES OF OLD-HOUSE PARTS

ANTIQUE HARDWARE COMPANY
P.O. Box 1592
Torrance, CA 90505

DECORATOR HARDWARE COMPANY
2760 North Highway 1
Fort Lauderdale, FL 33306

DRIWOOD MOULDING COMPANY
P.O. Box 1729, Dept. VH
Florence, SC 29503

THE EMPORIUM
2515 Morse Street
Houston, TX 77019

HALLELUJAH REDWOOD PRODUCTS
P.O. Box 669
Mendocino, CA 95460

MAC THE ANTIQUE PLUMBER
885 Fifty-seventh Street
Sacramento, CA 95819

OLD HOUSE CATALOG
Warner Books, Inc.
75 Rockefeller Plaza
New York, NY 10019

THE OLD-HOUSE JOURNAL CATALOG
(published annually)
The Old-House Journal Corporation
69A Seventh Avenue
Brooklyn, NY 11217

THE RENOVATOR'S SUPPLY
71A Northfield Road
Millers Falls, MA 01349

RESTORATION HARDWARE
438 Second Street
Eureka, CA 95501

SAN FRANCISCO VICTORIANA
606 Natoma Street
San Francisco, CA 94103

HOW-TO BOOKS

There are thousands of how-to books on the market; I believe the following to be among the best.

CARPENTRY AND BUILDING CONSTRUCTION
Wagner, Willis H. *Modern Carpentry.*
   (Illinois: Goodhart-Willcox Company,
   1976).

INTERIOR DESIGN
Faulkner, Ray and Sarah. *Inside Today's
   Home.* (New York: Holt, Rinehart,
   and Winston 1973).

INTERIOR FURNISHINGS
Seale, William E. *The Tasteful Inter-
   lude: American Interiors Through
   The Camera's Eye, 1860-1917.* (New
   York: Praeger Press, 1975).

PLASTERING
Van Den Branden, F. and Hartsell,
   Thomas. *Plastering Skill and Practice.*
   (Illinois: American Technical Society,
   1971).

TILING
Brann, Donald R. *How to Lay Ceramic
   Tile.* (New York: Directions Simpli-
   fied, 1975).

WIRING
Richter, H. P. *Wiring Simplified.*
   (Minnesota: Park Publishing, 1980).

WOOD FINISHING
Scharff, Robert. *The Complete Book of
   Wood Finishing.* (New York:
   McGraw-Hill, 1974).

NEWSLETTERS

Communique Newsletter of the Association for Preservation Technology
(APT). Published bimonthly, it lists
recent publications and articles, reviews
books, and announces preservation
happenings. APT, P.O. Box 2156,
Albuquerque, NM 87103.

Preservation News The monthly news-
letter of the National Trust for Historic
Preservation, 748 Jackson Place NW,
Washington, D.C. 20006.

VSA Bulletin A bimonthly newsletter
published by the Victorian Society in
America, 219 South Sixth Street,
Philadelphia, PA 19106.

History News Published monthly by
the American Association for State
and Local History, 1400 Eighth Avenue
S, Nashville, TN 37203.

OTHER PERIODICALS

Americana Published monthly by the
American Heritage Publishing Co.,
1221 Avenue of the Americas, New
York, NY 10020.

American Preservation Published bimonthly. Bracy House, 620 East Sixth,
P.O. Box 2451, Little Rock, AR
72203.

APT Bulletin Published quarterly for
Canadian-American preservationists by
the Association for Preservation Technology (APT), P.O. Box 2487, Station
D., Ottawa, Ontario K1P 5W6, Canada.

Nineteenth Century Published by the Victorian Society in America, 219 South Sixth Street, Philadelphia, PA 19106, this magazine contains feature articles concerning Victorian-era life and culture.

Old-House Journal Published monthly by the Old-House Journal Corporation, 69A Seventh Avenue, Brooklyn, NY 11217. A must for old-home aficionados. Loads of valuable historical information, tips, how-to features, and true-life experiences of single-family dwelling renovators.

Technology and Conservation This magazine is published by the Technology Organization, Inc., 1 Emerson Place, Boston, MA 02114. It is less technical than the *APT Bulletin*, but it devotes as much space to art and antiquities as it does to architecture.

Victorian Homes Published quarterly by Renovators' Supply, Inc., P.O. Fox 61, Millers Falls, MA 01349.

STATE HISTORIC PRESERVATION OFFICERS AND DEPUTY SHPOS

ALABAMA
Mr. F. Lawrence Oaks, Director
Alabama Department of Archives and History
Archives and History Building
Montgomery, AL 36104
(205) 832-6510

ALASKA
Mr. Ty L. Dilipane, SHPO
Division of Parks
Office of History and Archeology
619 Warehouse Avenue, Suite 210
Anchorage, AK 99501
(907) 274-4676

AMERICAN SAMOA
Mr. Avemaia I. A'asa
Territorial Historic Preservation Officer
Department of Public Works
Government of American Samoa
Pago Pago, American Samoa 96799

ARIZONA
Ms. Ann A. Pritzlaff, SHPO
Arizona State Parks
1688 West Adams
Phoenix, AZ 85007
(602) 255-4174

ARKANSAS
Mr. Wilson Stiles, SHPO
Arkansas Historic Preservation Program
Suite 500, Continental Building
Markham and Main streets
Little Rock, AR 72201
(501) 371-2763
DEPUTY: Barbara W. Heffington

CALIFORNIA
Dr. Knox Mellon, Director
Office of Historic Preservation
Department of Parks and Recreation
P.O. Box 2390
1220 K Street
Sacramento, CA 95811
(916) 445-8006
DEPUTY: Marion Mitchell-Wilson
(916) 322-8596

COLORADO
Mr. Arthur C. Townsend, SHPO
Colorado Historical Society
1300 Broadway
Denver, CO 80203
(303) 866-3391
DEPUTY: James E. Hartmann
(303) 866-3395

CONNECTICUT
Mr. John W. Shannahan, Director
Connecticut Historical Commission
59 South Prospect Street
Hartford, CT 06106
(203) 566-3005
DEPUTY: Clark J. Strickland

DELAWARE
Mr. Lawrence C. Henry, Director
Division of Historical and Cultural Affairs
Hall of Records
Dover, DE 19901
(302) 736-5314
DEPUTY: Daniel R. Griffith
(302) 736-5685

DISTRICT OF COLUMBIA
Mr. Robert L. Moore, Director
Department of Housing and Community Development
1133 North Capital Street, NE
Washington, D.C. 20002
(202) 535-1500

FLORIDA
Mr. L. Ross Morrell, Director
Division of Archives, History and Records Management
Department of State
The Capitol
Tallahassee, FL 32301
(904) 488-1480
DEPUTY: George W. Percy

GEORGIA
Dr. Elizabeth A. Lyon, Chief
Historic Preservation Section
Department of Natural Resources, Rm. 701
270 Washington Street, SW
Atlanta, GA 30334
(404) 656-2840
DEPUTY: Carole Griffith

GUAM
Mr. Joseph F. Soriano, Director
Department of Parks and Recreation
Government of Guam
P.O. Box 2950
Agana, Guam 96910
(Overseas Operator) 477-9620/21 ext. 4

HAWAII
Mr. Susumu Ono, SHPO
Department of Land and Natural Resources
P.O. Box 621
Honolulu, HI 96809
(808) 548-6550
DEPUTY: Ralston H. Nagata
(808) 548-7460

IDAHO
Dr. Merle W. Wells, SHPO
Idaho Historical Society
610 North Julia Davis Drive
Boise, ID 83702
(208) 334-3356
DEPUTY: Arthur A. Hart
(208) 334-2120

ILLINOIS
Dr. David Kenney, Director
Department of Conservation
602 Stratton Building
Springfield, IL 62706
(217) 782-6302
DEPUTY: William G. Farrar
Division of Historic Sites
405 East Washington Street
Springfield, IL 62706
(217) 782-1773

INDIANA
Mr. James M. Ridenour, Director
Department of Natural Resources
608 State Office Building
Indianapolis, IN 46204
(317) 232-4020
DEPUTY: Richard A. Gantz
Division of Historic Preservation
202 North Alabama Street
Indianapolis, IN 46204
(317) 232-1646

IOWA
Mr. Adrian Anderson, Director
Iowa State Historical Department
Divison of Historic Preservation
26 East Market Street
Iowa City, IA 52240
(319) 353-4186 or 353-6949
DEPUTY: R. Stanley Riggle

KANSAS
Mr. Joseph W. Snell, Executive Director
Kansas State Historical Society
120 West Tenth
Topeka, KS 66612
(913) 296-3251
DEPUTY: Richard D. Pankratz
(913) 296-4788

KENTUCKY
Ms. Mary Optel, SHPO
Department of the Arts
22 Capital Plaza Tower
Frankfort, KY 40601
(502) 564-6683

LOUISIANA
Mr. Robert B. DeBlieux, Asst. Secretary
Office of Program Development
P.O. Box 44247
Baton Rouge, LA 70804
(504) 925-3880
DEPUTY: Ann Jones
(504) 342-6682

MAINE
Mr. Earle G. Shettleworth, Jr., Director
Maine Historic Preservation Commission
242 State Street
Augusta, ME 04333
(207) 289-2133
DEPUTY: Robert J. Bradley

MARYLAND
Mr. J. Rodney Little, Director
Maryland Historical Trust
John Shaw House
21 State Circle
Annapolis, MD 21401
(301) 269-2851
DEPUTY: Nancy Miller
(301) 269-2438

MASSACHUSETTS
Ms. Patricia L. Weslowski, SHPO
Massachusetts Historical Commission
294 Washington Street
Boston, MA 02108
(617) 727-8470
DEPUTY: Valerie Talmage

MICHIGAN
Dr. Martha Bigelow, Director
Michigan History Division
Department of State
208 North Capitol
Lansing, MI 48918
(517) 373-6362
DEPUTY: Kathryn Eckert

MINNESOTA
Mr. Russell W. Fridley, Director
Minnesota Historical Society
690 Cedar Street
St. Paul, MN 55101
(612) 296-2747
DEPUTY: Nina Archabal

MISSISSIPPI
Mr. Elbert Hilliard, Director
State of Mississippi Department
    of Archives and History
P.O. Box 571
Jackson, MS 39205
(601) 354-6218
DEPUTY: Robert J. Bailey
(601) 354-7326

MISSOURI
Mr. Fred A. Lafser, Director
State Department of Natural Resources
1014 Madison Street
Jefferson City, MO 65102
(314) 751-4422
DEPUTY: Orval L. Henderson, Jr.
1001 Southwest Boulevard
P.O. Box 176
Jefferson City, MO 65102
(314) 751-4096

MONTANA
Dr. Robert Archibald, Director
Montana Historical Society
225 North Roberts Street
Veterans Memorial Building
Helena, MT 59601
(406) 449-2694
DEPUTY: Marcella Sherfy
(406) 449-4585

NEBRASKA
Mr. Marvin F. Kivett, Director
Nebraska State Historical Society
1500 R Street
Lincoln, NB 68508
(402) 471-3270
DEPUTY: William F. Munn

NEVADA
Ms. Mimi Rodden, SHPO
Division of Historic Preservation
    and Archeology
Department of Conservation and
    Natural Resources

Nye Building, Rm. 113
201 South Fall Street
Carson City, NV 89710
(702) 885-5138
DEPUTY: Charles D. Zeier

NEW HAMPSHIRE
Mr. George Gilman, Commissioner
Department of Resources and
    Economic Development
P.O. Box 856
Concord, NH 03301
(603) 271-2411
DEPUTY: Linda Ray Wilson
(603) 271-3483

NEW JERSEY
Mr. Robert Hughey, Commissioner
Department of Environmental Protection
P.O. Box 1390
Trenton, NJ 08625
(609) 292-2885
DEPUTIES: Lawrence Schmidt
Paul Arbesman
(609) 984-3732

NEW MEXICO
Mr. Thomas W. Merlan, SHPO
State Planning Division
Historic Preservation Bureau
505 Don Gaspar Avenue
Santa Fe, NM 87503
(505) 827-2108
DEPUTY: Lane Ittelson

NEW YORK
Mr. Orin Lehman, Commissioner
Parks and Recreation
Agency Building No. 1
Empire State Plaza
Albany, NY 12238
(518) 474-0444
DEPUTY: Ann Webster Smith
(518) 474-0468

NORTH CAROLINA
Dr. William S. Price, Jr., Director
Division of Archives and History
Department of Cultural Resources
109 East Jones Street
Raleigh, NC 27611
(919) 733-7305
DEPUTY: John J. Little
(919) 733-4763

NORTH DAKOTA
Mr. James E. Sperry, Superintendent
State Historical Society of
  North Dakota
Liberty Memorial Building
Bismarck, ND 58501
(701) 224-2667
DEPUTY: Louis N. Hafermehl
(701) 224-2672

NORTHERN MARIANA ISLANDS
Mr. Jesus B. Pangelinan, HPO
Department of Community and
  Cultural Affairs
Commonwealth of the Northern
  Mariana Islands
Saipan, Mariana Islands 96950
Saipan (Overseas) 9722 or 9411

OHIO
Mr. W. Ray Luce, SHPO
The Ohio Historical Society
Interstate 71 at Seventeenth Avenue
Columbus, OH 43211
(614) 466-1500

OKLAHOMA
Mr. C. Earle Metcalf, SHPO
Oklahoma Historical Building
2100 North Lincoln
Oklahoma City, OK 73105
(405) 521-2491
DEPUTY: Stephen Day

OREGON
Mr. David G. Talbot, State Parks
  Administrator
525 Trade Street SE
Salem, OR 97301
(503) 378-5019
DEPUTY: David Powers
(503) 378-5002

PENNSYLVANIA
Dr. Larry E. Tise, Executive Director
Pennsylvania Historical and
  Museum Commission
P.O. Box 1026
Harrisburg, PA 17120
(717) 787-2891
DEPUTY: Ed Weintraub
(717) 787-4363

COMMONWEALTH
OF PUERTO RICO
Mr. Rafael Rivera Garcia, SHPO
Office of Cultural Affairs
La Fortaleza
San Juan, Puerto Rico 00905
(809) 724-2100
DEPUTY: A. Gus Pantel

RHODE ISLAND
Mr. Frederick C. Williamson, Director
Rhode Island Department of
  Community Affairs
150 Washington Street
Providence, RI 02903
(401) 277-2850
DEPUTY: Eric Hertfelder
Rhode Island Historic Preservation
  Commission
Old State House
150 Benefit Street
Providence, RI 02903
(401) 277-2678

SOUTH CAROLINA
Mr. Charles Lee, Director
State Archives Department
1430 Senate Street
Columbia, SC 29211
(803) 758-5816
DEPUTY: Christie A. Fant
(803) 758-5816

SOUTH DAKOTA
Mr. Junius Fishburne, Director
Office of Cultural Preservation
Kneit Building
Pierre, SD 57501
(605) 773-3458
DEPUTY: Paul M. Putz
Historic Preservation Center
University of South Dakota
Alumni House
Vermillion, SD 57069
(605) 677-5314

TENNESSEE
Mr. Charles A. Howell, Commissioner
Department of Conservation
2611 West End Avenue
Nashville, TN 37219
(615) 741-2301

TEXAS
Mr. Curtis Tunnell, Executive Director
Texas Historical Commission
P.O. Box 12276, Capitol Station
Austin, TX 78711
(512) 475-3092

TRUST TERRITORY
OF THE PACIFIC ISLANDS
Mr. Scott Russell, Acting HPO
Trust Territory of the Pacific Islands
Saipan, CM 96950

UTAH
Dr. Melvin T. Smith, Director
Utah State Historical Society
300 Rio Grande
Salt Lake City, UT 84101
(801) 533-5755

DEPUTIES: Wilson G. Martin
(801) 533-7039
A. Kent Powell
(801) 533-6017

VERMONT
Mr. C. Harry Behney, Secretary
Agency of Development and
  Community Affairs
Pavilion Office Building
Montpelier, VT 05602
(802) 828-3231
DEPUTY: William B. Pinney
(802) 828-3226

VIRGINIA
Mr. H. Bryan Mitchell, Executive Director
Virginia Historic Landmarks Commission
221 Governor Street
Richmond, VA 23219
(804) 786-3143

VIRGIN ISLANDS
Mr. Roy E. Adamas, Planning Director
Virgin Islands Planning Board
P.O. Box 2606
Charlotte Amalie
St. Thomas, Virgin Islands 00801
(808) 774-1726

WASHINGTON
Mr. Jacob E. Thomas, SHPO
Office of Archeology and
  Historic Preservation
111 West 21 Street KL-11
Olympia, WA 98504
(206) 753-4011

WEST VIRGINIA
Mr. Norman Fagan, Acting SHPO
Department of Culture and History
Capitol Complex
Charleston, WV 25304
(304) 348-0244

WISCONSIN
Mr. Richard A. Erney, Director
State Historical Society of Wisconsin
816 State Street
Madison, WI 53706
(608) 262-3266
DEPUTY: Jeff Dean
(608) 262-1339

WYOMING
Ms. Jan L. Wilson, Director
Wyoming Recreation Commission
604 West Twenty-fifth Street
Cheyenne, WY 82002
(307) 777-7695
DEPUTY: Mark G. Junge

Glossary

BALLOON FRAME A method of frame house construction whereby the studs run continuously from floor to rafters. Used extensively from about 1860 to 1900.

BALUSTER A vertical member in a stairway or porch.

BALUSTRADE A porch, stairway, or balcony railing. Includes base, balusters, and continuous top railing.

BARGEBOARD (VERGEBOARD) A board along the roof edge of a gable.

BAY WINDOW A window that projects outward from the walls of a house.

BEVEL To cut at an angle other than 90 degrees.

BRACKET (CORBEL) An angled support or decoration under roof eaves, cornices, porches, etc.

BRIDGING Wooden or metal bracing affixed between joists to distribute the floor load and thereby increase structural support.

BROWNSTONE Brown sandstone used as house facing; also, a house faced with this sandstone.

CAPITAL The decorative top part of a column.

CASING Framing, including moldings and stops, for a window or door.

CAULKING Pliable material used to seal joints and crevices; especially useful for weatherproofing.

CLADDING See *siding*.

COLD CHISEL A chisel made from tempered metal alloys—extremely hard.

COLUMN A vertical support.

CORBEL See *bracket*.

CORNICE A horizontal projecting molding placed where a roof or ceiling meets a wall.

COURSE A horizontal row of bricks, blocks, or shingles.

CRAZING A network of small cracks on the surface of porcelain or pottery.

CRENULATION Notches or scallops.

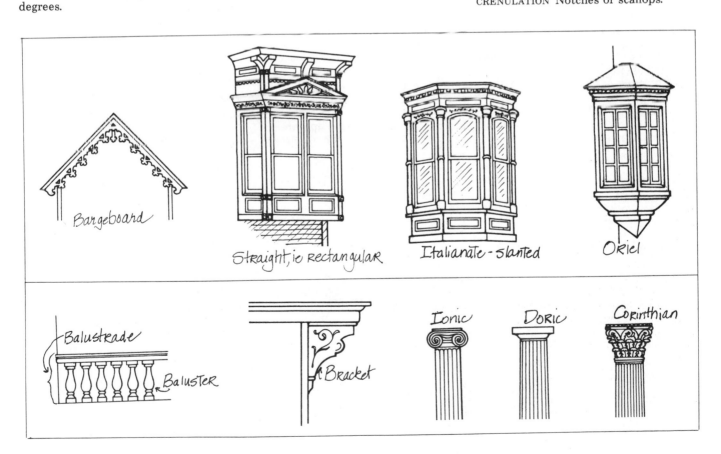

Bargeboard

Straight, ie Rectangular

Italianate - slanted

Oriel

Balustrade

Baluster

Bracket

Ionic

Doric

Corinthian

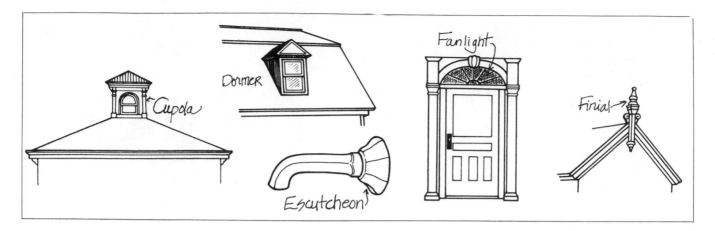

CROSS-CUTTING Sawing wood across the grain.

CUPOLA A small towerlike addition on the roof of a building.

DADO The lower portion of a wall, decorated differently from the rest of the surface.

DORMER A roofed structure covering an opening projecting from a roof.

DOUBLE-HUNG WINDOW Two sashes hung in vertical grooves. Sashes slide past each other when the windows are raised or lowered.

DOWNSPOUT A pipe, commonly metal, that carries water from the roof gutters down and away from the house.

DUCTING Pipes (metal or plastic) used to distribute air through the house from a heater or air conditioner.

EAVES The lower edges of a roof, projecting past the walls.

ESCUTCHEON A decorative plate that hides holes in the wall where pipes enter a room.

ETCHED GLASS Decorative patterning and frosting in glass created by cutting, sandblasting, or washing in acid.

FANLIGHT An arched, segmented window, often of leaded glass, above a window or door.

FIELD KILN BRICKS Bricks fired in kilns made on the construction site.

FINIAL An ornament, usually of iron or wood, at the top of a tower or gable.

FIRE STOP A plate or block used in the walls of a building (especially in balloon-frame construction) to retard the spread of fire within the walls.

FIVE-SIDED BAY WINDOW See *bay window*.

FLASHING Thin sheets of metal placed at joints between the roof and chimneys, vents, other roof slopes, walls, etc.

FLUE A passage within a chimney for exhumation of fumes and smoke.

FOUNDATION A small wall, usually concrete or masonry, on which a house sits.

FRIEZE A horizontal section under a cornice at the top of an interior or exterior wall.

FURRING STRIPS Strips of wood or metal affixed to a surface to render it even, so finish material can be applied over it.

GABLE The triangular peak at a roofline formed by a double-sloped roof.

GAMBREL ROOF A roof with two slopes on each of two sides.

GRAIN The direction, size, appearance, or quality of the fibers within a piece of wood.

GUTTER A wood, metal, or plastic trough attached to the edge of a roof to collect water and channel it away from the roof.

HALF-TIMBERING Exposed framing members in a structure.

HARDWOOD Wood from broad-leaved deciduous trees. The appellation *hard* has no relation to the actual hardness or softness of the wood.

HIP Where two sides of a roof meet to form an external angle. A hipped roof rises from all four sides of a building.

JACK POST A metal post with a screw end, used for lifting buildings.

JOINT COMPOUND A powder mixed with water and used for patching and finishing drywall.

JOIST A parallel framing member used to support floor and ceiling loads.

KILN-DRIED LUMBER Lumber dried at a controlled temperature and humidity so it will not shrink or warp.

LACQUER THINNER See *solvents*.

LANCET WINDOW A narrow window that comes to a point at the top.

LATH Wood, metal, or gypsum base for the application of plaster. Victorian-era houses commonly utilized wood lath: strips approximately 1-1/4 inches wide by 1/4 inch thick.

MASONRY Stone, brick, concrete block, or other similar materials bonded with mortar.

MINERAL SPIRITS (PAINT THINNER) See *solvents*.

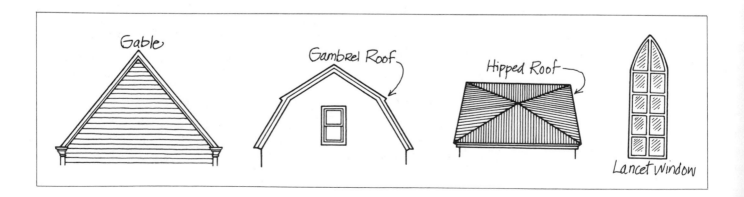

MITER A joint formed by fitting together two pieces cut at angles; to cut at an angle.

MOLDING A piece of wood cut with an ornamental contour or contours.

MULLION A vertical bar dividing a window.

MUNTIN A small strip dividing window panes.

NOSING A projecting, rounded edge, e.g., in moldings, stair treads, roof edges, etc.

ORIEL WINDOW See *bay window.*

PAINT THINNER See *mineral spirits.*

PEDIMENT The triangular face of a roof gable.

PIGMENT A powder used to color paint or dye.

PILASTER A pseudo column that projects only part way from a wall.

PLASTER A mixture of lime, cement, sand, and gypsum used for covering interior and exterior surfaces and for decorative embellishments.

PORTICO A covered entrance porch supported by columns or brackets.

QUOINS Stone or masonry blocks (or wood blocks used to simulate stone or masonry) placed at the exterior corners of some buildings. Stone and masonry quoins often added structural support to a building.

RABBET A longitudinal right angle groove along the edge of a board.

RAFTER A structural, load-bearing member of a roof.

RIPPING Sawing wood in the same direction as the grain.

RISER A vertical stair member between two treads.

ROUT To cut, mill, or gouge a groove in materials.

SASH A frame holding the glass in a window.

SASH WEIGHTS Cement or iron counterweights on double- or triple-hung windows.

SEPTIC TANK An underground tank into which a house's waste system empties if it is not connected to a sewer system. This tank holds the waste and decomposes it by bacterial action; then it is dispersed to the earth nearby.

SHEATHING Structural covering boards or sheets attached to roof rafters or wall studs.

SHELLAC A transparent coating composed of a secretion from an insect (the lacbug) dissolved in alcohol.

SHIM A small piece of wood or metal, sometimes beveled, used to level or bring something flush.

SIDING (CLADDING) The exterior finish covering of a frame house.

SILL A horizontal board that sits on the foundation and to which studs are attached. Also known as a sill plate.

SKIM COAT A thin, usually 1/8 to 1/4 of an inch, coat of a material such as plaster or stucco, on a surface.

SLANTED BAY See *bay window.*

SOFFIT A horizontal space underneath a boxed eave, an area for ducting, etc.

SOFTWOOD Wood that comes from trees having needles or scalelike leaves that are evergreen. The appellation *soft* has no relation to the actual hardness or softness of the wood.

SOLVENT A liquid that can dissolve other materials. Common solvents include mineral spirits (paint thinner), used for thinning and cleanup of oil-based paints and stains; and lacquer thinner, used for cleanup and for dissolving oil and grease.

SPAN The distance between structural members.

STAINED GLASS Glass colored by the addition or fusion of metallic oxides and pigments. It is usually cut into small pieces and put together with solder or lead came into a decorative design.

STENCILING Painting a repeating pattern, using a template.

STORY Part of a building between any one floor and the floor above it.

STRAIGHTEDGE A perfectly straight piece of wood, or a ruler, used to measure and assess the levelness or straightness of a surface.

STUD A wooden, vertical structural member of a house frame, forming the walls of the building.

SURFACED LUMBER Lumber that is finished by running it through a planer.

TACK RAG A piece of cloth moistened with solvent and used to clean surfaces.

TRACERY Ornamental work of interlacing or branching lines.

TRANSOM A small window or panel directly above a door or window.

TREAD The horizontal part of a stair, upon which one steps.

TRISODIUM PHOSPHATE (TSP) Used as a general cleaner, mixed with water.

TRUSS A structural unit, usually triangular in form, that provides rigid support over a wide span, i.e., on a roof.

TSP See *trisodium phosphate.*

URETHANE A type of clear plastic finish often used on wood.

VALLEY Where two slopes of a roof meet to form an internal angle.

VENEER A thin layer of wood, made by rotary-cutting a log; these sheets are glued to less-expensive types of wood.

VERGEBOARD See *bargeboard.*

VICTORIAN Of or during the reign of Queen Victoria in Great Britain (1837–1901).

WAINSCOT Protective or decorative boards covering the dado portion of a wall.

BIBLIOGRAPHY

Allen, Edith Louise. *American Housing as Affected by Social and Economic Conditions.* Peoria, Ill.: Manual Arts Press, 1930.

The Association for Preservation Technology. *APT Bulletin* vol. 5, no. 1 (1974); vol. 8, nos. 2 and 4 (1976); vol. 9, no. 2 (1977); vol. 10, no. 3 (1978).

Athenaeum Library of Nineteenth-Century America. *Exterior Decoration.* Philadelphia: Athenaeum, 1976.

Banov, Abel. *Paints and Coatings Handbook.* Farmington, Mich.: Structures Publishing Co., 1978.

Barnard, Julian. *The Decorative Tradition.* Princeton: Ryne Press, 1973.

Bicknell, A.J., and Comstock, William. *Victorian Architecture: Two Pattern Books by A. J. Bicknell and William Comstock.* New York: American Life Foundation and Study Institute, 1977.

Bode, Carl, ed. *American Life in the 1840s.* New York: University Press, 1967.

Boston Redevelopment Agency. *Revitalizing Older Houses in Charleston.* Boston: City of Boston Redevelopment Department, n.d.

Brown, Richard D. *Modernization: The Transformation of American Life, 1600–1865.* New York: Hill & Wang, 1976.

Bryant, Terry. "Protecting Exterior Masonry from Water Damage: Moisture Control Procedures and Products." *Technology and Conservation.* Vol. 3 (1978), pp. 38–42.

Buckley, Jerome Hamilton. *The Victorian Temper.* New York: Vintage Books, 1951.

Bullock, O. *The Restoration Manual.* Norwalk, Conn.: Silvermine Publishers, 1966.

Carroll, Margaret. *Historic Preservation Through Urban Renewal.* Washington, D.C.: Housing and Home Finance Agency, 1963.

Clark, Robert Judson, ed. *The Arts and Crafts Movement in America, 1876–1916.* New Jersey: Princeton University Press, 1972.

Cobb, Hubbard. *How to Buy and Remodel the Old House.* New York: Colliers, 1970.

Congam, Herbert. *Early American Homes for Today: A Treasury of Decorative Details and Restoration Procedures.* Rutand, Vt.: C. E. Tuttle Co., 1964.

Cooperative Architects of New York. *How to Build, Furnish, and Decorate.* New York: The Cooperative Building Plan Association, 1863.

Cummings, M., and Miller, C. *Architecture—Designs for Street Fronts, Suburban Houses, and Cottages.* New York: Orange, Judd, & Co., 1965.

Downing, A.J. *The Architecture of Country Houses.* New York: Da Capo Press, 1968.

Eastlake, Charles Locke. *Hints on Household Taste.* 1868. New York: Dover Publications, 1968.

Eastlake-Influenced American Furniture, 1870–1890. New York: The Hudson River Museum Publishers, 1973.

Edgerton, William H. *How to Renovate a Brownstone.* New York: Halsey Publishing Co., 1970.

Ferebee, Ann. *A History of Design from the Victorian Era to the Present.* New York: Van Nostrand Reinhold Co., 1970.

Florin, Lambert. *Victorian West.* Seattle, Wa.: Superior Publishing Co., 1978.

Forman, Henry. *The Architecture of the Old South.* New York: Russell & Russell, 1948.

Fowler, Orson S. *The Octagon House: A Home for All.* 1853. New York: Dover Publications, 1973.

Freudenlein, Leslie M., and Sussman, Elisabeth. *Building with Nature: Roots of the San Francisco Bay Region Tradition.* Santa Barbara, Calif., and Salt Lake City: Peregrine Smith, 1974.

From Tree to Trim. Oregon: Western Wood and Millwork Producers, 1975.

Garrigan, Kristine O. *Ruskin on Architecture.* Madison: University of Wisconsin Press, 1973.

Gebhard, David, and Von Breton, Harriette. *Architecture in California.* Santa Barbara: University of California Press, n.d.

Gillon, Edmund V., and Lancaster, Clay. *Victorian Houses—A Treasury of Lesser-Known Examples.* New York: Dover Publications, 1973.

Greater Portland Landmarks Advisory Service. *Living with Old Houses.* Washington, D.C.: National Trust Bookshop, n.d.

Green, Floyd, and Meyer, Susan. *You Can Renovate Your Own Home.* New York: Doubleday, 1978.

Halworth, Paul L. *The United States in Our Own Times, 1869–1920.* New York: Charles Scribner's Sons, 1920.

Handlin, David P. *The American Home: Architecture and Society, 1815–1915.* Boston and Toronto: Little, Brown, & Co., 1979.

Hitchcock, Henry Russell, et al. *The Rise of an American Architecture.* New York: Praeger Publishers, 1970.

Hunt, Gaillard. *Life in America One Hundred Years Ago.* New York: Harper & Brothers, 1914.

Hussey, E.C. *Victorian Home Building: A Transcontinental View.* New York: The American Life Foundation, 1976.

Hutton, Peter. *So You Want to Fix up an Old House.* Boston: Little, Brown & Co., 1979.

Jackson, Sir Thomas G. *Modern Gothic Architecture.* London: Henry S. King & Co., 1873.

Kerker, Harold. *California's Architectural Frontier.* Santa Barbara, Calif., and Salt Lake City: Peregrine Smith, 1973.

Ladies' Home Journal. Vols. 6 and 7, nos. 1–12 (1889–90).

Lancaster, Clay. *The Japanese Influence in America.* Japan: Walton A. Rawls, 1963.

Loftie, M.J., Orrinsmith, Lucy, and Barker, Lady. *The Dining Room, the Drawing Room, the Bedroom and Boudoir.* London: MacMillan & Co., 1878.

Loth, Calder, and Sadler, Julius T., Jr. *The Only Proper Style: Gothic Architecture in America*. Boston: Little, Brown & Co., 1975.

Maass, John. *The Victorian Home in America*. New York: Hawthorn Books, 1972.

Makinson, Randell L. *Greene and Greene*. Santa Barbara, Calif., and Salt Lake City: Peregrine Smith, 1977.

Malin, James C. *The United States, 1865–1917: An Interpretation*. Lawrence: Kansas University Press, 1924.

Millard, Richard. "Stained Glass Preservation: Guidelines for Repair and Restoration." *Technology and Conservation*. Vol. 4, no. 1 (1979).

Modern Architectural Designs and Details. New York: William Comstock, 1881.

Mumford, Lewis. *The South in Architecture*. New York: Harcourt Brace, 1941.

Naylor, Gillian. *The Arts and Crafts Movement*. Cambridge, Mass.: The MIT Press, 1971.

Nye, Russell Blaine. *Society and Culture in America, 1830–1860*. New York: Harper & Row, 1974.

Old-House Journal. Vols. 1–8 (1973–80).

Page, Charles Hall & Associates. *Santa Cruz Renovation Manual: A Homeowner's Handbook*. San Francisco, 1976, City of Santa Cruz.

Parloa, Maria. *Miss Parloa's Kitchen Companion*. Boston: Estes & Lauriat, 1883.

Phillips, Morgan W. *The Eight Most Common Mistakes Restoring Old Houses and How to Avoid Them*. Washington: National Trust Bookshop, n.d.

Plaster/Metal Framing Systems/Lath Manual. Los Angeles: Building News, 1977.

Putnam, R.E., and Carlson, G.E. *Architectural and Building Trades Dictionary*. Chicago: American Technical Society, 1974.

Rhoads, William B. "The Colonial Revival." Vol. 2. Master's thesis, Princeton University, 1977.

Richter, H.P. *Wiring Simplified*. St. Paul, Minn.: Park Publishing Co., 1975.

Rickey, Eleanor. *The Ultimate Victorians of the Continental Side of San Francisco Bay*. Berkeley: Howell-North Books, 1970.

Scharff, Robert. *Complete Book of Wood Finishing*. 2nd ed. New York: McGraw Hill, 1974.

Scherer, John L. *Complete Handbook of Home Painting*. Blue Ridge, Pa.: Tab Books, 1975.

Schmidt, Carl F. *The Victorian Era in the United States*. Scottsville, New York 1971.

Scott, Frank J. *The Art of Beautifying Suburban Home Grounds*. New York: D. Appleton & Co., 1870.

Scully, Vincent J., Jr. *The Shingle Style and the Stick Style*. New Haven and London: Yale University Press, 1971.

Seale, William. *Recreating the Historic House Interior*. Nashville: American Association for State and Local History, 1979.

Sherwood, Gerald E. *New Life for Old Dwellings: Appraisal and Rehabilitation*. U.S. Department of Agriculture publication no. 481. Washington, D.C.: U.S. Government Printing Office, 1975.

———. "Remodeling a House—Will it Be Worthwhile?" *U.S. Department of Agriculture 1978 Yearbook*. Washington, D.C.: U.S. Government Printing Office, n.d.

Sloan, Samuel. "Monthly Review: The Two Mansarts and the Mansard Roof." *Sloan's Architectural Review and Builders Journal*. August 1868, pp. 81–84.

Stanforthe, Dierdre, and Stamm, Martha. *Buying and Renovating a House in the City: A Practical Guide*. New York: Knopf, 1972.

Steegman, John. *Victorian Taste*. Cambridge, Mass.: The MIT Press, 1970.

Stephen, George. *Remodeling Old Houses without Destroying Their Character*. New York: Knopf, 1974.

Technical Preservation Services. Washington, D.C.: Department of the Interior. See these publications:

Curtis, John O. *Moving Historic Buildings*.

Frangiamore, Lynn. *Wallpapers in Historic Preservation*.

Historic Preservation Grants-in-Aid for Acquisition and Development Projects.

Mack, Robert C. *Preservation Brief No. 1: The Cleaning and Waterproof Coating of Masonry Buildings*.

———. *Preservation Brief No. 2: Repointing Mortar Joints in Historic Buildings*.

Tax Incentives for Rehabilitating Historic Buildings.

Thomas, Samuel W., and Morgan, William. *Old Louisville: The Victorian Era*. Louisville: Data Courier, 1975.

Thorne, Mrs. James Ward. *American Rooms in Miniature*. Chicago: Chicago Art Institute, 1941.

Tucci, Douglass Shand. *Built in Boston*. Boston: New York Graphic Society, 1978.

Vail, Wesley D. *Victorians: An Account of Domestic Architecture in Victorian San Francisco*. San Francisco: Brandes Printing Co., 1964.

Van Rensselaer, Mrs. Schuyler. *Henry Hobson Richardson and His Works*. Cambridge, Mass.: The Riverside Press, 1888.

Waite, Diana S. *Architectural Elements*. Princeton: The Pyne Press, n.d.

Waldhorn, Judith Lynch. *An Amateur's Guide: Victorian Research in San Francisco*. Palo Alto, Calif.: Stanford Research Institute, 1974.

———, and Woodbridge, Sally B. *Victoria's Legacy*. San Francisco: 101 Productions, 1978.

Whiffen, Marcus. *American Architecture Since 1780: A Guide to the Styles*. Cambridge, Mass.: The MIT Press, 1969.

Wright, Lawrence. *Clean and Decent*. New York: Viking Press, 1960.

Notes & Index

NOTES

1. Richard A. Biggs, "A Personal Experience," U.S. Department of Agriculture Publication No. YS-78-3, p. 79.

2. *California Architect and Building News,* letter from Charles Eastlake, April 1882, p. 49.

3. Loftie, Orrinsmith, and Barker, *The Dining Room* (London: MacMillan & Co., 1878), pp. 2–3.

4. Harriet Beecher Stowe and Catharine Beecher, *The American Woman's Home* (New York, Boston: J. B. Ford, 1869.)

5. Robert C. Mack, *Repointing Mortar Joints in Historic Brick Buildings* (Washington, D.C.: 1969), p. 4.

6. *Plaster/Metal Framing Systems/Lath Manual* (Los Angeles: Building News, 1977), p. 100.

7. Department of the Interior, National Park Service, *Publication No. 12* (Washington, D.C.: n.d.).

Katherine Knight Rusk is no stranger to the joys and frustrations of working on and living in old houses. Her first renovation project, shown at right, was a 1901 Queen Anne, which had been converted into a commercial building, in Sacramento, California. Other projects include a rural Italianate mansion in California's central valley and a turn-of-the-century farmhouse, where she presently lives with her two children and her husband, John Tosney.

Ms. Knight has been a freelance writer since 1975. For the past five years her column, "Old House Overhaul," has appeared in *The Sacramento Bee.* Her articles also have been published in many local and statewide periodicals and another book, *The River City Renovator's Guide,* is soon to be released.